# MAKING THINGS HAPPEN

# MAKING THINGS HAPPEN

## On *Casablanca* and Other World War II Icons

*Richard Raskin*

*Characters who make things happen are more interesting than characters things happen to.*

for my daughters Adina and Melanie
– international women of mystery –
with gratitude and love

*Making Things Happen*
On Casablanca *and Other World War II Icons*
Richard Raskin

© Richard Raskin and U Press 2017

Graphic design and cover: Ordered by Colour
Typesetting: Narayana Press
Type: Adobe Caslon Pro
Paper: Munken Premium Cream 90g
Printed by Narayana Press, Denmark
Printed in Denmark 2017
ISBN: 978-87-93060-69-2 (pbk.)
ISBN: 978-87-93060-70-8 (E-book)

No part of this book may be reproduced,
stored in a retrieval system, or transmitted in any
form or by any means, including mechanical, electronic,
photocopying, recording, or otherwise, without the
prior written permission of the publisher.

U PRESS
Rådhuspladsen 16
DK-1550 Copenhagen
www.upress.dk

Published with the financial support of
THE VELUX FOUNDATIONS

# Content

Introduction   9

**1**
*Casablanca* and United States Foreign Policy   13

**2**
Bogart's Nod in the *'Marseillaise'* Scene: A Physical Gesture in *Casablanca*   35

**3**
A Note on a Wartime Function of the Bogart Image   41

**4**
Two *'Marseillaise'* scenes: From Michael Curtiz's *Casablanca* (1943) to Ziad Doueiri's *West Beirut* (1998)   45

**5**
From Leslie Howard to Raoul Wallenberg: The Transmission and Adaptation of a Heroic Model   55

**6**
Interview with Alain Resnais on *Night and Fog*   77

**7**
Reflections on Art and the Holocaust: Elie Wiesel versus Alain Resnais   93

**8**
An Iconic Holocaust Photo in Context   101

**9**
*Bad Day at Black Rock* and the Overcoming of Evil   113

**10**
The Moth in *Merry Christmas, Mr. Lawrence*   129

**11**
The Role of the Birds in *Seven Minutes in the Warsaw Ghetto*   137

**12**
'*Le Chant des Partisans*': Functions of an Underground Song   153

**13**
On Barbara's Need to Write the Song '*Göttingen*'   179

**14**
Camus' Critiques of Existentialism   189

**15**
Five Explanations for the Naming of Malta's Gloster Gladiators 'Faith', 'Hope' and 'Charity' in 1940-1941   197

**16**
Far from where? A Classic Jewish Refugee Joke   209

**17**
*The Ghost Army* (2013) and Deception as Performance   217

**18**
The King of Denmark and the Yellow Star: Changing Forms and Functions of an Irresistible Myth   235

Acknowledgments   255

# Introduction

For over forty years I have been writing about films, songs, poems, novels, photos, jokes and concepts related to World War II, with the resulting studies scattered in a number of journals and books. Here, along with four new studies, many of those writings are assembled within the covers of a single volume for the convenience of the reader who – like myself – finds that these films and other cultural icons representing the war are an inexhaustible source of nourishment and have lost nothing of their magic.

That the Second World War remains a compelling frame of reference for us, regardless of our age or background, is undeniable.

At a White House press briefing on April 11, 2017, Sean Spicer – wishing to emphasize how disgraceful it was that Bashar al-Assad used poison gas against civilians in northern Syria – oddly claimed: "We didn't use chemical weapons in World War II. You had someone as despicable as Hitler who didn't even sink to using chemical weapons" (Smith 2017). When reminded by a journalist that countless Jews had been gassed by Hitler, the press secretary awkwardly improvised a reply that earned him further ridicule: "Thank you. I appreciate that. There was not, in the, he brought them into the 'Holocaust centers,' I understand that." As this bizarre incident illustrates, not only does it seem perfectly natural to gauge present-day villainies in relation to those of Hitler, but it is also clear that uninformed references to the Second World War will be recognized as such by today's audiences, with some degree of astonishment.

But a focus on artworks and other evocations of that war is not the only common denominator of the essays in this book, which whenever possible and at least implicitly ascribe a positive value to purposeful action, to taking charge of one's own story – to making things happen. Many years ago, when deterministic models of the Marxist and psychoanalytic varieties were widely embraced in university research, I was greatly inspired by this old Jewish legend used by David Rapaport (1967: 724) to illustrate his views on ego autonomy:

> Moses' portrait was brought to an Oriental king whose astrologers and phrenologists concluded from it that Moses was a cruel, greedy, craven,

self-seeking man. The king, who had heard that Moses was a leader, kindly, generous, and bold, was puzzled, and went to visit Moses. On meeting him, he saw that the portrait was good, and said: "My phrenologists and astrologers were wrong." But Moses disagreed: "Your phrenologists and astrologers were right, they saw what I was made of; what they couldn't tell you was that I struggled against all that and so became what I am."

With this basic, life-affirming outlook in mind while studying each work, I have tried whenever appropriate to focus on moments of meaningful, purposive choices designed to change the course of events or to enable a character or a creative artist to shape more fully his or her own story.

Another shared aspect of these studies worth a passing mention is the deliberate avoidance of jargon, and the attempt to present things in as clear and down-to-earth a manner as possible. The general reader will at no point feel excluded by specialized terms accessible only to initiates.

While the studies reprinted here have not been updated with respect to subsequent research, they will not – I believe – be experienced as less interesting or less pioneering than newer work. The only changes I have made in relation to their originally published form are: 1) the addition of footnotes enabling viewers to see French, Danish or Swedish quotations and their English translations on the same page; 2) the relocation of all other footnote references into the text; 3) some stylistic or cosmetic improvements; and 4) the insertion of visual documentation and other necessary background material.

It is gratifying to see gathered in one place – where they can be conveniently considered in relation to one another – these older and some new studies. This is particularly true of the essays on Michael Curtiz's *Casablanca* (1943), three of which illuminate the memorable *Marseillaise* scene from very different perspectives, including a critical one inspired by Ziad Doueiri's film *West Beirut* (1998). This applies as well to the articles dealing with the Holocaust, whether in relation to four films – Leslie Howard's *Pimpernel Smith* (1941), Kjell Grede's *Good Evening, Mr. Wallenberg* (1990), Alain Resnais' *Night and Fog* (1956) and Johan Oettinger's *Seven Minutes in the Warsaw Ghetto* (2012); to an iconic Holocaust photo taken by the SS in 1943; to the myth of the Danish king wearing a Star of David; and to the divergent views on the relation between art and the Holocaust proposed by Elie Wiesel and Alain Resnais. Armed struggle against the Nazis is discussed in essays on the main song of the French Resistance movement, *Le Chant des Partisans* (1943); on Camus' novel *The Plague* (1947) as it relates to colonial issues, to his critiques of existentialism and to the postwar settling of scores with collaborators; on the obsolete biplanes that were cheered from rooftops as they defended Malta in 1940; and in connection with Rick Beyer's documentary film *The Ghost Army* (2013), about a secret U.S. army unit that was aptly called a "traveling roadshow of deception." Postwar Jewish attitudes toward the Germans and other nations are evoked both in Barbara's poignant song *Göttingen* (1967) and in a classic Jewish refugee joke (1948). And two essays are devoted to films that deal with very different aspects of the war in the Pacific: John Sturges' *Bad Day at Black Rock* (1954) and Nagisa Oshima's *Merry Christmas, Mr. Lawrence* (1983).

I am grateful to Mads Julius Elf at U Press for believing in this project from the start, and also wish to thank Francesco Caviglia for a chance remark that gave me the idea for this book; former Chief Rabbi Bent Melchior for precious information, kindness and inspiration; and Aage Jørgensen for tireless proofreading. As always my daughters, Adina Raskin Teplin and Melanie Raskin Nielsen, gave me the encouragement I needed and without the wise editorial advice and life-support provided by my wife, Marilyn Shepard Raskin, this book would never have seen the light of day.

Aarhus, Denmark
24 August 2017

# References

Rapaport, David (1967). "The Theory of Ego Autonomy" (1958) in Merton M. Gill (ed.), *Collected Papers of David Rapaport*. New York and London: Basic Books, pp. 722-744.

Smith, David et al (2017), "Sean Spicer apologizes for 'even Hitler didn't use chemical weapons' gaffe," *The Guardian,* 12 April, https://www.theguardian.com/us-news/2017/apr/11/sean-spicer-hitler-chemical-weapons-holocaust-assad Accessed 20 May 2017.

# 1

# *Casablanca* and United States Foreign Policy

At the Casablanca Conference, January 1943. Left to right: General Henri Giraud, President Franklin D. Roosevelt, General Charles de Gaulle and Prime Minister Winston Churchill. Roosevelt's approval of the Vichy-minded Giraud as French High Commissioner of North Africa, and systematic exclusion of de Gaulle – leader of the Free French – from all authority, meant that people like Victor Laszlo were being hunted down and imprisoned under Allied auspices in North Africa when U.S. audiences were watching *Casablanca*.

# Introduction

*Casablanca,* directed by Michael Curtiz, opened at New York's Hollywood Theater on Thanksgiving Day, 1942 – in the aftermath of the Allied landings in French North Africa. The general release of the film, several months later, occurred at a time when Casablanca was in the headlines again: after Roosevelt's return from the Casablanca Conference, which was held in secret in January 1943.

Discussions of *Casablanca* customarily include one or two paragraphs on the film's timeliness with regard to the Allied landings and the Casablanca Conference. In that context, two interpretations of the film's political significance have been suggested, neither of which takes into account the film's role in shaping public assumptions regarding American policy toward the Free French.

After showing how the Free French are evoked in *Casablanca*, both explicitly and indirectly, and then reviewing U.S. policy toward Vichy and the Free French, particularly with regard to French North Africa, the present study will present and refute the two main interpretations of the film's political significance already proposed in the literature, and will in their place give a new assessment of the political function the film is likely to have fulfilled for American audiences in late 1942 and early 1943.

NB. De Gaulle changed the name of his organization from "*La France Libre*" [Free France] to "*La France Combattante*" [Fighting France] in July 1942. In *Casablanca*, the filming of which began in May of that year, only the terms "Free France" and "Free French" are used. In order to avoid appearing to discuss two different organizations, I have used only those terms in this essay, even when discussing the period when "Fighting France" or "Fighting French" would be the more appropriate designations.

# I. Evocations of the Free French in *Casablanca*

At three points in *Casablanca* are the Free French explicitly invoked by name or emblem or both.

This first occurs in one of the earliest scenes in the film, when 'suspicious characters' are rounded up by French and Moroccan officers, in search of documents stolen from murdered German couriers – the missing 'letters of transit' which will play an important role in the story. A suspect who is shot while fleeing from two Moroccan officers collapses at a wall bearing an oversized portrait of Philippe Pétain, whom the viewer may or may not recognize as the head of the collaborationist Vichy government and who seems to be presiding over this scene. On papers pried from the dead suspect's hand, we see the Cross of Lorraine, which serves as the letter 'F' in the words 'Free France,' while mournful strains of the *'Marseillaise'* are heard – the music serving as a sound bridge to the Republican motto Liberté, Égalité, Fraternité on a plaque over the entrance to the Palais de Justice.

In this way, less than four minutes into the film, the Cross of Lorraine has been identified for the viewer as the emblem of the Free French and linked to the *'Marseillaise'* and the Republican motto, which any adult American movie-goer would immediately perceive as embodiments of French nationhood.

The second invocation occurs about 25 minutes into the film, soon after the Czech resistance leader Victor Laszlo and his companion, Ilsa Lund, enter Rick's Café. A man approaches their table and to Laszlo's polite disinterest persists in showing him a ring he appears to be selling. When the ring's secret compartment is opened, a Cross of Lorraine appears, which – thanks to the earlier scene discussed above – the viewer now recognizes as the emblem of the Free French. Laszlo's dismissive attitude suddenly changes and the look of reverence in his and his companion's eyes when they see the hidden emblem impresses on the viewer of *Casablanca* that this political symbol is almost sacred (it is in fact a cross) and is worthy of the deepest possible respect. In this way, the Cross of Lorraine and the movement it represents are invested with unlimited prestige in the eyes of the viewer.

The bearer of the ring is a Norwegian named Berger, who explains that Ugarte, the man Laszlo was supposed to meet, has been arrested: "But we who are still free will do all we can. We are organized, monsieur. Underground like everywhere else." The "we" in this statement encompasses both the Free French organization whose emblem Berger carries in his ring, and the Underground understood in the broadest possible sense, suggesting that the Free French, the Norwegian and Czech resistance networks, as well as the North African Underground, are all facets of one and the same valiant movement.

As the film nears its conclusion, the Free French are explicitly invoked for a third and last time, after Rick and Renault each undergoes a fundamental transformation, rising above cynical self-interest and embarking upon a new life of moral commitment.

In place of "I stick my neck out for no one" – the line he used when assuring Renault he would not help Laszlo escape and when Ugarte desperately pleaded for help – Rick now lives up to the heroic potential we knew he had in him from the start, when running guns to Ethiopia, fighting on the Loyalist side in Spain and earning himself a place of honor on the Nazi blacklist. He arranges for Victor and Ilsa to board the plane bound for freedom while he remains behind to deal with the consequences. When handed the letters of transit, Victor tells Rick: "Welcome back to the fight. This time I know our side will win." Rick's transformation is complete. Having to shoot Major Strasser in order to ensure Victor's and Ilsa's safe getaway, Rick expects Renault to have him arrested, as had been threatened moments earlier, but it is Renault's turn to rise to the occasion and take sides. He therefore tells his men when they arrive on the scene: "Major Strasser has been shot. Round up the usual suspects," after which he contemptuously drops a bottle of "Vichy Water" into a wastepaper basket. Having both become patriots and rejoined the fight against the Nazis, Rick and Renault will now have to leave Casablanca. In Renault's words: "There's a Free French garrison over at Brazzaville." And the *Marseillaise* is appropriately heard as the two men walk off into the fog together to join the Free French – that organization defined here once again as embodying the one true France.

In addition to these three explicit references to the Free French, it is clear that the spirit of that movement is most powerfully, though indirectly, evoked in the *'Marseillaise'* scene, which is undoubtedly the emotional summit of this film.

The scene is carefully prepared at an earlier point when a beautiful young French woman, Yvonne, previously jilted by Rick, shows up at the Café Américain accompanied by a German officer. The German puts his arms around her as they sit at the bar, and a French officer sitting nearby challenges Yvonne for betraying her country. A fight ensues between the German and French officers and Rick's intervention is required to put an end to the disturbance: "Either lay off politics or get out!" But the Frenchman gets in an additional insult and political remark, warning that the day of reckoning is coming. This set-up will be followed by a pay-off about eight minutes later.

As Rick and Victor Laszlo are speaking in Rick's private office, they hear a group of German officers singing *'Die Wacht am Rhein'* in the café below. Rick and Victor stand at the top of the stairway, surveying the scene. They exchange glances and Victor Laszlo takes the situation in hand. He walks quickly to the bandstand and instructs the musicians to play the *'Marseillaise.'* The musicians look over to Rick for a sign. Rick nods affirmatively and the band plays. Laszlo sings *"Allons enfants de la patrie..."* A woman guitarist and others join in the singing of the *'Marseillaise,'* which is now drowning out the sound of the German song. Soon virtually all of the non-Germans in Rick's café are singing the *'Marseillaise,'* and Colonel Strasser and his fellow officers, who had competed as long as they could, finally give up singing *'Die Wacht am Rhein.'* Even Yvonne is now singing the *'Marseillaise'* with tears running down her cheek and Ilsa – with deep admiration in her eyes – watches her husband lead the singing. After the last line is sung, Yvonne cries out *"Vive la France! Vive la démocratie!"* Strasser, exasperated at having suffered a symbolic defeat, demands that Rick's café be closed down by Renault. Meanwhile the victorious Victor Laszlo is toasted by admirers, including uniformed French officers.

Among the premises of the film is that deep within all Frenchmen – including those officially in the service of Vichy or momentarily led astray – a spark of the true France remains alive. To whatever degree their patriotism comes to the fore, they recover both their self-respect and a defiant posture vis-à-vis the Germans – and of course, become embodiments of the true France in the eyes of the viewer. As their dormant patriotism is awakened and exalted in this act of singing the *'Marseillaise,'* and submission to Vichy and to the Germans as well as all personal considerations are imperiously superseded, France is momentarily reborn in the midst of Vichy. And though no Cross of Lorraine appears in this scene, we know that in gallantly bringing France back to life in this symbolic moment, it is the spirit of the Free French that Victor Laszlo champions, to the Nazis' displeasure.

## II. U.S. Foreign Policy

### 1. Recognition of Vichy

In the summer of 1940, when Pétain founded his new collaborationist government, the U.S. established diplomatic relations with Vichy. In January 1941, Roosevelt strengthened U.S. ties to Vichy by elevating American representation to the full ambassadorial level. On presenting his credentials at the ceremony filmed by newsreel cameras, Ambassador Leahy "received the definite impression that Roosevelt's action in sending a full-fledged ambassador to Vichy had given Pétain a lift in moral[e]" (Leahy 1950: 21). Leahy had been instructed by Roosevelt to gain the confidence first of Pétain and then of Admiral Darlan, who controlled the French fleet. Leahy was to be a watchdog, "to try to prevent France from extending any aid to Germany beyond what was required by the Armistice agreement." He was also "to seek renewed pledges that under no circumstances would the [French] fleet fall into German hands."

> The president already had told Vichy bluntly that if the fleet were to be surrendered to the Axis, France would forfeit the longstanding good will and friendship of the United States. I was to renew that warning whenever it seemed necessary to do so. The president wanted me to include hostile operations against the British in that warning (18).

A growing concern of Roosevelt's was that Vichy might comply with German demands for North African bases, particularly after Darlan casually accorded to Japan the use of bases in Indo-China in July 1941. In a strongly worded letter to Pétain on September 12, 1941, Roosevelt urged the head of the Vichy government "to prevent German penetration into French North Africa" (Langer and Gleason 1953: 774-775).

The rationale of U.S. recognition of Vichy was thus first and foremost to be able to exert pressure on Pétain, particularly concerning the French fleet and sovereignty of French North Africa. When the State Department was under fire for maintaining diplomatic relations with Vichy, department spokesmen would answer that thanks to the influences exerted on Pétain though diplomatic channels, the fleet never fell into German hands and the Germans were never allowed to establish bases in French North Africa, and that any affront to Vichy might have jeopardized both of those crucial interests (*New Republic* 5 January 1942: 3 and 9 February 1942: 189).

A second justification for diplomatic recognition of Vichy was that the level of U.S information concerning developments in France was considerably higher than it would have been if there were no diplomatic personnel present at the seat of Pétain's government (Langer 1947: 387).

At no point did the U.S. suspend diplomatic relations with Vichy. When the Germans succeeded in imposing Laval as premier in April 1942, Admiral Leahy was recalled but diplomatic relations remained intact. And the State Department apparently encouraged members of the French diplomatic and consular staffs in the U.S. *not* to resign and join de Gaulle when Laval took over the government (*New Republic* 8 June 1942: 785). It was Laval who severed the ties between the U.S. and Vichy in November 1942, at German insistence after the Allied landings in North Africa (Aron 1954: 235-237).

Roosevelt publicly implied that U.S. policy toward Vichy was formulated at the State Department rather than at the White House. For example at a press conference given on April 14, 1942, at the time the Germans were still maneuvering Laval into place as the head of the Vichy government, the following exchange took place (Roosevelt 1972: vol. 21, no. 819, p. 279):

– Mr. President, are our relations with Vichy going to be changed as a result of the difficulties there?
– Oh, I think you will have to ask the State Department.

## 2. The 'Deal with Darlan'

When the Allies landed at Casablanca, Algiers and Oran at daybreak on November 8, 1942, they met active opposition from the Vichy French who could not be prevented from firing upon the Anglo-American forces by the small number of 'conspirators' who had been encouraged – and misinformed about the timing of the operation – by State Department representative Robert Murphy. Admiral Darlan, former Vichy premier and designated successor to Pétain, happened to be in North Africa at the time of Operation TORCH (the definitive code name for the Allied landings). General Mark Clark, acting on orders from General Eisenhower, persuaded Darlan to declare a ceasefire in Algiers on November 8, and subsequently – after Darlan had received instructions from Pétain – to end the fighting at Casablanca and Oran as well. In exchange for his cooperation in ordering the ceasefire, Darlan was appointed French High Commissioner of North Africa in late November 1942 (Funk 1974). The Free French, who had been totally excluded from Operation TORCH, were also passed over in the establishment of a French administration in North Africa, under Allied auspices.

In a press conference given on November 17, 1942, Roosevelt justified the U.S. 'deal with Darlan' by insisting that: 1) it was only temporary; 2) it saved American, British and French lives; 3) it avoided the loss of vital time on a 'mopping up' operation; 4) the U.S. had requested the release of all persons arrested in North Africa for opposition to Nazism and had asked for the abrogation of all Nazi-inspired racial laws and decrees in the territories under Darlan's jurisdiction; and 5) according to an old Balkan proverb, "you are permitted in time of great danger to walk with the Devil until you have crossed the bridge" (Roosevelt 1972: vol. 20, no. 861, pp. 244-247).

However, as Christmas approached, Darlan was apparently still unwilling or unable to comply with Roosevelt's requests for a democratization of French North Africa (Smith 1972: 61-62):

Allied correspondents in Algiers reported in devastating detail the true conditions of life under the Darlan regime – Jews still persecuted under anti-Semitic Vichy decrees that remained in force, concentration camps still filled with political prisoners, fascist political groups still allowed to flourish. No attempt had been made to expunge reactionary elements from the government bureaucracy. The Vichy-appointed generals of Darlan's 'Imperial Council' who had openly resisted the TORCH landings freely declared their intention to recreate an authoritarian Pétain regime-in-miniature in Algiers.

Darlan was assassinated on December 24, 1942, and General Henri Giraud was appointed his successor by the Imperial Council and acknowledged as the new French High Commissioner by the U.S. The wave of anti-Gaullist terror Giraud unleashed in the wake of Darlan's assassination, and Giraud's continued reliance on Vichy officials, exposed U.S. policy-makers to continued criticism. Giraud himself provided some new arguments Roosevelt would use in a press conference on February 2, 1943 to justify U.S. backing of the Giraud administration in North Africa: 1) swift reversals are impossible to make in countries like Algeria and Morocco; 2) Vichy men are needed in the administration because of the shortage of trained administrative personnel in North Africa; 3) having held office under the Vichy regime doesn't mean that someone is necessarily a 'man of Vichy'; and 4) the main thing is to get on with the war and not engage in politics (Roosevelt 1972: vol. 21, no. 876, pp. 109-111). At the same press conference, Roosevelt also flatly denied stories about political prisoners under Giraud's regime, claiming that "practically all of them have been released, unless there's something else 'agin' them" (116).

Roosevelt's positive attitude toward Giraud was not shared by members of the Anglo-American Psychological Warfare Branch, who were pro-Free French, wore the Cross of Lorraine in their lapels, and did their best to rescue leaders of the Gaullist underground from Vichy police under Giraud's orders (Smith 1972: 65). Nor was Roosevelt's attitude shared by the OSS Research and Analysis group in Algiers, or by Arthur Roseborough, head of espionage operations in North Africa. Roseborough, who saw Giraud as essentially a puppet with no popular backing, repeatedly sought support for members of the Free French who had helped the Allies at great personal risk and remained imprisoned by Giraud. Eisenhower's command refused "to worry about the Jews and communists who helped us," and General Patton said of 19 French soldiers at Oran who had dismantled their artillery on the day of the TORCH landings and were under arrest for having done so: "They got what they deserved. It *was* treason, wasn't it?" (Smith 1972: 71).

## 3. Refusal to recognize the Free French

Despite direct appeals made by the Free French to the State Department, explaining in human terms why the support of the U.S. was essential for the spirit of resistance in France (de Gaulle 1954: vol. 1, p. 523), despite a declaration sent to the Allied governments and signed by representatives of the three resistance movements of the "unoccupied zone" – *Combat*, *Libération* and *Franc-Tireur* – assuring that "*le général de Gaulle est le chef incontesté de la résistance et, plus que jamais, groupe tout le pays derrière lui*"[1] (de Gaulle 1954: vol. 2, p. 53), and despite the fact that even Laval was aware that de Gaulle was supported by 80% or 90% of the French population in November 1942 (Aron 1954: vol. 2, p. 269), the United States government refused to recognize the Free French and systematically excluded de Gaulle from Operation TORCH and from the administration of French North Africa in the months following the Allied landing.

Numerous reasons have been given for the administration's unwillingness to recognize the Free French. Admiral Leahy, who continued as Roosevelt's chief of staff after serving as ambassador to Vichy, alleged that de Gaulle had little backing and was "a paid British agent," and that the Free French organization was "impregnated with German spies" and "closely tied in with communists" (Leahy 1950: 56, 162, 175). Leahy also suggested characteristically that the pressure on Roosevelt to receive de Gaulle for a conference was instigated by a group of "Jews and Communists" (165). De Gaulle's representative Texier reported hearing rumors that the Free French were reactionary or fascist (de Gaulle 1954: vol. 1, p. 517).

On another level, it was argued that recognition of de Gaulle would constitute an affront to Vichy and would thereby jeopardize the French fleet and North Africa, from the Allied point of view (Langer and Gleason 1953: 772); or that "de Gaulle can be given no authority regarding the sovereignty of France because the people of France have not had the opportunity to give such authority"(Aandahl et al 1968: 514) – and why should de Gaulle be recognized instead of Giraud (Roosevelt 1972: vol. 21, no. 879, 12 Feb. 1943, pp. 140-141); or that the incident of the Saint Pierre and Miquelon islands of

---

1 "General de Gaulle is the undisputed head of the resistance and, more than ever, has the entire country backing him."

December 1941 showed that the "so-called Free French" were underhanded and not to be trusted (Funk 1974: 17; de Gaulle 1954: vol. 1, p. 184). It was Secretary of State Cordell Hull who launched the "so-called Free French" slur.

De Gaulle agreed to meet with Giraud during the final days of the Casablanca Conference of January 14-26, 1943, despite resentment over a number of political blows, the last of which was Giraud's appointment of Marcel Peyrouton as governor of Algeria. Peyrouton, as Vichy minister of the interior, had reportedly signed de Gaulle's death warrant (Funk 1974: 72). The 'shotgun wedding' Roosevelt and Churchill had hoped to bring about between Giraud and de Gaulle never came off. The meeting resulted in little more than the signing of a relatively meaningless communiqué and in a photograph of Giraud and de Gaulle shaking hands, at Roosevelt's request. According to one commentator, Roosevelt had made it abundantly clear at Casablanca that he was thoroughly committed to Giraud and "was prepared to hinder de Gaulle from gaining political or military control of North Africa" (Funk 1974: 89). Roosevelt finally accorded de Gaulle official recognition on October 23, 1944 – two months after the liberation of Paris – and even then, according to Admiral Leahy, it "must have been a difficult decision for Roosevelt" (Leahy 1950: 322).

## 4. The liberal critique of the State Department

Liberals argued that the U.S. should have broken with Vichy and recognized the Free French from the start. Such a policy would have "given the Free French invaluable moral support" and "immeasurably heartened the forces of antifascism around the world" (*New Republic* 27 April 1942: 556).

During the period extending from the American recognition of Vichy in the summer of 1940 to the Allied landing at North Africa in November 1942, liberals accused the State Department of following a course of "appeasement" and suspected that the architects of U.S. policy – such as Cordell Hull and Sumner Welles – secretly sympathized with Vichy. Allusions were accordingly made to the State Department as "a sinister outfit bent on encouraging the forces of fascism" (*New Republic* 5 January 1942: 3) and "a nest of antidemocrats" – the appeasement of Vichy being "a case of like calling to like" (*New Republic* 9 February 1942: 189).

Once Operation TORCH was carried out, Cordell Hull apparently expected his liberal critics to apologize for their harsh words, acknowledging that behind the scenes, the State Department had been working all along to prepare the Allied breakthrough in North Africa. For a while, the criticism did in fact subside, and even the temporary acceptance of Darlan was seen by some liberals as "probably a wise move" (*New Republic* 30 November 1942: 699). But others, exasperated by the sovereignty argument still used by Roosevelt for withholding recognition from the Free French, pointedly asked: "Has General Giraud or has Admiral Darlan received more of a mandate from the French people than the General de Gaulle?" (*New Republic* 23 November 1942: 659).

And perhaps even more significant was the growing conviction that the State Department made its policies, not on the basis of moral principle, but purely out of considerations of national self-interest, manipulating in Machiavellian fashion whomever might be used to further American strategic or political objectives (*New Republic* 7 December 1942: 730).

In all of these respects, the liberal American viewpoint corresponded essentially to that of de Gaulle. With regard to the sovereignty argument, de Gaulle bitterly stated (de Gaulle 1954: vol. 2, p. 24):

> Comment prendre au sérieux les scrupules affichés par Washington, qui affectait de tenir à distance le général de Gaulle sous prétexte de laisser au Français la liberté de choisir un jour leur gouvernement et qui, en même temps, conservait des relations officielles avec la dictature de Vichy et s'apprêtait à traiter avec quiconque ouvrirait aux troupes américaines les portes de l'Afrique du Nord.[2]

And concerning a moral as opposed to a manipulative policy, de Gaulle appealed to Cordell Hull in the following terms (de Gaulle 1954: vol. 1, p. 523):

> Si la guerre était simplement un jeu d'échecs, où les pièces sont des objets sans âme, la position actuelle du State Department en ce qui concerne la France, pourrait être comprise par nous. Mais la guerre est une chose morale. Pour que les hommes fassent la guerre, il est nécessaire qu'ils se croient moralement obligés de la faire, et, qu'en la faisant, ils soient moralement soutenus.[3]

---

2   How can one take seriously the scruples evoked by Washington, which claimed to distance itself from the General de Gaulle on the pretext of giving the French people the freedom to choose their government and which, at the same time, maintained official relations with the Vichy dictatorship and prepared to deal with whomever would open the ports of North Africa to the American troops.

3   If war were simply a game of chess in which the pieces were soulless objects, we might understand the present position of the State Department regarding France. But war is

The Free French suffered not only from the withholding of official recognition by the State Department and White House, but also from the denial of the slightest moral prestige to de Gaulle's organization. This led some liberals to suspect that the State Department had made a secret agreement with Vichy, promising "not to do anything to increase the prestige and authority of the Free French" (*New Republic* 8 June 1942: 785). The acute sensitivity of the Free French to the mental picture Americans held of them can be seen in the disheartening statement René Pleven made to de Gaulle, in a telegram from Washington on July 1, 1941 (de Gaulle 1954: vol. 1, pp. 472-473):

> Il est étonnant de voir combien le mouvement de la France Libre est peu connu par le public américain et que ce qui en est connu est, très souvent, en sa défaveur. Une propagande puissante a sans doute été faite par Vichy pour jeter une lumière fausse sur le mouvement et sur les intentions de son chef. Un grand effort serait nécessaire pour mettre le mouvement dans sa véritable lumière et pour montrer qu'il incarne l'esprit de la France, et à quel point il est appuyé par la nation.
>
> …Il nous faut convaincre les Américains que la France Libre est la France qu'ils ont aimée.[4]

## III. On the political significance of *Casablanca*

### 1. Previous interpretations

Citing the timeliness of *Casablanca* with respect to the Allied landings in North Africa and the Casablanca Conference, Nathaniel Benchley has suggested that these contemporary events "tended to point up the allegorical similarity between Rick and Roosevelt: the uncommitted American who stands by while others do the fighting, and then, at the proper time, steps in and turns the tide" (Benchley 1975: 45).

---

something moral. For men to engage in war, they have to believe they are morally obligated to do so and that in so doing, they have moral support.

4  It is astonishing to see how little the Free French movement is known by the American public and that what is known about it is often unfavorable. A powerful propaganda effort has undoubtedly been undertaken by Vichy in order to cast the movement and the intentions of its leader in a false light. A great effort would have to be made to place the movement in its proper light and to show that it embodies the spirit of France and to what degree it is backed by the nation. …We have to convince the Americans that Free France is the France they have loved.

Similarly, Barry Day described *Casablanca* as (Day 1974: 24):

> A topical thriller to suit an emerging national mood veering sharply from isolationism to international involvement in World War II. (Indeed another current interpretation is that *casa blanca* stands for White House with Rick and Roosevelt being persuaded to take sides).

Richard Corliss also mentioned the theory that (Koch 1973: 186-187):

> *Casablanca* is a political allegory, with Rick as President Roosevelt (*casa blanca* is Spanish for "white house"), a man who gambles on the odds of going to war until circumstance and his own submerged nobility force him to close his casino (read: partisan politics) and commit himself – first by financing the Side of Right and then by fighting for it. The time of the film's action (December 1941) adds credence to this view, as does the irrelevant fact that, two months after *Casablanca* opened, Roosevelt (Rick) and Prime Minister Winston Churchill (Lazlo) met for a war conference in Casablanca.

This apparently widespread interpretation of the political significance of the film – that is, of Rick's change of heart as symbolizing Roosevelt's and the nation's shift from isolationism to involvement in the war – is perfectly justified as far as it goes. But in addition to that shift, the film also and more specifically contrasts two political (and ethical) alternatives: accommodation with Vichy and opting for the Free French. As shown at the start of this study, the Free French are evoked in the film as heroic embodiments of the true France of the '*Marseillaise*' and of the republican values of *Liberté, Égalité, Fraternité*. According to the premises of *Casablanca*, Vichy and the Free French represent respectively the interests of Nazi Germany and America's natural ally in the war. The isolation/involvement interpretation of *Casablanca* simply fails to take into account the central role of the Vichy/Free French polarity within the film. And especially since the issue of U.S. indulgence toward Vichy and refusal to recognize the Free French was bitterly debated at the time the film was being shown to American wartime audiences, the isolationist/involvement interpretation cannot be defended as adequately covering the political meaning of *Casablanca*.

I have found only one discussion of *Casablanca* in relation to Roosevelt's embattled French policy. In an analysis dealing principally with the film from a psychoanalytic perspective, Harvey Greenberg suggested that *Casablanca* was in harmony with a new, pro-Free French policy decided by Roosevelt in late 1942. Greenberg wrote (1975: 82):

> Despite his opposition to the Gaullist cause, Roosevelt significantly elected to show *Casablanca* at the White House on New Year's Eve, December 31, 1942. The president, I believe, may very well have been telegraphing a change in strategy, for soon thereafter the controversial connection with Vichy was severed.

According to Greenberg, it was "not long after the Casablanca Conference" that Roosevelt was to accept de Gaulle, "however unhappily," as "unquestioned commander of the Free French," and news of this change in strategy may or may not have been leaked to Warner Brothers. Assuming that the studio was *not* aware of Roosevelt's new pro-Free French policy, Greenberg's argument continues (82-83):

> ...one may speculate that Rick Blaine's refusal to take up the sword at a time when Hollywood had become a haven for talented émigrés fleeing Nazi persecution was intended to be symbolic of the Roosevelt administration's vacillation in North Africa. Rick's change of heart at the end would then forcibly point out to our equivocating leaders the path of honor.

One way or another – either in consciously confirming in advance a new and as yet unpublicized pro-Free French policy, or in attempting to influence policy-makers in a pro-Free French direction they had in fact already elected to follow – the makers of *Casablanca* are seen by Greenberg as being on the same political wavelength as Roosevelt. One way or another, the film is viewed as in harmony with a new U.S. policy.

This argument sounds plausible but is not borne out by the facts. To begin with, if by "the controversial connection with Vichy," Greenberg referred to diplomatic relations between Washington and Vichy, that connection had already been severed in November 1942, and by Laval, not Roosevelt. Secondly, neither the Allied intervention in North Africa nor any decision Roosevelt made immediately prior to or during the Casablanca Conference changed the U.S. position with regard to the Free French, who were not to be accorded diplomatic recognition by Washington until October 1944. As I have shown, the Allied military breakthrough in North Africa paradoxically resulted in the reconstituting of a pro-Vichy administration in Morocco and Algeria. At the time *Casablanca* was playing in movie theaters across the

U.S., men like Victor Laszlo were hunted down by the police of Darlan and Giraud, the French High Commissioners kept in power by Roosevelt. The White House and State Department were to continue to frustrate the Free French, despite the pressure from "Jews and Communists," as Roosevelt's chief of staff characteristically put it.

## 2. A political function of *Casablanca* in 1942-1943

*Casablanca* is pro-Free French and anti-Vichy. The film was obviously designed to pattern in the mind of the viewer a totally positive picture of the Free French as America's natural ally in the fight against the Nazis and as embodying the spirit of democracy, of resistance, and the true France. Similarly the film was designed to pattern a negative image of Vichy as unprincipled and as serving the interests of Nazi Germany.

It is possible that the film was *intended* to correct unfavorable American attitudes toward the Free French, to influence policy-makers, or to strengthen the hand of Roosevelt's critics who reproached the State Department for basing policy decisions on assessments of national self-interest rather than moral principle. In any event, and whatever the motivations of the producer, director, scriptwriters and actors may have been, there is every reason to believe that the film led millions of American movie-goers to experience a strong political and emotional identification with the Free French in 1942-1943.

When *Casablanca* first played in theaters across the United States, policies actually being implemented under Allied auspices in French North Africa were pro-Vichy and anti-Free French. The reader is reminded for example that the Free French, who had been systematically excluded from Operation TORCH, were also bypassed in the establishment of a French administration in North Africa. The first French High Commissioner appointed under U.S. auspices was Darlan, formerly Vichy premier and designated successor to Pétain. Darlan reconstituted a Vichy regime in North Africa. After his assassination in December 1942, the U.S. acknowledged Giraud as the new French High Commissioner. Giraud unleashed a wave of anti-Free French terror, and in a press conference of February 1943, in response to criticism, Roosevelt justified U.S. backing of the Giraud administration in North Africa. As already suggested, men like Victor Laszlo were being arrested by the police of the administrators the U.S. supported in North Africa.

Roosevelt's choice to have *Casablanca* shown on December 31, 1942 was at least in part a private joke, savored by those few guests at the New Year's Eve party who knew that the president was secretly arranging to depart for

Casablanca (Sherwood 1948: 665). But the White House screening of *Casablanca* may have been politically significant as well. Greenberg's suggestion has already been discussed and rejected. Another hypothesis concerning the political significance of this event would be useful.

In a review that appeared in *The New Republic*, one of the major organs of liberal criticism of the Roosevelt administration's French and North African policies, no mention whatsoever is made of the portrayal of the Free French in *Casablanca* (Farber 1942: 793-794). Max Lerner, who ardently criticized Roosevelt for pursuing a "blind and illiberal" foreign policy (1945: 205), referred to *Casablanca* in 1943 without even mentioning its political significance (Lerner 1945: 28). Bosley Crowther, in a *New York Times* review, did say of the film that "it certainly won't make Vichy happy – but that's just another point for it" (1942: 27). However that does not suggest that anyone felt in any way challenged by the film. In other words, *Casablanca* was not perceived as politically controversial.

The film was advertised in *The New York Times* with such slogans as "Nothing could be more timely" and "As exciting as the landing at Casablanca!" (22 November 1942: section VIII, 4; 25 November 1942: 19). The reader is reminded that the Allied landings began on November 8, 1942, and that *Casablanca* opened at the Hollywood Theater in New York on November 26. It was originally announced for release in June 1943 but the "Warners sales department rushed the film into New York [...] in time for a Thanksgiving opening" (Haver 1976: 27). The Casablanca Conference ended on January 24, 1943 and was publicized immediately after Roosevelt's return. The film's general release occurred on January 23, and by mid-February 1943, *Casablanca* was being shown at 200 theaters across the U.S.

# Conclusion

Appearing in the wake of the Allied landings, the film seemed to explain why those landings were made and thereby served to disseminate, within a broad American public, a sense that the values embodied by Victor Laszlo and adopted by Rick and Renault at the end were the values the Allies brought with them to North Africa. Movie-goers uninformed about or uninterested in the 'deal with Darlan' probably left screenings of the film with a feeling that current U.S. involvement in such places as Casablanca must have been in complete harmony with the attitudes presented as admirable in the film.

Paradoxically then, in conferring unlimited prestige to the Free French and militant anti-fascism, *Casablanca* contributed to a blurring of public awareness of the essentially anti-Free French orientation of U.S. policy and of American support for Vichy leaders in North Africa. One small but significant piece of evidence I have found in support of this hypothesis is a sentence Howard Barnes wrote in his review of *Casablanca* in the *New York Tribune* in November 1942: "[*Casablanca*] exposes the intrigue, political shilly-shally and anti-Fascist resentment which must have been the background for the present Allied offensive in Northwest Africa" (Koch 1973: 201-203).

*Casablanca* captured the heart of the American public – even standing room was sold out when it played at the Hollywood Theater in New York, and it was to win three Academy Awards (Best Picture, Best Directing and Best Screenplay). The film's pro-Free French orientation undoubtedly left its mark on audiences, and precisely because it 'got through' to the public in that respect, it probably led millions of movie-goers to assume that Operation TORCH and the Casablanca Conference were fulfillments of the democratic values celebrated in the '*Marseillaise*' scene, in Laszlo's idealism, in Renault's unexpected conversion and in Rick's return to the fight. One cannot help but wonder why politically informed commentators – such as Max Lerner – were apparently uninterested in drawing on the film's immense popularity as an additional weapon in their critique of Roosevelt's illiberal French policies, and whether it would have made any difference if they had. One also wonders whether Roosevelt was so politically cunning that he not only understood the unintentionally misleading impact of the film, but also deliberately reinforced that impact by having *Casablanca* shown at the White House, as if to confirm that *Casablanca* was an endorsement of his policies.

# Chronological Overview

|  | **U.S. FOREIGN POLICY** | *CASABLANCA* |
|---|---|---|
| **Summer 1940** | The newly constituted Vichy regime is accorded diplomatic recognition by the U.S. American liberals protest. De Gaulle establishes the Free French organization in London. French Equatorial Africa (Brazzaville) rallies to the Free French in late August. | "Everybody Comes to Rick's," a three-act play, is written by Murray Burnett and Joan Alison. |
| **January 1941** | U.S. representation at Vichy elevated to ambassadorial level. | |
| **May 1941** | De Gaulle sends René Pleven to Washington, to organize support for the Free French. In July, Pleven is shocked by negative image of the Free French in the U.S. | |
| **December 1941** | U.S. enters the war after Japanese attack on Pearl Harbor. Incident at Saint Pierre and Miquelon Islands off the Newfoundland shore, governed by a pro-Vichy admiral; the inhabitants were apparently pro-Free French. Against specific instructions from Washington, de Gaulle had a Free French naval chief who was in the area with corvettes and a submarine land on the islands and claim them for the Free French. Secretary Hull lashes out against "so-called Free French." | Hall Wallace of Warner Brothers buys the screen rights for "Everybody Comes to Rick's," never produced as a play. Michael Curtiz is to direct; Philip and Julius Epstein are to write the screenplay. |
| **January 1942** | De Gaulle appeals to State Department for moral support in the form of diplomatic recognition, to no avail. | |

| | | |
|---|---|---|
| **Late March 1942** | | First draft of the Epsteins' screenplay is completed. Howard Koch is to revise it. |
| **April 1942** | Laval is imposed as head of Vichy government. Ambassador Leahy is recalled by Roosevelt, but diplomatic relations are not broken. | |
| **25 May 1942** | | Shooting of *Casablanca* begins. |
| **13 July 1942 8 November 1942 and thereafter** | *La France Libre* is renamed *La France Combattante* by de Gaulle. Operation TORCH: Allied landings at Casablanca, Algiers and Oran. Deal with Darlan, recognized as French High Commissioner of North Africa. A Vichy administration is reconstituted in North Africa, under American auspices. The Free French – excluded from Operation TORCH – are bypassed in the establishment of North African administration. Delegates of major resistance movements declare to Allied governments that the Free French have full backing of the French Resistance and the French people. Laval is forced by the Germans to sever diplomatic ties with the U.S. | |
| **Thanksgiving 1942** | | *Casablanca* opens at the Hollywood Theater in New York. 31,000 paid admissions in the first week alone. |

| | | |
|---|---|---|
| **24 December 1942** | Darlan is assassinated. The pro-Vichy Imperial Council appoints Giraud as Darlan's successor. A wave of anti-Free French terror is unleashed in the wake of the assassination. | |
| **31 December 1942** | Roosevelt has *Casablanca* shown at the White House. | |
| **14-24 January 1943** | Casablanca Conference held in secret. Roosevelt, Churchill, Giraud and de Gaulle confer. The Conference is publicized upon Roosevelt's return to the U.S. | |
| **February 1943** | | *Casablanca* is shown at 200 theaters across the U.S. |
| **March 1944** | | *Casablanca* wins three Academy Awards (Best Picture, Screenplay and Directing) |
| **23 October 1944** | Roosevelt finally accords diplomatic recognition to de Gaulle, two months after the liberation of Paris. | |

## References

Aandahl, F., Franklin, W. M. and Slany, W. (eds) (1968). *Foreign Relations of the United States, The Conferences at Washington, 1941-1942, and Casablanca, 1943*. Washington: U.S. Government Printing Office.

Aron, Robert (1954). *Histoire de Vichy*. Paris: Fayard.

Benchley, Nathaniel (1975). "Here's Looking at You, Kid," *The Atlantic Monthly*, no. 235, February, pp. 39-48, 81-84.

Corliss, Richard (1973). "*Casablanca*. An Analysis of the Film," in H. Koch, *Casablanca: Script and Legend*, pp. 186-187.

Crowther, Bosley (1942). *New York Times*, 27 November, p. 27.

Day, Barry (1974). "The Cult Movies: *Casablanca*," *Films and Filming*, vol. 20, no. 11, August, pp. 20-24.

De Gaulle, Charles (1954). *Mémoires de guerre*. Paris: Plon.

Farber, Manny (1942). "The Warner Boys in Africa," *The New Republic*, no. 107, 14 December, pp. 793-794.

Funk, Arthur Layton (1959). *Charles de Gaulle – The Crucial Years, 1943-1944*. Norman: University of Oklahoma Press.

Funk, Arthur Layton (1974). *The Politics of TORCH – The Allied Landings and Algiers Putch*. University Press of Kansas.

Greenberg, Harvey (1975). "*Casablanca* – If It's So Schmaltzy, Why Am I Weeping?," in *The Movies on Your Mind. Film Classics on the Couch, from Fellini to Frankenstein*. New York: Saturday Review Press/Dutton, pp. 79-105.

Haver, Roland (1976). "Finally the truth about *Casablanca*," *American Film*, June, vol. 1, no. 8, pp. 10-16.

Koch, Howard (1973). *Casablanca: Script and Legend*. Woodstock, New York: Overlook Press.

Langer, William L. (1947). *Our Vichy Gamble*. New York: Knopf.

Langer, William L. and Gleason, S. Everett (1953). *The Undeclared War 1940-1941*. New York: Harper.

Leahy, W. D. (1950). *I Was There*. London: Gollancz.

Lerner, Max (1945). "Confessions of a Movie Addict" [1943] and "The Enigma of FDR" [1944] in *Public Journal. Marginal Notes on Wartime America*. New York, Viking.

*New Republic* (1942). Unsigned articles appearing in the following issues: 5 January: 3; 9 February: 189; 8 June: 785; 23 November: 659; 30 November: 699; 7 December: 730.

*New York Times* (1942). Advertisements appearing on 22 November: section VIII, 4; 25 November: 19.

Roosevelt, Franklin D. (1972). *FDR: Complete Presidential Press Conferences*. New York: Da Capo.

Sherwood, Robert E. (1948). *Roosevelt and Hopkins: An Intimate History*. New York: Harper.

Smith, R. Harris (1972). *OSS*. Berkeley: University of California Press.

2

# Bogart's Nod in the *'Marseillaise'* Scene: A Physical Gesture in *Casablanca*

When the stage has been properly set, the simplest physical gesture can be charged with meaning in a film. Bogart's nod in the *'Marseillaise'* scene in *Casablanca* stands out as perhaps the most striking example of this important resource in cinematic storytelling, and one particularly deserving of a closer look.

## The situation

Rick (Humphrey Bogart) and Victor Laszlo (Paul Henreid) are upstairs in Rick's office, with Laszlo offering to buy the letters of transit that would enable him and his wife, Ilsa, to escape from Casablanca. Rick refuses, and in reply to Laszlo's question as to why, Rick tells him to ask his wife. They then hear German officers singing '*Die Wacht am Rhein*' in the main room below. Rick and Laszlo go out on the balcony and look down at the Germans singing. Renault is watching from the bar, his eyebrow raised. Laszlo, listening tight-lipped, finally walks down the steps and goes decisively over to the band, telling them: "Play the '*Marseillaise*'! Play it!" The band members look down, then up toward Rick, who nods to them. Having obtained Rick's approval, the band then begins to play the '*Marseillaise*,' and one of the most electrifying scenes in film history unfolds.

## Earlier nods in the film

On meeting Rick for the first time, we observe two things he does before we actually see his face: 1) approving a customer credit slip handed to him by an employee and on which he writes "OK Rick," thereby identifying him for us as the owner of the café and defining him as the man in charge, the one the people working at the café go to when approval is needed; and 2) playing chess with himself, suggesting an enjoyment of strategy, intellectual challenge and self-sufficiency (in a positive sense). Soon after we see Rick's face and the intensity of his involvement in the game, he looks up and sees another of his employees, Abdul, on guard at the entrance to the room and asking with a glance whether the couple standing in the doorway may be admitted. Rick nods 'yes.' After they enter, another person appears in the doorway and again Abdul, now with a sneer on his face, looks to Rick for a signal. This time Rick nods 'no,' and when the man protests, Rick walks over and – as Ugarte (played by Peter Lorre) slips in – Rick confirms that the guest is unwelcome in this part of the café and lucky that his money is good at the bar. In the ensuing dialogue between Rick and Ugarte, we learn to our delight that the man Rick had excluded was a representative of the Deutschebank.

Nodding 'yes' or 'no' to an employee looking to him for a signal is one of the first things Rick does in this film, and Bogart's nod in the '*Marseillaise*' scene is therefore grounded in our experience of Rick from the very start. Though the relation of the earlier to the later nods is hardly one of set-up to pay-off, the earlier nods nevertheless help to prepare us for the later one, by defining Rick as the one who calls the shots.

## The significance of the nod in the *'Marseillaise'* scene

### 1 Marking a new stage in Rick's development

Rick's overall evolution, including what we know of his past and can foresee of his future, can be divided into three periods:

- an early idealistic period, when – as both Renault and Victor Laszlo point out – Rick ran guns to the Ethiopians and fought on the Loyalist side in the Spanish civil war, earning himself a place of honor on the Nazis' blacklist;
- a central period, filling most of the present time-frame of the film, characterized largely by a cynical and selfish neutrality, as expressed by the line spoken twice by Rick – "I stick my neck out for nobody"; yet even here, there are flashes of profound integrity, as when Rick tells Ferrari (Sidney Greenstreet) that he doesn't buy or sell human beings; presumably, Rick's fall into cynicism was triggered by what he experienced as a betrayal at the Paris railroad station when he received Ilsa's farewell note;
- a final period, in which Rick overcomes his selfish and self-pitying stance and returns to the fight against oppression.

In the dialogue between Rick and Victor Laszlo just before the *'Marseillaise'* scene, we are reminded that Rick is at present squarely rooted in his neutrality stance, telling Laszlo for example: "I'm not interested in politics. The problems of the world are not in my department. I'm a saloon keeper."

Yet moments later, when the boundaries are clearly drawn between resistance and oppression, and the possibility of delivering Victor Laszlo's liberating response to the German song is dependent on a choice that only Rick can make, the saloon keeper risks everything and nods 'yes.' As one commentator wrote (Greenberg 1975: 96):

> The die is cast. At Rick's behest, a line has been drawn between good and evil in a place where moral ambiguity, also at Rick's behest, has been the order of the day.

The Rick the band members knew was the one who had stood by passively as Ugarte was arrested, and who consistently put the interests of the café above politics. This is why, when confronted with Laszlo's command to play the '*Marseillaise*' in defiance of the Germans, the band could not take it for granted that Rick would allow them to comply.

If any moment in this film might be called a *point of no return*, this is it. Here, for the first time, in nodding his approval, Rick takes a stand against the representatives of the Third Reich, and places himself on the side of resistance.

All of this is in the nod, which marks Rick's transition from neutrality to commitment. It is here that the ground is broken for future moves Rick will undertake, such as devising and carrying out a plan for getting Victor and Ilsa out of Casablanca, ultimately shooting Major Strasser in the process, and going off to join the Free French in Brazzaville along with Captain Renault, who – inspired by Rick – undergoes his own parallel conversion from neutrality to commitment. Renault's line "Round up the usual suspects" in the final airport scene plays the same point-of-no-return role in his development as the nod does for Rick in the '*Marseillaise*' scene.

## 2 Status and power

Paul Henreid did not want the part of Victor Laszlo when he was first assigned the role as a contract player at Warner Brothers. His initial response was that the script was terrible and he didn't "want to be the second lover in a film, second to Humphrey Bogart!" But he allowed himself to be talked into the role, provided among other things that he get Ilsa at the end, as befits a leading man (Henried 1984: 120-121). In other words, from the very start, he experienced a fundamental rivalry with respect to Humphrey Bogart's Rick.

This feeling of rivalry was dramatically reactivated when Henreid learned whom the band members were to look at before beginning to play the '*Marseillaise*,' as the following passage in Henreid's autobiography makes abundantly clear:

> I am described by the Germans as a great leader of the masses, a man who can command obedience. That's the reason the Germans don't want me to leave Casablanca, and it's also the plot hinge. There's a scene in Rick's Café, one of the high points, when I order the band to play '*La Marseillaise*' to counter the Germans' singing '*Die Wacht am Rhein*,' a very patriotic military

song. The musicians look away, then back to me before they start playing, and I conduct them, singing myself.

After the rehearsal, I asked Curtiz, "What the hell is going on? Why do they look away and then back at me?"

"Oh, yes," Curtiz said, "That – I told them to look at Bogie. I'll have a cut of Bogie nodding, giving them the order to play."

"But why?" I asked, confused.

"Because in the picture Bogie pays their salary, and they don't want to do anything that could get them fired."

"But for heaven's sake," I protested, "I'm supposed to be a leader of the masses, and here I have a stinking little band, and I can't get them to do what I want!"

Curtiz laughed. "Oh, it'll be all right. It will establish that Bogie is on your side" (Henried 1984: 122).

So much for the relative status of Laszlo and Rick in this scene, as experienced from Paul Henreid's perspective, as well as the manner in which Curtiz pacified Henreid.

But there is another hierarchical relationship in play here as well: namely that involving Curtiz and Bogart, the latter being just as unaware as Henreid had been as to exactly what happens when Laszlo orders the band to play. And in this connection, it is ironic that the very shot that invests Rick with so much power in the scene was directed in such a way as to make Bogart feel as powerless as possible (Benchley 1975: 44):

One day, when Bogart appeared for shooting, Curtiz told him, 'You've got an easy day today. Go on that balcony, look down and to the right, and nod. Then you can go home.' 'What am I nodding at?' Bogart asked. 'What's my attitude?' 'Don't ask so many questions!' Curtiz replied. 'Get up there and nod and then go home!' Bogart did as he was told, and didn't realize until long afterward that that nod had triggered the famous '*Marseillaise*' scene, where Henreid leads the nightclub orchestra in drowning out some Germans who'd been singing '*Die Wacht am Rhein*.' It's a scene that, even after thirty years, prickles the scalp and closes the throat, and for all Bogart knew he was nodding at a passing dog.

There was no artistic justification whatsoever for holding back from Humphrey Bogart the shred of information he requested. In not letting him in on the meaning of the nod and instead insisting on blind obedience, Curtiz indulged in an arbitrary exercise of power at the expense of an actor who merely wanted to understand what was happening.

## References and other works consulted

Benchley, Nathaniel (1975). "Here's looking at you, kid," *Atlantic Monthly*, February, pp. 39-48, 81-84.

Day, Barry (1974). "The Cult Movies: *Casablanca*," *Films and Filming*, vol. 20, no. 11, August 1974, pp. 20-24.

Greenberg, Harvey R. (1975). "*Casablanca*. If It's So Schmaltzy, Why Am I Weeping?," in *The Movies on Your Mind. Film Classics on the Couch, from Fellini to Frankenstein*. New York: Saturday Review Press/Dutton, pp. 79-105.

Harmetz, Aljean (1992). *Round Up the Usual Suspects: The Making of Casablanca*. New York: Hyperion.

Haver, Roland (1976). "Finally, the Truth About *Casablanca*." *American Film*, June 1976, vol. 1, no. 8, pp. 11-16.

Henreid, Paul and Fast, J. (1984). *Ladies' Man. An Autobiography*. New York: St. Martin's Press.

Koch, Howard (1992). *Casablanca: Script and Legend*. 50th Anniversary Edition. London: Aurum Press.

Lebo, Harlan (1992). *Casablanca: Behind the Scenes*. New York: Simon & Schuster.

McArthur, Colin (1992). *The Casablanca File*. London: Half Brick Images.

Miller, Frank (1992). *Casablanca: As Time Goes By*. London: Virgin Books.

Raskin, Richard (1990). "*Casablanca* and U.S. Foreign Policy," *Film History*, vol. 4, no. 2, pp. 153-164.

Siegel, Jeff (1992). *The Casablanca Companion*. Dallas: Taylor Publishing Co.

# 3
# A Note on a Wartime Function of the Bogart Image

In an article entitled "Humphrey Bogart – Epitaph for a Tough Guy" (1978: 138), Alistair Cooke suggested that Bogart's immense popularity was "due in the main to the rise of Hitler." Noting that Bogart graduated from gangster parts "just when parliamentary Europe was caving in to gangsters on a grand scale, Cooke wrote (141):

> There was nothing now to offend the most respectable suburban patriot in a hero who used the gangster's means to achieve our ends. And this character was suddenly very precious in the age of violence, for it satisfied

a quiet, desperate need of the engulfed ordinary citizen. When Hitler was acting out a script more brutal and obscene than anything dreamed of by Chicago's North side or the Warner Brothers, Bogart was the only possible antagonist likely to outwit him and survive. What was needed was no knight of the boudoir, no Ronald Coleman or Leslie Howard (whose movie careers compensatingly slumped) but a conniver as subtle as Goebbels. Bogart was the very tough gent required, a murderously bland neutral who we knew, if the Germans didn't, would in the end be on our side.

In the context of *Casablanca*, one scene stands out as having been tailor-made to fulfill the psychological function Cooke attributed to the Bogart image: the scene in which Rick and Major Strasser – hero and villain – first encounter one another. The setting is a table at the Café Américain, and Captain Renault as well as a subordinate of Major Strasser's – a Herr Heinz – are also present. Throughout this encounter, Rick is portrayed as neither submissive, nor afraid, nor at a loss in answering the Nazi's questions. In fact, Rick answers with an intriguing mixture of politeness and flippancy which enables him to maintain the upper hand.

> Strasser: Are you one of those people who cannot imagine the Germans in their beloved Paris?
> Rick: It's not particularly *my* beloved Paris.
> Heinz: Can you imagine us in London?
> Rick: When you get there, ask me.
> Renault: Oh! Diplomatist!
> Strasser: How about New York?
> Rick: Well, there are certain sections of New York, Major, that I wouldn't advise you to try to invade.

Describing a subsequent portion of this scene, Richard Corliss wrote (1973: 192):

> We know that Rick ran guns to Ethiopia in 1935, and fought for the Loyalists in 1936 [...]. But when Strasser tries to intimidate Rick by reading him a Nazi-researched dossier of these adventures, Rick simply glances at the German's little black book and, with a bland expression that perfectly reveals his contempt for the obviousness of Strasser's methods, asks, "Are my eyes really brown?" This blending of the modest and the arrogant, the

casual and the ballsy, stamps Rick as a man of courage as indelibly as will his climactic heroism.

From the Nazi point of view, Americans were characterized by "democratic degeneracy," and were consequently soft and spineless. Furthermore, there is some evidence that anxieties did in fact exist on the home front as to whether or not the American male was sufficiently tough to function effectively against a formidable enemy. In a sermon given at a Manhattan synagogue some two weeks after the Allied landings in North Africa, a Rabbi stated: "It becomes evident that our boys, reared in the fresh air of democracy, far from being 'soft and coddled,' are soldiers, sailors and airmen as tough as any and as good as the best" (*New York Times* 22 November 1942: 28). Even more explicit indications that such anxieties had existed can be found in a *New York Times* article on the U.S. troops in Algeria and Morocco: "They're Tough and Fighting Mad" (Kluckholm 1942: 38). The heading of this article read: "A correspondent with our soldiers in Africa reports that we at home need have no fear that they are too soft for the job they must do." And in the body of his article, Kluckholm wrote: "the boys from America have not grown soft, as many feared they would … these men are prepared to stand up to anything." Such statements are ample evidence that the American public needed reassurance about the toughness of its fighting men.

Both the sermon and the article just quoted date from the time *Casablanca* first opened in a New York theatre. From this perspective, it is reasonable to suggest that *Casablanca* contributed to the public's confidence in the American male, embodied by Humphrey Bogart, as more than adequately equipped – both mentally and physically – to stand up to any threat and to emerge as the victor in any confrontation.

# References

Cooke, Alistair (1977). *Six Men*. Hammondsworth: Penguin.
Corliss, Richard (1973). "*Casablanca*: An analysis of the film," in Howard Koch (1973), *Casablanca: Script and Legend*. Woodstock. New York: Overlook Press, pp. 183-198.
Kluckholm, Frank L (1942). "They're Tough – and Fighting Mad," *The New York Times*, 29 November, Magazine Section, pp. 1, 38.
*The New York Times* (1942). "Victory Themes Inspire Sermons." 22 November, p. 28.

# 4

# Two 'Marseillaise' scenes: From Michael Curtiz's *Casablanca* (1943) to Ziad Doueiri's *West Beirut* (1998)

*In Ziad Doueiri's* West Beirut, *high school pupils in Lebanon are led in the singing of the* 'Marseillaise.'

## Introduction

The '*Marseillaise*' scene in *Casablanca* has moved successive generations of movie-goers to tears since 1943. Even Murray Burnett, the man who first conceived of the scene as part of his never-to-be-produced stage play *Everybody Comes to Rick's*, wept as he scripted the duel of national songs: "I cried when I wrote it. I literally cried when I wrote it. Tears, actual tears. I was writing and I cried. It was that powerful to me. And it was that powerful in the film" (Burnett 1992).

45

In earlier studies, I tried to show how this scene helped to shape the attitudes of U.S. audiences toward the Free French (Raskin 1982/1990), as well as looking closely at the role of Bogart's nod in the scene (Raskin 2002). In the present study, it is in relation to French colonialism that I want to focus on this scene and on the film more generally. And I would like to suggest that Ziad Doueiri's '*Marseillaise*' scene in *West Beirut* (1998) might be considered a reply to its counterpart in *Casablanca*.

The critical light in which *Casablanca* will be discussed in these pages – specifically in connection with French colonialism – is not meant to detract one iota from anyone's love and appreciation of the film in all other respects.

## *Casablanca* and colonialism

In describing her own experience of the '*Marseillaise*' scene in *Casablanca*, Judith Mahoney Pasternak wrote (2000):

> The 'Marseillaise' comes to its stirring conclusion, and with tears in their eyes the patriots in the bar cry out, "Vive la France!"

> Watching, tears in my own eyes, I always murmur along, "Vive la France." It took 40 years for me to notice that they're shouting "Vive la France!" *on African soil.*

This important point has been missed by many commentators over the years.

As has been shown elsewhere (Raskin 1982/1990), much of the storytelling in *Casablanca* is designed to elevate the Resistance and the Free French in the eyes of the viewer, at a time when U.S. policy was utterly unaccommodating toward representatives of these movements. And as numerous commentators have pointed out, the film casts in a positive light the transition from neutrality to engagement. But while serving those laudable purposes, the storytelling in *Casablanca* also represses the reality that "French Morocco" as a colonialist construct involved for an indigenous people: a) subjection to French rule and exploitation; b) the frustration of their own sense of nationhood; and c) the overshadowing of their own Arabian-Berber culture by another.

The film defines the city of Casablanca as "French soil" in an unequivocally positive way, meaning that as such, it is – at least in principle – free from

German authority. Victor Laszlo, the most politically admirable character in the film, does this when first confronted by Major Strasser at Rick's:

STRASSER
[…] you are a subject of the German Reich!

LASZLO
I've never accepted that privilege, and I'm
here now on French soil.

and then again at the Prefect's office:

LASZLO
You won't dare to interfere with me here.
This is still Unoccupied France.

And what a curious Casablanca we have in this film, in which not a word of Arabic is heard, though we are treated to smatterings of Italian, French, Spanish, German and even a bit of Russian. And there is only one character with an Arabic name in this film: Abdul, the doorman at Rick's.

Is it unfair to expect a greater recognition of the colonial realities in a film made in 1942? Not if one considers the following facts.

As early as 1924-1925, the Berber leader Abd al-Karim Al-Khattabi led "a resistance movement against French and Spanish colonial rule in North Africa," and curiously, the Spanish and French forces fighting against him were commanded by none other than Francisco Franco and Marshal Henri Philippe Pétain, respectively (Kechichian 2011).

On August 14, 1941, Franklin D. Roosevelt and Winston Churchill issued an important statement, the third provision of which commits the signatories to "respect the right of all peoples to choose the form of government under which they will live; and they wish to see sovereign rights and self government restored to those who have been forcibly deprived of them" (Atlantic Charter 1941).

This provision would soon be cited by groups calling for Moroccan independence from French rule, such as the Istiqlal (Independence) Party, officially established in 1944. Furthermore, Roosevelt expressed his own views on the necessity of Moroccan independence at the Casablanca Conference held in January 1943, when – at about the time of *Casablanca*'s general release – the following meeting took place (Copson 2002):

> On the evening of January 22, the president [Roosevelt] invited Churchill and Morocco's Sultan Sidi Muhammad to dinner. [...] In deference to the sultan's Islamic faith, Roosevelt served no alcohol, much to Churchill's chagrin. The prime minister's dismay increased when Roosevelt steered the conversation toward colonialism, a particular sore point between the president and Churchill, who wanted to maintain Britain's colonies after the war. Morocco had been a French protectorate since 1912, and Roosevelt sketched out for the sultan the role that America could play in post-colonial Morocco. Churchill knew that Roosevelt's views on France's colonies applied to Britain's as well, and the prime minister moved uneasily in his chair until the conversation changed to another subject.

Those who might argue that the wartime situation made it inappropriate even to consider the issue of colonialism in North Africa, would be at odds with the views held by Roosevelt himself at the time *Casablanca* was first shown in movie theaters all across the United States.

Before returning to the '*Marseillaise*' scenes in the two films, I would like to cite one of Conor Cruise O'Brien's comments on Albert Camus' allegorical novel, *La Peste/The Plague* (1947). The action in this novel takes place in the Algerian city of Oran, where a plague sets in and is fought, against all odds, by teams of medical workers. To some degree at least, the characters who fight against the plague – the doctor Rieux and other key figures in the "*équipes sanitaires*" such as Tarrou and Grand – symbolize French Resistance groups in their struggle against the Nazis. O'Brien incisively wrote (1970: 47-48):

> The difficulty derives I believe from the whole nature of Camus' relation to the German occupiers on the one hand and to the Arabs of Algeria on the other. It comes natural to him, from his early background and education, to think of Oran as a French town and of its relation to the plague as that of a French town to the Occupation. But just below the surface of his consciousness, as with all other Europeans in Africa, there must have lurked the possibility of another way of looking at things – an extremely distasteful one. There were Arabs for whom 'French Algeria' was a fiction quite as repugnant as Hitler's new European order was for Camus and his friends. For such Arabs, the French were in Algeria in virtue of the same right by which the Germans were in France: the right of conquest. The fact that the conquest had lasted considerably longer in Algeria than it was to last in France changed nothing in the essential resemblance of the relations between conqueror and conquered. From this point of view, Rieux,

Tarrou and Grand were not devoted fighters against the plague: they were the plague itself.

The same point could be made regarding *Casablanca*: that from the point of view of those Moroccans who wished to see an end to the colonial occupation of their country, the glorification of France in the singing of the '*Marseillaise*' might be viewed more as an affront to freedom than as a true expression of it.

In this respect, the '*Marseillaise*' scene in *Casablanca* is an unfinished situation since it leaves unexpressed and unacknowledged an important aspect of the realities in play. Those very realities, kept from surfacing in *Casablanca*, are given full expression in a corresponding scene in Ziad Doueiri's *West Beirut* (1998).

## The '*Marseillaise*' scene in *West Beirut*

As this film begins, the setting is the schoolyard of a French *lycée* in Beirut on April 13, 1975, and after an initial scene in which the pupils observe a dogfight of two military jets in the sky overhead, resulting in the explosion of one of the planes, the children are called to order and told to line up for assembly.

The headmistress, Mme Vieillard, walks toward the flagpole. Tarek, a 15-year-old boy, observes her then suddenly puts his books on top of his friend Omar's and rushes off without saying where he is going. Mme Vieillard arrives at the flagpole and begins to lead in the singing of the '*Marseillaise*.'

Tarek ascends a staircase inside the school building, enters a room, and emerges from it again a moment later carrying a megaphone. He then walks quickly along a balcony, smiling. In the courtyard below, the children continue singing the '*Marseillaise*.' Tarek, now standing on a balcony overlooking the schoolyard, raises the megaphone to his mouth and begins to sing the Lebanese national anthem. Both songs can now be heard. Children who had been facing Mme Vieillard and singing the '*Marseillaise*' now turn to face Tarek. There is a moment of confusion as Mme Vieillard tries to understand what is happening. The other children now join in Tarek's singing of the Lebanese national anthem. Mme Vieillard calls out to Tarek and orders him to "come down from there." Ignoring her protests, Tarek and his schoolmates finish their singing and Tarek waves the victory sign to his enthralled and cheering classmates below. Omar can barely contain his admiration for

Tarek. As the cheering continues, Mme Vieillard makes her way through the crowd, heading for an entrance to the building

1
2
3
4
5
6

In the scene that follows and that takes place inside the classroom, Tarek has been called up to the blackboard to answer for his rebellious behavior, but responds to Mme Vieillard's orders and questions in a way that indirectly mocks her and the French culture she represents. He is reprimanded and thrown out of the classroom. While Tarek stands in the corridor and looks through a window, Mme Vieillard says to the boy's classmates (in French):

Mme VIEILLARD
We must not forget that France created your country. France gave you your borders. We taught you peace. We prepared your civilization and your constitution. Know that education, French education in particular, is the only means for freeing you from your primitive customs ...

While looking down at the street, Tarek notices masked gunmen taking up positions along the sidewalk, waiting in ambush for a bus carrying Palestinians on whom they will soon open fire – an event marking the start of the civil war that was to devastate Lebanon for the next fifteen years.

# Ziad Doueiri's own comments on the scene (2004)

RR. *West Beirut* has been described as 90% autobiographical. Does that apply to the '*Marseillaise*' scene? Did you actually do what Tarek does in this scene?

ZD. No, actually it's probably the most fictional scene in the film. Because [in the French *lycée*] we were never asked to do that. The school never performed this singing period. The reason we did it was because for me, dramatically it worked. For several reasons, which I'll explain in a moment. And also because it's symbolic. It shows that the Lebanese students at that time, in this particular school, had their own identity which they wanted to display in front of French authority. So it was a way to say that we are ready to rebel against you, basically.

But mainly the reason I did that scene ... You know, in feature films, in drama, you can say whatever you want. You're not bound by any responsibility except to make a film that works. I wanted to show that the main character, Tarek, is a rebel. He does not like authority, period, whatever it is. And I thought that that scene was a good manipulative way for me to achieve that.

Now, I got a lot of hassle for that scene when the film was shown here. There are a lot of pro-French people, people who think very highly of the French and who are francophone, who travel to France for all of their vacations. Mainly the *bourgeoisie*. They really protested. They said: "How can you do that? We never did that!" They took it literally. They could not separate reality from fiction. And I kept on saying: "Well you know, this is just a fictional thing." They were pretty upset. Also some of the French diplomats who were invited from the embassy were more civilized and diplomatic about it, but they said: "You know, we never taught you this." The current principal of the Lycée Français, the scene where this is supposed to happen, – he was not the principal when I was a teenager – he also said "I don't think that's part of our agenda at our school ... to teach any form of nationalism or patriotism." I had to explain to him again that this was just an idea, to dramatically help the scene and help this character, whose rebelliousness I wanted to show. I said that if it had been an American setting in Lebanon, I would have had him sing against the American national anthem.

So that's basically what it was. But I still got a lot of shit for it. [*Laughter.*]

RR. There is an obvious comparison to be made with the '*Marseillaise*' scene in *Casablanca*. Did that play any role at all for you, in imagining your own '*Marseillaise*' scene?

ZD. No. Not at all.

## Conclusion

Though not intended as such, the '*Marseillaise*' scene in *West Beirut* – involving as it does a duel of national anthems – can be understood as a fitting reply to the corresponding scene in *Casablanca*, finally drawing into open view an implicit colonial element in that scene that generations of Western movie-goers and commentators have missed, presumably as a result of a cultural blind spot which even today is difficult to recognize.

The *Casablanca* scene will always remain a cinematic masterpiece, and will continue to thrill audiences around the world. But it is also a record of an outlook that focuses on one occupation while repressing all awareness or acknowledgement of another.

## References

Anon (2006). "The Notes of the Rif Revolt," 22 March. http://www.agraw.com/2006/03/notes-rif-revolt/ Accessed 24 April 2017.

Atlantic Charter (1941). Joint statement issued by Franklin D. Roosevelt and Winston Churchill on 14 August 1941. http://web.ics.purdue.edu/~wggray/Teaching/His300/Handouts/Atlantic-Charter.pdf Accessed 22 April 2017.

Burnett, Murray (1992). Interviewed in Scott Benson's *You Must Remember This: A Tribute to 'Casablanca'*.

Camus, Albert (1947). *La Peste*. Paris: Gallimard.

Curtiz, Michael (1943). *Casablanca*. Warner Brothers: U.S.A.

Copson, Raymond W. (2002). "Summit at Casablanca," *American History*, vol. 37, no. 1, April. http://www.historynet.com/franklin-d-roosevelt Accessed 22 April 2017.

Doueiri, Ziad (1998). *West Beirut*. 3B Productions: France et al.

Doueri, Ziad (2004). Interviewed by Richard Raskin on 14 August.

Kechichian, Joseph A. (2011). "Father of guerilla warfare," *Gulf News*, 15 April. http://gulfnews.com/news/mena/father-of-guerrilla-warfare-1.790991 Accessed 24 April 2017.

O'Brien, Conor Cruise (1970). *Camus*. London: Fontana.

Pasternak, Judisth Mahoney (2000). "The Shifting Sands of Righteousness," *Nonviolent Activist, The Magazine of the War Resisters League*, May-June. No longer available on the magazine's website.

Raskin, Richard (1982/1990). "*Casablanca* and U.S. Foreign Policy," first published in *The Functional Analysis of Art. An Approach to the Social and Psychological Functions of Literature, Painting and Film* (Aarhus: Arkona, 1982), pp. 277-315, and subsequently reprinted in abridged form in *Film History*, vol. 4, no. 2 (1990), pp. 153-164.

Raskin, Richard (2002). "Bogart's Nod in the *Marseillaise* Scene: A Physical Gesture in *Casablanca*," *P.O.V. – A Danish Journal of Film Studies*, no. 14, December, pp. 136-142.

# 5

# From Leslie Howard to Raoul Wallenberg: The Transmission and Adaptation of a Heroic Model

*Professor Horatio Smith (Leslie Howard) dealing with the Gestapo in* Pimpernel Smith.

## Introduction

While it is widely known that seeing Leslie Howard's film *Pimpernel Smith* in 1942 may have played a role in inspiring and shaping Raoul Wallenberg's rescue mission in Budapest two years later, the connection between the two events has never been discussed at any length, and even the most comprehensive study of *Pimpernel Smith* to date (Aldgate and Richards 1994: 63) simply mentions Wallenberg in passing, just as accounts of Wallenberg's activities in Budapest do not go beyond a brief reference to *Pimpernel Smith* when the film is mentioned at all.

The purpose of the present article is to look more closely at the model found in Leslie Howard's film and the ways it was adapted by Raoul Wallenberg to the situation in Budapest in 1944.

But first, a brief discussion of an earlier work, *The Scarlet Pimpernel* first as novel (Orczy 1968; orig. pub. 1905) and then as film (Young 1934), will provide some useful back-story.

Baroness Emmuska Orczy, Hungarian-born but residing in England, wrote *The Scarlet Pimpernel*, both as a play performed in London's West End in 1903 and as a novel published in 1905.

The action, set in 1792, concerns a band of daring Englishmen who make forays into France during the Reign of Terror, "snatching away lawful victims destined for Madame la Guillotine" (Orczy 1968: 11). These Englishmen (12):

> seemed to be under the leadership of a man whose pluck and audacity were almost fabulous. Strange stories were afloat of how he and those aristos whom he rescued became suddenly invisible as they reached the barricades and escaped out of the gates by sheer supernatural agency.

The leader of this band is Sir Percy Blakeney, a baronet who pretends to be a mindless and effeminate fool, affecting a "perpetual inane laugh," in order to prevent anyone from suspecting that he is the legendary rescuer of French aristocrats. Even Lady Blakeney, his French-born wife, is deceived by his foppish pose and has no idea as to the identity of the Scarlet Pimpernel, so named because he sends those he will rescue as well as their persecutors a slip of paper "signed with a device drawn in red – a little star-shaped flower, which we in England call the Scarlet Pimpernel" (12). Acting on behalf of the *Comité de salut public*, Citoyen Chauvelin is the Scarlet Pimpernel's arch enemy. Chauvelin blackmails Lady Blakeney into helping him lay a trap for the mysterious rescuer, by threatening to have her brother Armand arrested. Ultimately, of course, Lady Blakeney discovers her husband's secret identity, bitterly regrets having unwittingly laid a trap for him, Sir Percy cunningly outwits Chauvelin once again and, along with his now adoring wife, makes a getaway from revolutionary France and a safe return to England.

In 1934, *The Scarlet Pimpernel* was filmed with Leslie Howard as Sir Percy Blakeney, cast in that role by producer Alexander Korda only after protests erupted over his original and somewhat incomprehensible choice of Charles Laughton for the lead (Orczy 1947: 165).

However, Baroness Orczy did not consider Leslie Howard ideal for the part because "he was short and could not look strong enough to dominate certain situations, nor could he tower over Chauvelin, played, as it happened, by a very tall man [Raymond Massey]" (1947: 166). And although she disapproved of the film's ending, she stated that all things considered: "I think I may safely say that my pleasure in the presentation of my romance on the cinema outweighed any disappointment I may have felt" (166).

The film, directed by Harold Young, picked up no awards of distinction, but did win high praise from contemporary critics (Sennwald 1935; Variety Staff 1933 [sic]).

## *Pimpernel Smith*

In January 1938, on a skiing holiday in Kitzbühel, Leslie Howard met a painter named Alfons Walde who told him "disquieting stories of friends liquidated by the Nazis." In the wake of this meeting, imagining an escape story for this painter "was to become the germ of the idea for the film *Pimpernel Smith*" (R. Howard 1981: 63-64; L. R. Howard 1959: 228-229, 249). In late 1940, after the Battle of Britain and during the Blitz, that individual escape story seemed too limited a framework for the film Leslie Howard wanted to make as part of his contribution to the war effort, which would eventually include: a role in Michael Powell's *49th Parallel* (1941); producing, directing and starring in *The First of the Few* (1942), released in the U.S. as *Spitfire*; a voice-over (uncredited) in Noel Coward's *In Which We Serve* (1942); 27 radio broadcasts to the U.S. in the BBC's *Britain Speaks* series, beginning in July 1940; and speaking tours in Spain and Portugal on behalf of the British Council.

While trying to flesh out this new rescue story with the help of a friend, the Scottish novelist Archibald MacDonell, the idea emerged of an archeology professor who would lead rescue operations in Nazi Germany, and it was MacDonell who suggested: "Why not a modern Pimpernel?" Not keen on the idea of exploiting the Pimpernel name in this new film, Leslie Howard replied, "Well – not exactly. Let's just call him Smith." (R. Howard 1981: 77-78). And according to his son, he "never cared much for the finally selected title *Pimpernel Smith*, finding it catchpenny and trivial" (77-78). Yet as the following synopsis will show, the storyline of the film – which Leslie Howard produced, directed and starred in, and which was released in the U.K. in July 1941 – is in many ways a transposition of the *Scarlet Pimper-*

*nel* story from one "reign of terror" to another, even with regard to such details as a distinctive calling card, the blackmailing of the woman who is in love with the hero, and her unwitting though ultimately inconsequential betrayal of him.

## Synopsis

In the spring of 1939, a mysterious rescuer, referred to in the press as the Shadow, manages to save a number of scientists and artists from the clutches of the Nazis, getting them safely out of Germany. His calling card, given to prisoners he is about to liberate, is a note with the words "The mind of man is bounded only by the universe." The arch villain of the film, General von Graum (played by Francis L. Sullivan and clearly modeled on the equally corpulent Hermann Goering) is obsessed with capturing the mysterious Shadow, and is also preoccupied with debunking the idea that humor is a secret weapon of the British. In the summer of 1939, the bespectacled and absent-minded Professor Horatio Smith (Leslie Howard) conducts archeological excavations in Germany. The six Cambridge students he has brought along on the dig are unaware that he is in fact the Shadow. He slips away from time to time on his secret rescue operations, in one striking scene disguised as a scarecrow. Smith's students eventually discover that the Shadow is none other than their "prof," and from then on, assist him in his secret operations.

Meanwhile, Ludmilla Koslowski, daughter of a Polish newspaper editor, has been blackmailed into working for von Graum, who is holding her father prisoner. Her assignment: to help capture the Shadow, whom von Graum knows will be attending a specific banquet at the British Embassy in Berlin. At this banquet, von Graum and Smith meet for the first time and Smith replies with wit and persistence to the general's absurd claims, e.g. that Shakespeare was a German. It is also here that Ludmilla first sees Smith and immediately suspects that he is the Shadow, informing von Graum of her guess, which the general dismisses as ridiculous. She visits Smith's room that night, asking him to rescue her father, but he denies being the Shadow. The next day, having verified that she is in fact Sidimir Koslowski's daughter, Smith agrees to help free her father, whom he tells her is being held at the concentration camp in Grossberg. When Ludmilla tells von Graum that she was mistaken about Smith's being the Shadow, she inadvertently reveals that he must in fact be the mysterious rescuer, since she now knows where her father is being held.

Von Graum expects a rescue attempt, but not on the day it is deftly carried out by Smith, in the guise of a revolting Nazi propagandist calling himself Vodenschatz, who intimidates and rudely bosses people around at the Ministry of Propaganda. Through this elaborate bluff, Smith manages to free Koslowski as well as several other prisoners at Grossberg. Von Graum is unable to confirm that Smith and Vodenschatz are one and the same and lets Smith and Ludmilla go, though under surveillance. Smith promises Ludmilla that he will not leave Germany without her. He then arranges for her father and the other prisoners he has freed to escape from Germany to France by train. When the Nazis interrogate Ludmilla, claiming that Smith has left Germany for good and that her father has been recaptured, she admits that Smith is the rescuer. Smith now returns for her, she is distraught but forgiven for having revealed his identity, and the two of them set out on their own getaway by train. At the border station, von Graum's men arrest Smith, and Ludmilla is sent back on the train to France. It is now that Smith is led into a waiting room at the station where von Graum takes charge of his prize prisoner.

What follows is a memorable monologue in which Smith replies to the general's claim that Germany will soon rule the world:

"You will never rule the world because you are doomed. All of you who have demoralized and corrupted a nation are doomed. Tonight you will take the first step along a dark road from which there is no turning back. You will have to go on and on, from one madness to another. Leaving behind you a wilderness of misery and hatred. And still you will have to go on because you will find no horizon and see no dawn 'til at last you are lost and destroyed. You are doomed, Captain of Murderers. And one day, sooner or later, you will remember my words."

The general then has Smith placed at the flimsy wooden gate marking the frontier, where he can be "shot while trying to escape." But once again, Smith slips through the general's fingers, disappearing behind the barrier when the general turns away for a moment. Von Graum fires his pistol in the direction of the puff of smoke Smith has left behind from his cigarette, and when von Graum shouts "Come back," Smith – no longer visible and safely on the other side of the wooden gate – calmly replies: "Don't worry, I'll be back. We'll all be back."

## The Vodenschatz episode

In the opening sequence of *Pimpernel Smith*, a scientist named Dr. Beckendorf is safely smuggled out of Germany by the mysterious Shadow, but exactly how that feat is accomplished is left entirely to the viewer's imagination. The same is true of Karl Plancke's escape at the Swiss frontier, and also of the pianist Karl Meyer's rescue following the remarkable scarecrow scene. In all these cases, not a clue is given as to how the Shadow operates.

However, in the Vodenschatz episode we are clearly shown and in rich detail at least some of the ways in which Professor Smith gets the better of the Nazis.

In order to carry out a plan he has devised for liberating Sidimir Koslowski and several other prisoners being held at the Grossberg camp, Smith needs six official permits for visiting the camp and a high-ranking officer to accompany him when he enters Grossberg in the guise of Herr Vodenschatz, along with his six students posing as American journalists. He will have to get the permits and the officer he needs at the Ministry of Propaganda, and his visit there is prepared by one of the his students who taps into the ministry's private telephone line and says:

> Propaganda Ministry? Gestapo Headquarters speaking. Department X2. About those six American journalists. We are permitting their visit to Grossberg … The journalists who wish to accompany Herr Vodenschatz … Your representative of the Bund … What do you mean you don't know? Then find out! *(Hangs up the phone.)*

Professor Smith, unrecognizable thanks to a fake mustache and wads of cotton stuffed in his cheeks, and wearing a bowler hat and matching suit, then strides busily into the Ministry, puffing on a cigar.

At several points, when he needs to cross a threshold of some kind within the Ministry, he brushes off the guard who tries to question or stop him:

> SMITH (*walking briskly past the entrance guard*): Heil Hitler.
> GUARD: Who do you wish to see?
> SMITH (*without stopping*): I've seen.

Or again at an inner gate, he turns the situation around, putting the guard on the defensive and defining his role as someone who is there to assist him:

> SMITH: Heil Hitler.
> GUARD: No visitors, except by appointment.
> SMITH (*curtly*): How long have you been here? You don't know me? Ever heard of the American Department?
> GUARD: Ah, yes sir. I thought …
> SMITH (*interrupting him*): Don't apologize. See if you can find my umbrella. I left it behind the other day. Vodenschatz is the name.

After more encounters of this nature, but in which he begins pressing for the permits he needs, Smith finally barges into the office of department head Steinhof, along with a subordinate named Graubitz. As this somewhat longer quotation will illustrate, Smith captures and holds the initiative at every turn, confusing and bullying his adversary, and meeting any hesitation to comply with his demands by threatening to complain to a feared superior, in this case Josef Goebbels:

> SMITH: Now look here Steinhof, where are the permits for the six American journalists.
> STEINHOF: Permits?
> SMITH: Yeah, don't you say Heil Hitler any more?
> STEINHOF (*rising from his chair*): Heil Hitler.
> SMITH: Heil Hitler.
> STEINHOF: I don't think I know you.
> SMITH: Then what do you know? Have you ever heard of America?
> STEINHOF: Yes.
> SMITH: Good. Then where are the permits?
> STEINHOF: But I … I …
> SMITH: Now listen. I'm Vodenschatz. The man who got the Nazi Party those nice headlines in America where they don't like you. I'm the man who put the Nazi American Bund on the map. And you never even heard of me. Let this be a lesson to you, Gentlemen.
> STEINHOF: But ah …
> SMITH: No, no, no, no. Let me speak. I've come all the way from New York to correct your blunders with the American correspondents. I've spent two whole weeks with them, trying to nurse them into a better humor. This afternoon I was taking them to the Grossberg camp so they could cable

the United States and tell them not to believe those stories they hear about the German concentration camps. And you've got to spoil everything. I ask for permits and you haven't got any permits.

STEINHOF (*to Graubitz*): No one told me anything about this.

GRAUBITZ: The Gestapo did telephone.

STEINHOF: Oh.

SMITH: So now you're deliberately obstructing the Gestapo.

GRAUBITZ: That would be the last thing I'd do. Perhaps if you'd come back tomorrow …

SMITH (*to Graubitz*): Tomorrow? Do you want me to keep the representatives of six of the biggest newspapers in America waiting outside this building until tomorrow? Unless I get those permits in two minutes, you'll be responsible.

GRAUBITZ: I'll be responsible?

SMITH: Right! I know what I'll do! (*Pointing to the phone.*) Get me Dr. Goebbels.

STEINHOF: No, no, Herr Vodenschit … uh, Vodenschatz. I … I … I'll find the permits.

SMITH: Find them, find them.

GRAUBITZ (*to Steinhof*): There are some here, Sir.

SMITH: That's better. Now you can fill them out as we go.

STEINHOF: As we go?

SMITH: Certainly. Didn't I say you are coming with us?

STEINHOF: No, no. I have …

SMITH: Oh, this is too much. Please. Get me Dr. Goebbels (*picking up the phone*).

STEINHOF (*rising from his seat*): No, no. I can finish the work at home.

SMITH: Ya, that's right. And we've been waiting long enough. Come along. Come along.

*Smith leads Graubitz and Steinhof from the inner office.*

SMITH: You know, the trouble with you propaganda boys … You've got so used to telling lies … you don't recognize the truth when you hear it.

STEINHOF: Orders are orders.

SMITH (*to someone walking in the other direction*): Heil Hitler …. You know, Graubitz, you're a smart boy.

GRAUBITZ: Thank you, Sir.

SMITH: Yes, you can do something for me. Ring up the Grossberg camp and tell them we're on the way. Have them prepare everything in the usual

Ministry of Propaganda style. And remember: America is a soft-hearted democracy. Get me?
GRAUBITZ: Leave it to me, Herr Vodenschatz.
GUARD (*seen earlier in the scene and now holding out two umbrellas*): Your umbrella, Sir.
SMITH: Oh, umbrella. (*Taking one*). Thank you.
*Smith leading Steinhof toward the exit, stops for a moment pointing at a guard's boots with his umbrella.*
SMITH (*to guard*): Dirty boots.
*Exit.*

Shortly after arriving at Grossberg with Steinhof and with his six students posing as journalists, Smith has Steinhof knocked out, and his uniform donned by Koslowski while the other prisoners to be freed put on the clothing of the "journalists," who later pretend to have been beaten unconscious. Smith makes an easy getaway in two cars with the prisoners he has rescued, remarking as he removes the fake mustache: "Well, goodbye Vodenschatz. You were the quintessence of all the objectionable men I ever met but you served a noble purpose."

# Raoul Wallenberg

*Raoul Wallenberg in 1944*

In 1942, Raoul Wallenberg, son of a wealthy family of Swedish bankers and industrialists, and who had been educated as an architect, was working as a junior partner in an import-export firm based in Stockholm. During his business trips throughout Europe, including Germany and Nazi-occupied countries, Wallenberg had seen with his own eyes how Jews were being murdered and he became increasingly frustrated over not being able to do anything about the unbearable scenes he was witnessing. One of his friends stated: "he seemed a little depressed at that time. I had the feeling he wanted to do something more worthwhile with his life" (Bierman 1981: 27). It was at this time that seeing *Pimpernel Smith* apparently gave a new direction to Wallenberg's plans for the future, as John Bierman reported in these terms (29):

> In the grim winter of 1942 Raoul Wallenberg spent an evening in the company of his half-sister at a private film show put on by the British embassy in Stockholm. The attraction was *Pimpernel Smith*, an updated version of Baroness Orczy's classic novel *The Scarlet Pimpernel*. In it the British star Leslie Howard played an apparently effete and absent-minded university professor who nevertheless outwits the Nazis and rescues dozens of prospective victims from their clutches.
>
> Wallenberg identified strongly with Howard's quiet, pipe-smoking Professor Smith, whom he physically resembled. "On the way home he told me that was just the kind of thing he would like to do," Nina Lagergren recalls. By an astonishing twist of fate, Wallenberg was to get his chance.

Two years later, having been accepted by representatives of President Roosevelt's War Refugee Board to carry out a rescue mission in Budapest where he would serve officially as First Secretary of the Swedish legation, Wallenberg carried out in reality the kinds of daring exploits his role-model had performed in *Pimpernel Smith*.

On July 9, 1944, the day of his arrival in Budapest, Wallenberg asked Per Anger, Second Secretary at the Swedish legation, what documents he had issued to the Jews. Anger showed him the array of materials that had been used until then, with varying degrees of success (Anger 1981: 50):

> I showed him the provisional passports, the visa certificates and the Red Cross protection letters. Wallenberg looked at the documents and said, after a pause: "I think I've got an idea for a new and maybe more effective document."

In this way, the idea of the so-called protective passports was born at our first meeting. These were the identification papers in blue and yellow with the three crowns emblem on them that would come to be the saving of tens of thousands of Jews.

These homemade but visually striking "passports" with their official emblems, seals and signatures, stated that "the bearer awaited emigration to Sweden and, until his departure, enjoyed the protection of that government" (Morse 1968: 293).

The issuing of these protective passports was just one of many plans Wallenberg put into practice as part of his rescue mission, which included the creation of "safe houses"; the hiring of hundreds of Jews as embassy staff; providing food, medicine and clothing, even during death marches to the Austrian border; and threatening to have the supreme commander of German forces in Hungary, General Gerhard Schmidhuber, hanged when the advancing Red Army arrived in Budapest, unless he prevented the slaughter that had been planned by the Arrow Cross (Hungarian Nazis) of the approximately 70,000 Jews then clinging onto life in the ghetto.

Returning now to the protective passports, we can consider one of the most dramatic ways in which they were used: namely as a pretext for extracting Jews from freight cars bound for Auschwitz. While written accounts could be cited to illustrate these remarkable events, the account that does the greatest justice to them is an unforgettable scene in the award-winning Swedish film, *Good Evening, Mr. Wallenberg*, written and directed by Kjell Grede and released in 1990.

As the scene opens, a truck is seen driving alongside railroad tracks on which a single freight car is being pushed toward a station by a locomotive. Seated in the cab of the truck are Wallenberg (Stellan Skarsgård) and his driver, Szamosi (Károli Eperjes). All dialogue in the scene is in German, provided here in English translation based mainly on the film's subtitles. Stills are reproduced with the kind permission of Kjell Grede and Sandrew Metronome.

1

2

3

SZAMOSI: Everyone in the Spanish Embassy has gone home. I'm the only one left. But I'm not even employed there. We have embassy stamps, flags, and official cars at our disposal. So the Spanish Embassy ... is me.

WALLENBERG (*smiling*): Not bad for a Jew with false papers.

SZAMOSI: Lies and deception lead to success. With real papers, you die. (*He looks over at the Arrow Cross guards holding on to ladders at the back of the freight car.*) Here they are supposed to be transferred. If they leave with the next train they'll never come back. (*As the train comes to a halt, Szamosi parks the truck in a position perpendicular to the tracks.*) How many have Swedish passports?

WALLENBERG: Five.

SZAMOSI: Five. Out of fifty-two.

WALLENBERG (*putting on white gloves*): We have to do it in less than two minutes. Otherwise it's no use.

SZAMOSI: Put on the fur cap. Without it you're lost.

*Wallenberg fits a fur cap onto his head. They both look through the rear window of the cab, as Arrow Cross guards pull open the sliding doors of the freight car.*

4

5

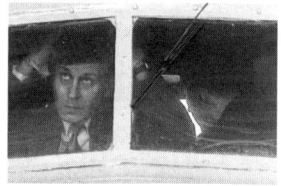
6

SZAMOSI: Now?
WALLENBERG: Now!

*Szamosi backs the truck, so that the loading platform is flush against the opening of the freight car, then hurries out of the cab and climbs up onto the platform. Wallenberg, who has also descended from the cab, hands him a paper. Arrow Cross soldiers approach, led by a sergeant.*

WALLENBERG (*in a loud angry voice, addressing the sergeant*): This is a very serious mistake for a minor official.

*Meanwhile Szamosi is now inside the freight car, coaching the men who all have yellow stars sewn onto their coats.*
WALLENBERG (*begins calling out names on a list*): Schönberger.

*In the freight car, Szamosi instructs a man to say "Ja, Ja" and pushes him out toward the platform. The sergeant puts his hand on Wallenberg's arm.*

WALLENBERG (*to the sergeant*): Be quiet. (*Then resuming the roll-call.*) Weiss.
SZAMOSI (*off-screen*): Ja!

*Wallenberg circles around, waving the sergeant over and beckoning him with his gloved hand, so that the sergeant, in following Wallenberg's instructions and changing his position, now has his back to the truck.*

WALLENBERG (*in a reproachful, lecturing tone*): Herr Sergeant. A labor battalion that is supposed to carry out repairs at the Swedish and Spanish Embassies. Repairs that cannot be delayed. (*Waving a handful of protective passports.*) They have Swedish passports. Understood? (*The sergeant, who can't get a word in edgewise, looks exasperated. Wallenberg resumes the roll-call.*) Fischer!

13  14  15

16  17  18

SZAMOSI: Ja! (*He grabs a man, has him raise his hand, and pushes him out toward the platform.*)
WALLENBERG (*now yelling at the sergeant*): The repairs can't be delayed. Do you understand what that means? Herr Sergeant! (*Resuming roll-call.*) Fingelmann!
SZAMOSI: Ullman? (*He looks around.*) Ja, Ullmann.
WALLENBERG (*handing his pack of protective passports to the sergeant*): Here, check for yourself. (*He turns toward the rest of the squad, then back to the sergeant.*) I want the names of all of your men. (*The sergeant is now facing the truck once again and looking at the protective passports. Wallenberg walks over to him, snatching the papers from his hand.*) What is it with you? Answer me! Don't you speak German? (*He gets the sergeant to look away from the truck.*)
SERGEANT: There should be ... should be a ...
WALLENBERG (*off-screen*): Are we supposed to do the repairs ourselves?
*Szamosi hurries into the driver's seat in the cab of the truck.*
WALLENBERG (*keeping an eye on the truck, which the sergeant cannot see*): How do you imagine that? You're going to pay for your lies.

*The sergeant begins to reply but has trouble formulating a single word in German, then turns to see the truck pull away, with all 52 Jews on the loading platform.*

19  20  21

22  23  24

WALLENBERG (*off-camera, and still haranguing the sergeant*): That was a very unusual transfer. Very unusual and you're gonna pay for it. (*Now Wallenberg sees his embassy car pull up, with a small Swedish flag mounted on the fender.*) You're totally unreliable. You don't say a single true word. (*Getting into the car.*) One asks oneself if you know what honesty means. (*As the car pulls away, Wallenberg removes his fur cap. Now viewed from inside the car, Wallenberg, looking weary, quietly addresses the unseen driver while removing his gloves.*) You were late. 30 seconds.

25  26  27

In this scene, a kind of composite based on a variety of accounts in the literature describing Wallenberg's activities in Budapest (including Anger 1981), it isn't difficult to see how Wallenberg might have taken what he needed from Leslie Howard's Professor Smith and adapted it to the present circumstances – above all, the use of bullying and insults, of a constant stream of threats and blame, keeping the adversary on the defensive at every turn and never letting him capture the initiative, the verbal and gestural flourish, the hammering away with an elaborate pretext, the perfect or near perfect timing of efforts coordinated with confederates, etc. There are also of course important differences, since here for example no disguise was needed; there was no secret identity to hide. But the spirit and manner of the two performances unmistakably share the same essential qualities.

By the way, Kjell Grede had seen *Pimpernel Smith* some ten or twenty years before he wrote the script for *Good Evening, Herr Wallenberg*, but now [2009], approximately twenty years after the writing of that script, he has no memory of the Vodenschatz episode (Grede 2009).

## Leslie Howard's death

Leslie Howard didn't live to learn about the rescue operations in Budapest that *Pimpernel Smith* may have helped to inspire. The *Ibis*, the civilian aircraft in which he was returning to England from a speaking tour in Spain and Portugal on June 1, 1943, was shot down by eight Luftwaffe fighter planes. There is no consensus in the literature on this subject as to why the routine BOAC flight was intercepted on that occasion, and three main explanations have been proposed.

One is that German spies mistook another passenger, Alfred Chenhalls – Leslie Howard's cigar-smoking, heavy-set, balding accountant – for the British Prime Minister. Churchill himself believed this to be case, and when describing his return to England from Gibraltar at about the same time, he wrote (1953: 666-667):

> Eden and I flew home together by Gibraltar. As my presence in North Africa had been fully reported, the Germans were exceptionally vigilant, and this led to a tragedy which much distressed me. The regular commercial aircraft was about to start from the Lisbon airfield when a thickset man smoking a cigar walked up and was thought to be a passenger on it. The German agents therefore signaled that I was on board. Although these passenger planes had plied unmolested for many months between Portugal and England, a German war plane was instantly ordered out, and the defenceless aircraft was ruthlessly shot down. Thirteen passengers perished, and among them the well-known British actor Leslie Howard, whose grace and gifts are still preserved for us by the records of the many delightful films in which he took part. The brutality of the Germans was only matched by the stupidity of their agents. It is difficult to understand how anyone could

imagine that with all the resources of Great Britain at my disposal I should have booked a passage in an unarmed and unescorted plane from Lisbon and flown home in broad daylight. We of course made a wide loop out by night from Gibraltar into the ocean, and arrived home without incident. It was a painful shock to me to learn what had happened to others in the inscrutable workings of Fate.

Ian Colvin also believed this to be the reason for the attack on the BOAC flight (1957).

Another explanation is that the Luftwaffe pilots were unaware that the plane they shot down was a civilian aircraft. This at least was claimed by one of the pilots who had taken part in the operation – Oberleutnant Herbert Hintze – who stated that it was only after they had opened fire that the air crews discovered that the enemy aircraft they had attacked was a civilian plane (Goss 2001: 54).

And a third explanation is that the Nazis specifically targeted the flight because they knew that Leslie Howard was on board. Though Ronald Howard believed the mystery of the attack would never be solved, he also suggested that the presence of his father on the plane, as well as that of T. M. Shervington (Chief of Shell Oil), "may well have been the main motive, the basis for the [Luftwaffe's] search and final interception of *Ibis*" (1984: 230). Ronald Howard offered another argument in possible support of this explanation, namely (231-232):

> Goebbels' hatred of [Leslie Howard] for making fools of the Germans in *Pimpernel Smith* and for his truculent, anti-*Herrenvolk* broadcasts. He was, after all, Goebbels' principal propaganda opponent in Britain. And to this the insidious Goebbels would not be slow in adding the racial element, perhaps the lynchpin of his hatred. […] Though Leslie's point of view was scarcely predominantly Jewish he was tainted, in Goebbels' eyes, by the fact that he had a Hungarian-Jewish father.

Furthermore, in discussing reactions to his father's death, including those published in Germany, Ronald Howard wrote (225):

> News of the death of Leslie Howard was given special prominence in Goebbels' newspaper *Der Angriff*. It was celebrated almost like a victory. Under banner headlines, larger than those accorded 'the strategic withdrawal' of

Hitler's armies in Russia, the front page bore the words: 'Pimpernel Howard has made his last trip!'.

Unfortunately, Ronald Howard cites no date for this article, which would presumably have appeared during the first week of June 1943. However, it did not in fact appear on the front page of any issue of *Der Angriff* in the period June 1-12, 1943 (as confirmed by the Berliner Stadtbibliothek in an email to this author on August 31, 2009). Nor did it appear on the front page of *Der Stürmer* or *Völkischer Beobachter* in the relevant period. Numerous references to the headline, attributing the article to *Der Angriff*, must all stem from Ronald Howard's bibliographically incomplete discussion of it in his book.

In this context, as well as in the relationship between *Pimpernel Smith* and Raoul Wallenberg, the boundaries between life and art, reality and fiction, are not nearly as clear-cut as they are generally thought to be.

Finally, Raoul Wallenberg also met a tragic fate soon after fulfilling his mission in Hungary, and the mystery as to why he was arrested by the Russians in January 1945 – and the fate he met while in their custody – now appears to be as insoluble as the mystery surrounding the Germans' attack on the *Ibis*. These tragic endings for two lives, each dedicated in its own way to the outwitting of Nazi executioners, constitute yet another parallel between Leslie Howard and Raoul Wallenberg.

# Epilogue

After completing the above discussion, I was able to contact Nina Lagergren, who graciously responded to a number of questions and helped to clarify an important issue. As the reader will recall, it was to his sister, Nina Lagergren, that Raoul Wallenberg said "that was just the kind of thing he would like to do," after seeing *Pimpernel Smith* at the British Embassy in Stockholm in 1942.

In a telephone conversation on September 22, 2009, Nina Lagergren said that to her knowledge, Raoul Wallenberg did not think of carrying out rescue operations in Budapest until the Spring of 1944, when he was chosen to organize a rescue mission for Hungarian Jews by Iver Olsen, who had been sent by Roosevelt to Stockholm as an official representative of the War Refugee Board. According to Nina Lagergren, it was therefore not the case that seeing *Pimpernel Smith* in 1942 gave Wallenberg the idea of taking on the Pimpernel role in Budapest in 1944. Nor did he subsequently mention *Pimpernel Smith* to his sister. So much for what now appears to be too simplistic a view of the effect of the film on Wallenberg when he first saw it.

However, if the film was not the catalyst that first set Wallenberg's plans in motion, it can still have defined the dramaturgy that would ultimately be in play. On the basis of Wallenberg's statement to his sister in 1942 and the striking similarities pointed out above between Leslie Howard's performance, particularly in the Vodenschatz episode, and Wallenberg's *modus operandi* in Budapest, there is every reason to believe that once committed to his mission at the Swedish legation in Hungary, Wallenberg found in *Pimpernel Smith* a role-model he could adapt to the situation at hand when facing down Nazi and Arrow Cross guards and snatching prisoners from their grasp.

It is in this respect that the remarkable rescue of countless lives in Budapest involved at least in part the transmission of a heroic model from Leslie Howard to Raoul Wallenberg.

| PRINCIPAL CREDITS *PIMPERNEL SMITH* | |
|---|---|
| Director and producer | Leslie Howard |
| Screenplay and scenario | Anatole de Grunwald |
| Story | A. G. Macdonald, Wolfgang Wilhelm |
| Novel *The Scarlet Pimpernel* | Baroness Emmuska Orczy |
| Scenario | Roland Pertwee |
| Co-writer (uncredited) | Ian Dalrymple |
| Cinematographer | Mutz Greenbaum |
| Editor | Douglas Myers |
| | |
| Professor Horatio Smith | Leslie Howard |
| General von Graum | Francis L. Sullivan |
| Ludmilla Koslowski | Mary Morris |
| David Maxwell | Hugh McDermott |
| | |
| Shoot at Denham Studios | January-April 1941 |
| Release date U.K. | 26 July 1941 |
| Release date U.S. (New York) | 12 February 1942 |

| PRINCIPAL CREDITS<br>*GOOD EVENING MR. WALLENBERG*<br>*GOD AFTON HERR WALLENBERG – EN PASSIONSHISTORIA FRÅN VERKLIGHETEN* ||
|---|---|
| Director and writer | Kjell Grede |
| Producer | Katinka Faragó |
| Executive producer | Klas Olofsson |
| Cinematographer | Esa Vuorinen |
| Editor | Darek Hodor |
| Raoul Wallenberg | Stellan Skarsgård |
| Marja | Katharina Thalbach |
| Szamosi | Károly Esperjes |
| The Rabbi | Erland Josephson |
| Release date Sweden | 5 October 1990 |
| Release date U.S. (New York) | 23 April 1993 |

## References and other material consulted

Aldgate, Anthony and Jeffrey Richards (2007). *Britain Can Take It: The British Cinema in the Second World War.* London/New York: I. B. Taurus. Orig. pub. 1994.

Anger, Per (1981). *With Raoul Wallenberg in Budapest. Memories of the War Years in Hungary.* Translated from the Swedish by David Mel Paul and Margareta Paul; preface by Elie Wiesel. New York: Holocaust Library.

Bierman, John (1981). *Righteous Gentile – The Story of Raoul Wallenberg, Missing Hero of the Holocaust.* Harmondsworth: Penguin.

Bo, Michael (2008). "Reddede Leslie Howard Europa fra fascismen?" *Politiken*, 14 October.

Brown, Gordon (2007). *Courage. Eight Portraits.* London: Bloomsbury.

Churchill, Winston S. (1953). *The Second World War. Volume Four: The Hinge of Fate.* London: The Reprint Society.

Colvin, Ian (1957). *Flight 777. The Mystery of Leslie Howard.* London: Evans Brothers.

Coniam, Mathew (n.d.). "Pimpernel Smith." *BFI Screenonline* http://www.screenonline.org.uk/film/id/476656/ Accessed 8 May 2017.

Coward, Noel (1942). *In Which We Serve.* U.K.: Two Cities Films et al.

Fox, Jo (2007). *Film Propaganda in Britain and Nazi Germany: World War II Cinema.* Oxford/New York: Berg.

Furhammer, Leif (1971). *Politik och film.* Stockholm: Pan/Norstedts.

Goss, Christopher (2001). *Bloody Biscay: The Story of the Luftwaffe's Only Long Range Maritime Fighter Unit, V Gruppe/Kampfgeschwader 40, and Its Adversaries 1942-1944*. Manchester: Crécy. Orig. pub. 1997.

Grede, Kjell (1990). *Good Evening, Mr. Wallenberg / God afton Herr Wallenberg*. Sweden, Hungary, Norway: Film Teknik, Filmhuset, Hungarian Filmproduction.

Grede, Kjell (2009). Personal communication to the author, 24 August.

Grey, Amber (n.d.). "Leslie Howard's Propaganda Films." *BellaOnline* http://www.bellaonline.com/articles/art36901.asp Accessed 8 May 2017.

Howard, Leslie (1941). '*Pimpernel*' *(aka Mr. V) Smith*. U.K.: British National Films.

Howard, Leslie (1942). *The First of the Few* (aka *Spitfire*). U.K.: British Aviation Pictures.

Howard, Leslie Ruth (1959). *A quite remarkable father*. London: Longmans.

Howard, Ronald (1984). *In Search of My Father: A Portrait of Leslie Howard*. New York: St. Martin's Press.

Morse, Arthur D. (1968). *While 6 Million Died. A Chronicle of American Apathy*. New York: Ace.

Orczy, Baroness (1905/1968). *The Scarlet Pimpernel*. New York: Lancer.

Orczy, Baroness (1947). *Links in the Chain of Life*. London: Hutchinson.

Powell, Michael (1941). *49th Parallel*. U.K.: Ortus Films.

Richards, Jeffrey (1976). "Leslie Howard: the thinking man as hero," *Focus on Film*, vol. 25, Summer-Autumn, pp. 37-50.

Sennwald, André (1935). "Leslie Howard as the Scarlet Pimpernel in a Fine British Screen Version of the Famous Novel," *New York Times*, 8 February. http://www.nytimes.com/movie/review?res=9500E2DD113FE53ABC4053DFB466838E629EDE Accessed 23 October 2017.

Strauss, Theodore (1942). "'Mr. V,' a British Melodrama, Opens at Rivoli," *New York Times*, 13 February.

Tremblett, Giles (2008). "British film star was secret agent, claims author," *The Guardian*, 6 October.

Variety Staff (1933 [sic]). "Review: The Scarlet Pimpernel," 31 December. Since according to IMDb the film was released in the U.S. on February 7, 1935, it is unlikely that a review could have appeared in *Variety* on December 31, 1933. http://variety.com/1933/film/reviews/the-scarlet-pimpernel-1200410810/ Accessed 8 May 2017.

Young, Harold (1934). *The Scarlet Pimpernel*. U.K.: London Film Productions. https://archive.org/details/TheScarletPimpernel Accessed 8 May 2017.

# 6

# Interview with Alain Resnais on *Night and Fog*

Recorded in Paris, on February 18, 1986, this interview appeared in French in my book *Nuit et Brouillard by Alain Resnais. On the Making, Reception and Functions of a Major Documentary Film* (Aarhus University Press, 1987), pp. 47-63. Here it is published in English for the first time, in my translation from the French.

| | |
|---|---|
| ***first contacts between producer and director*** | In a phone call one night, Anatole Dauman suggested that I make a short film about the concentration camps. But my first reaction was obviously to decline because I had never been deported and I thought that only a director who himself had been deported could make such a film. It was simply beyond my capabilities. |
| ***Alain Resnais' situation at the time*** | I should add that it was quite chivalrous of Anatole Dauman to make that phone call, because […] my latest film, made in collaboration with Chris Marker, *Statues Also Die*, had had a lot of problems with the censors, who didn't give it their approval. And in commercial terms I was in a slump. Producers didn't actually 'distrust' me. It wasn't that. They thought, "Okay, Resnais is fine. He has made films about painting but there are always problems with him. It's just too complicated…" So the idea of working with me showed a lot of willfulness on Dauman's part. I was not in a very good place with respect to public relations. And I was considered – not quite 'dangerous,' that's not what I'm saying – but rather: "Oh, that's going to mean trouble." So it was courageous of him to offer me work. I told him that I was very moved by his kind offer but that taking on that work was out of the question. |
| ***Jean Cayrol as a guarantor of authenticity*** | So then Anatole Dauman tried again and I think I answered: "Listen, I'll think about it but in that case it would require… I'm acquainted with Jean Cayrol who is a writer I greatly admire and a friend of Chris Marker's. He works at Seuil. And *he* was deported. If Jean Cayrol agreed to work on this project, I could reconsider. I need someone who can back me up, or provide a guarantee of authenticity, because I can't do that on my own." Then some negotiations must have taken place. |

| | |
|---|---|
| ***Commission for the History of the Second World War – Henri Michel and Olga Wormser*** | In any event it was an order from the Commission for the History of the Second World War, directed by the historian Henri Michel, in collaboration with the historian Olga Wormser. I guess the three of us met along with Dauman and I must have explained my position by saying: "If I don't have Jean Cayrol's agreement, I can't make this film." And I think we all agreed on that. |
| ***starting the work*** | At that point I began the usual work involved in making a short film. Let's say that I learned the basic facts, actually with a good deal of misgivings because I felt I was on shaky ground in working with these things. |
| ***the reticence of Jean Cayrol*** | But I went to see Jean Cayrol who in turn was reticent because he had no desire to plunge back into all that. But he said to me: "I can't say 'no' to you, Alain. In any event, it would be without pleasure or enthusiasm. But when you have done your work, show it to me and then we'll see." That's the way I remember it. Maybe Chris Marker also had to insist in order to convince Jean Cayrol to agree. Yes, that must have happened. |
| ***Henri Michel and Olga Wormser – historical advisors*** | From that point on, there were many conversations with Henri Michel and especially with Olga Wormser, with whom I spoke a lot and I told her about my reading, about the documents I had assembled, and she helped me to find photos and other documentation, or at least guided my efforts. And we got on very well. |

***limited time***　　　　And I remember having typed something in order to tell Anatole Dauman how I wanted to make the film. That must have lasted four or five months. But I know there was a major problem: that because of a matter of money I think, the film had to be ready before Christmas. So there was very little time. We couldn't say: "we'll take our time making this film." If the copy could not be ready by Christmas, and at that time it must have been March or April, then the film could not be made because Anatole Dauman did not have the necessary funds. It had to qualify for a kind of premium of quality to be feasible. I think Dauman already believed that the film he wanted to make would not be commercially profitable. I think the Commission for the History of the Second World War owed part of the film and Anatole Dauman negotiated. They were three partners: Anatole Dauman, Samy Halfon and Lifschitz. Three associates who got along beautifully and all three of them were extremely interesting and likeable.

***the initial concept for the film: human Folly***　　　　I remember typing up the thoughts that occurred to me and telling them to Anatole Dauman, saying: "That's it, that's how we're going to make the film." He agreed. I know that the first version was especially focused on the notion of Folly, with a capital 'F.' You understand, Folly as something dreadful. The horror of human imbecility. That was the initial concept I had … And also a film that lasted thirty minutes, which was a bit longer than anticipated – it was supposed to run twenty to twenty-five minutes – thirty minutes would be a problem. But Anatole Dauman went along with that length. Only all that could not be done in thirty minutes and that initial aspect practically disappeared from the film as our work progressed.

*not a 'memorial in remembrance of the dead'*

The idea that I latched on to and that seemed most important, was that I did not want to make a film of the type 'memorial in remembrance of the dead'. That's what I feared, making a film declaring 'Never again,' 'No, that will not happen again,' 'It's because it was the evil Germans, but now that Hitler is defeated, it's over, it won't recur and let's make sure it doesn't.' I felt a film of that type would solve nothing. And so I tried to push the film toward the question mark that it represents: the fact that something like that occurred at that time, but that in the past it had taken other forms.

*the Algerian war*

We were in the midst of the Algerian war in France, a war that began in France, and there were already zones in the middle of France where people were rounded up – agreed, they were not concentration camps – but where drivers passing by were not allowed to stop their cars. There were already gendarmes and all the rest. So we made the film, or at least I made the film, with this idea that in a way it was starting again in France. Already, you see, there was that perspective, and that made me even more worried about an aspect of the 'memorial to the dead' type and 'everyone agreed about that horrible past that could never happen again.' Because I was feeling precisely that it could happen again.

*the problem of form*

Another problem we had was that of the form of the film: how to handle a subject of that kind? Personally I was completely crushed by it (and still am now, for that matter). So I said to myself: alright, there have been a number of films on the concentration camps. Everyone says that they are very good but they don't seem to have made very much impact on people. Now since I am a formalist, maybe I should override my misgivings and in the making of this film, despite its subject, engage in form experiments (*recherches formelles*).

For example, the mixing of black-and-white and colour, which today is common but at that time it was … And in fact, when I asked Anatole Dauman about this, I said: "Okay, listen. I want to make this film but I want to do it by alternating between black-and-white and colour. So making prints will be much more expensive. Do you agree?" And I think within two minutes, Anatole Dauman told me: "Yes, I go along with that." That was yet another proof of his courage. And Samy Halfon and his associates immediately agreed as well. They spent a great deal of money and effort on getting this film ready.

*in Poland*

After that, we reached an agreement with Poland which took care of our expenses and travel, nothing more but it was enormous. And we set out, filming two or three weeks in Poland. Then we came home and I obtained some documents thanks to Henri Michel, who had found them in Holland.

*the film services of the British and French armies*

I had a terrible feeling: that another year of research would have been needed, that there were other documents available. But our time was limited. So we couldn't continue … And there wasn't enough money for us to travel to Germany, to go to many other places, even just in the hunt for documents. The British were approached, I believe. But we were told that they did not wish to give us any documents. And as for the Film Service of the French Army, which had very little, they showed us nothing of any real interest, just official ceremonies and things of that type. But we did choose three or four shots. We requested them and then received a letter stating that "given the character of the film" – meaning the character of the director – it would not be possible to provide us with the documents we had requested.

So I had the feeling that there was an understanding between the armies, whether French or English (or even German, almost) that meant they did not want anyone to talk about these things. Maybe I'm exaggerating a bit, but there was something of that in play. If the documents we requested had been exciting, we might have asked people to intervene and help us obtain them, but there was no point.

*Jean Cayrol's commentary*

After that, when I brought back all my material, I made a rough cut that I showed to Jean Cayrol. And he was very shaken by it. It made him ill to see all that reappearing, returning to the surface. And he told me: "I can't work directly in the cutting room. It's too painful for me. I'll write a text for you." And he did just that. And obviously the text he wrote was not completely adapted to the film, since he had written it on the basis of what he could remember of that rough cut. Then Chris Marker reappeared on the scene and helped me out by restructuring Cayrol's text. And Cayrol, apparently recovered in the days that followed, completed the rewriting Chris Marker had begun, and completely rewrote the text himself. So all of that was involved in the writing process. I make that point because there have been some myths in circulation about this commentary.

*Michel Bouquet*

Then Michel Bouquet recorded it. It may seem odd now but at the time we thought that putting the name of an actor in the credits might be inappropriate, given the nature of the film. I thought it was a mistake, but okay, that's what we did. And Michel Bouquet said: "I prefer that my name not be listed," and we said alright. But his voice was so easily recognizable that there really was no point.

*unexpected success*  Then we finished the film and Anatole Dauman came to the laboratory to see the first projection of the first print. He said to me, and this I remember clearly: "My dear Alain, I think we have made a beautiful film. But I can guarantee that given its character, it will never be shown in any movie theatre. But I don't regret having made it." But that's not at all what happened. The film was shown in movie theatres and was one of the very few short films ever to be announced at the entrance to movie theatres, and drawing the public in to see the feature film. So it was the exact opposite of what we expected.

*another surprise*  And I remember another surprise as well. The first foreign country to buy the film was Germany – West Germany. (East Germany bought it but only after thinking about it for four years because the commentary wasn't exactly to their liking.)

*the story of the kepi [French military cap]*  Then there was a series of hitches with the control commission, called 'the board of censorship,' which asked me before the release to cut the scenes near the end where we see cadavers, because it was too violent. And there was a shot I hadn't noticed, which is the famous story of the gendarme's kepi. There is this shot lasting about three seconds I believe, in which different camps are named, and against the sunlight – I assure you that we hadn't seen this, it was entirely unintentional – one can see a French gendarme from the top of a watchtower. I think he is keeping watch over the camp. It lasts a few seconds. It was the camp of Pithiviers. So the censorship board tried to blackmail us about that ... What was amusing is that on the back of the photo we used, there was the German eagle and swastika and "authorized by the *Propagandastaffel*." So what was authorized by the *Propagandastaffel* was prohibited by the French government.

It was a great story! I was then told: "If you don't cut this shot …" "No, I won't cut it on my own. It's not the role of the director to remove shots from his film. It's up to the censorship board to require it. As long as I have not received an official letter demanding that I cut the shot, I will never do it …" "Oh, no. It's not that at all. But I warn you that if you don't cut that shot, you will not be allowed to use the last reel. Take it or leave it." At that point, even the producers told me: "Alain, shouldn't you give in all the same?" Because the meaning of the film was more important, etc. And I replied: "No, I can't. Not without a letter. I want a letter from the control commission demanding the cuts and I won't do it without that proof." Because in effect after a phone call, there is no trace. So in the end they prohibited the release of the film because of this two-second shot of the gendarme that no one would have noticed. No viewer would have noticed it.

*the kepi was 'beamed' from view*

Then for I think for about two or three weeks, the film remained in a kind of no-man's-land. And there were bargaining sessions I did not attend. A deal was made. A strip was painted over the gendarme's kepi, since it had not been our intention to compromise the gendarmerie, about which we couldn't care less. But I wanted to keep the name: 'Camp of Pithiviers,' because it was important to show that France had organized points of departure for the camps. 'Camp of Pithiviers,' I insisted, not on the gendarme's kepi. And they didn't cut anything from the end of the film. They didn't dare. The ending remained intact.

*The original photo*   *The doctored version*

**two communist perspectives**

There were also quarrels at the start with – I don't dare say 'the Communist Party,' that's too important – because the final sentences of the film suggested … Personally I was thinking of the camps for Algerians that were being set up in France. And certain communists in film told me: "Yes, but people will think that there are camps in Russia. So listen: you join us and we are going to rewrite the commentary with you, we're going to change it because it's important that no one thinks you had Russia in mind." They were not very pleased.

**Louis Daquin**

Then fortunately, Louis Daquin, a French director who was communist, saw the film and was very moved by it. He said to me: "Listen, I know what certain of my comrades see in this story, but I don't think you should change a thing because if there are Frenchmen who believe there are camps in Russia, they are going to believe that anyway. And if by any chance there are camps in Russia, then too bad for them. It's the Russians who are at fault." And that was the end of it. Thanks to Louis Daquin, there was no trouble, we did not rewrite the commentary. Those periods were something. You have to put yourself in [the mentality of] the 50s.

*"You have omitted the terrible images"*

Another thing I'd like to mention and that struck me at the time is that people saw the film in private screenings, and many said to me: "Obviously you were afraid of the violence and you have omitted the terrible images we saw at the Liberation, etc." And that is completely wrong. I had access to all of the French films that were shown at the Liberation and I omitted no violent document. They had simply imagined they had seen things in 1944 and 1945 that had struck them, but this myth circulated that I had deliberately watered the film down to make it more commercial. No, I made no effort to omit hyper-violent images. I simply hadn't found any. I'm not sure what I would have done if I had. There were rumors. Some people said there were shots which showed what happened in a gas chamber at the moment of annihilation and that all that had been filmed by the Germans. I think it's a myth. In any event, I never saw any such documents.

*"The contrast between movement and immobility for certain dramatic aspects seems very mannered, I was even ashamed of it during the editing."* **Alain Resnais, 1956**

Yes, actually. I would say the same thing now. It's true that in the editing room, sometimes, in that way, I was ... Yes, I remember evenings (because I edited at night in order to win some time since we were so pressed) when I had the strange impression that I was manipulating documents of cadavers or, even worse, of people still alive – when they are dead it's less serious than when they are living – with a view to carrying out form experiments (*recherches formelles*).

*Hanns Eisler*

Likewise, asking Hanns Eisler for the music – which for me was of the utmost importance – exasperated many people. I took a lot of flak, even now, about that. I was told that it was wrong to ask a real musician to provide the music, that silence is what was needed.

| | |
|---|---|
| *form experiments* | But after all, the films that were made according to that formula, let's call it of sobriety, have disappeared. What I am saying is very pretentious. But people have spoken of *Night and Fog* and not about the other films. So maybe form experiments are necessary for people to be receptive to something. I don't know. |
| *the final sentences of the commentary* | …there was this idea of posing a question. That's what it was. I wanted a film that said to people, not 'Don't forget' – that didn't interest me – but rather 'Try to understand why this happens. And don't wait for it to happen before you become concerned.' I often spoke in fact of a wake-up call. Out of a fear that it would happen again. Today I'll tell you that what strikes me – and I don't have a solution, maybe there are philosophers who do – is this kind of proportion (because balance matters when speaking of the human race) between those who destroy, who torture, who oppress, who draw pleasure from dominating other human beings, and those who derive pleasure from sacrifice, from atonement, from edification, etc. As though there are these two extremes of – I don't know: maybe it's called a Gaussian curve? Maybe that's it. I'm not sure about the term. I wish some attention was given to the reasons for which there are these two forces that seem to nourish the human race, at least have for the last six thousand years. I don't dare talk about before then … It's really a great question mark, the issue of "Who is responsible?" |
| *a realization?* | No, it's a film that leaves me feeling profoundly troubled, still to this day. And even – I'm going to contradict myself – there were moments while I was working on it when I almost forgot who I was, along with my reasons for having initially refused to make it because I considered myself unworthy of the task, and when I thought this film might shake up the world. I told myself: "After all, once they have seen this, they are going to … It's going to make something happen." |

At that time I hadn't foreseen the film's commercial success (since it was sold to practically every country in the world). I thought it might bring people to a kind of realization. And then the commercial and even critical success of the film, absorbed as it turned out … It became accepted, digested … And that raises a new question. (If the film hadn't been released, that would not have been a victory either.)

**the problem of evil**

Personally I believe that science is making progress in the study of the brain, in the study of the central nervous system, in the study of what drives us – to quote Henri Laborit – especially over the last twenty years. It's a very young science. Maybe there is a pathway there. But I don't think the way out will reside in grand humanitarian reasoning, in great declarations that I still hear now on the radio, nor in the writings of editorialists for whom I have the highest regard, who still wrote just a few months ago: "Evil will have to be torn from the heart of man." Yes, agreed. But why is this evil there to begin with, in the human heart? Maybe there are chemical or other explanations. Are all torturers people who don't have a normal sexual life and who can't achieve satisfaction in other ways? But at the same time, when you consider the running of the Nazi concentration camps, you get the impression that for so many people it was simply routine, complete with boredom and everything else. No, I have no answers to these questions.

**the idea**

I think the idea, the very core of the film and the desire to see it made, all stem from Henri Michel, who brought Olga Wormser into the picture, who in turn invested it with all her enthusiasm and poetic sense. I have a good rapport with Henri Michel but we have lost contact by force of circumstances.

***the producers*** And of course there is Dauman, along with Samy Halfon and Lifschitz, all three – as a group and I insist on that because subsequently these associates separated and each went his own way. But at the time of *Night and Fog*, they worked in complete harmony. I remember Samy Halfon, at 10 o'clock at night, bringing cases himself that he had looked for in the laboratory. Things that would usually be done by an assistant were taken on by a producer who wanted to be ready; he really gave it all he had. And I have nothing but admiration for the work that Dauman does.

***a vile argument*** I'll mention something else that has to do with human folly and imbecility. It's something I have heard several times and that has always left me feeling indignant and also aroused Cayrol's indignation. I have heard people say: "Yes, but Anatole Dauman is perfectly vile because this film is very successful. And he made a lot of money with *Night and Fog* and enriched himself at the expense of deportees." Now that's a very serious charge because what does it mean? It implies that if you want to make 'message' films that are courageous, that defend the ideas that mean a lot to you, which was certainly the case for Anatole Dauman and Samy Halfon, then it can only be done on the condition that it loses money. What a beautiful lesson! Because in fact people say: "It's terrible, political films are never made in France, etc." Okay, so if a political film is at all profitable, then no, that's immoral. So you can only be a good producer if you lose money when dealing with noble issues. You see how stupid that argument is? It's a good argument for discouraging any enterprise of this nature... It is not worth taking seriously, but people say it.

***the support***
***of deportees***

But fortunately from the very start we had the support of associations of deportees. The film was not in competition of course but was screened at the Cannes festival. But of course, the festival committee said: "No, we won't screen it because it's too political a film." And the deportees of the region of Nice and Cannes replied: "Okay, but if you don't screen it, we will show up wearing our deportee uniforms and will occupy the festival quarters. Take it or leave it."

***to share***

There was a time when the director was hardly ever cited in discussions of films. That was going a bit too far. But now I find that people are going too far in talking only about the director. Because if you love cinema, you have to accept sharing. Unless you are a total auteur, who acts and writes and does everything else. That's fine. There are other ways. I don't know who is most responsible for *Night and Fog* as a film. I would personally say that Hanns Eisler is of utmost importance, that Cayrol is of utmost importance. That's an issue I won't [try to] settle.

# 7

# Reflections on Art and the Holocaust: Elie Wiesel versus Alain Resnais

*Elie Wiesel*

*Alain Resnais*

Born only six years apart in the 1920s and admirers of each other's work, Elie Wiesel and Alain Resnais had a great deal in common and are among the most highly respected figures to have worked with representations of the Holocaust. Yet for all they shared, they held radically different views of the relationship between art and the Holocaust. This essay will focus on two of the ways in which their approaches differed.

# (1)

Death-camp survivor Elie Wiesel drew a sharp distinction between fiction and non-fiction. He singled out such feature films as *The Night Porter* (Cavani 1974) and *Sophie's Choice* (Pakula 1982) as well as the TV mini-series *Holocaust* (Chomsky 1978) as vulgarly exploitative examples of (Wiesel 1989):

> cheap and simplistic melodramas [offering] a little history, a heavy dose of sentimentality and suspense, a little eroticism, a few daring sex scenes, a dash of theological rumination about the silence of God and there it is: let kitsch rule in the land of kitsch, where at the expense of truth, what counts is ratings and facile success.

And in the same article, he praised for their authenticity such documentaries as *Night and Fog* (Resnais 1956) and *Shoah* (Lanzmann 1985).

Because of the very nature of the creative process, Wiesel believed that fiction must necessarily be misleading, exploitative, voyeuristic and trivializing, as though the esthetic concerns in play when a work of art is fashioned would inevitably interfere with an authentic portrayal of the Holocaust. He once stated his position this way (Wiesel 1977: 7):

> A novel about Treblinka is either not a novel or not about Treblinka. A novel about Majdanek is about blasphemy. Is blasphemy. Treblinka means death, absolute death, death of language and of hope, death of trust and of inspiration. Its secret is doomed to remain intact. How can one write about a situation which goes beyond its very description? How can one write a novel about the Holocaust?

And using a similar formulation once again, he affirmed that fiction and authenticity are mutually exclusive when death-camps are portrayed (Wiesel 1983b: 12):

> Auschwitz defies imagination and perception. It submits only to memory. It can be communicated by testimony, not by fiction. A novel on Majdanek is either not a novel or not about Majdanek.

Whenever Wiesel returned to this dichotomy between documentary and fiction, he invariably singled out Resnais' *Night and Fog* for special praise, writing for example: "Certain productions dazzle with their authenticity; others shock with their vulgarity. *Night and Fog* on one side, *Holocaust* on the other" (Wiesel 1983a: xii).

From Wiesel's perspective, fiction is governed by esthetic concerns which inevitably undermine the truthfulness of its representations, and it is implicit in his remarks that he considered the process of making a documentary film to be exempt from the pernicious effects of artistic creation, as though its transmission of testimony somehow circumvented the esthetic concerns of a work of art. This would be consistent with such titles of Wiesel's articles as "Does the Holocaust lie beyond the reach of art?" (1983) and "Art and the Holocaust: Trivializing Memory" (1989) – articles in which only documentaries were acknowledged as authentic. For Wiesel, the relationship between esthetics and authentic representation was that of a zero-sum game: the more artistic creation was involved in a depiction of the Holocaust, the more exploitative and trivializing that depiction would inevitably become.

Yet despite Wiesel's admiration for *Night and Fog*, that film was made on a basis that differed radically from his own view of the relationship between art and the Holocaust. When, in 1954 or 1955, Resnais was asked by producer Anatole Dauman to direct a film on what was then called 'the deportation,' Resnais initially refused because he felt unqualified to make a film about the death-camps of which he had no first-hand experience. But Dauman persisted and Resnais finally gave in when Jean Cayrol, who had survived imprisonment at Mauthausen, agreed to write the narration for the film, which from Resnais' perspective would serve as "une garantie d'authenticité" (Raskin 1987: 27-28, 48-49). However, he felt strongly that the new documentary would have to be made, not as yet another cinematic pamphlet of the kind that other filmmakers had produced, but rather as an esthetically interesting work of art, in order to have any lasting impact. He stated in an interview (Raskin 1987: 52, my translation):

> Another problem was the form of the film: how to handle a subject of that kind? I was completely crushed by it (and still am) and I said to myself: Alright, there have been a number of films on the concentration camps. Everyone approves of them but they don't seem to have made very much impact on people. And since I am a formalist, maybe in this film and despite its subject, I should override my misgivings and try to carry out form experiments (*des recherches formelles*).

Needless to say, the kind of formalism Resnais practised in no way marginalized the importance of the content of this film. As he once observed (Benayoun 1980: 231, my translation):

> The dichotomy between form and content has always seemed to me to be based on an absurd reasoning. The idea that a formless film expressing noble sentiments would be superior to a purely formal film is ridiculous. Communication can only occur through form. If there is no form, you cannot create emotion in the viewer.

In making *Night and Fog*, the creative process involving form experiments was not an easy one for Resnais to perform. He stated, for example, that when editing in the evenings to save time, it was often unnerving for him to carry out form experiments with images of cadavers or of people in agony; but he knew that unless he did precisely that, those images would not get through to the audience with the power they deserved (Raskin 1987: 58-59).

For Resnais then, *Night and Fog* had to be made as an innovative work of art with careful attention to formal esthetics if it were to have any effect, and stir the viewer; in this respect, he and Wiesel held diametrically opposed views as to the salutary or noxious role of artistry in representations of the Holocaust. However, since Wiesel repeatedly cited *Night and Fog* as exemplifying authenticity in its representation of the Holocaust, in this case at least esthetics and authenticity were in no way mutually exclusive.

## (2)

Another important difference between Elie Wiesel's and Alain Resnais' outlooks concerns the functions their depictions of the Holocaust were intended to fulfill.

For Wiesel, it was primarily a matter of keeping alive the memory of those who had perished. In his acceptance speech for the Nobel Peace Prize in Oslo on December 10, 1986, he said (Wiesel 1986):

> I have tried to keep memory alive, I have tried to fight those who forget because if we forget, we are guilty, we are accomplices. We could not prevent their death the first time. But if we forget them, they will be killed a second time and this time, it will be our responsibility.

And in 2009, he stated (cited by Heffner 2009):

> The word "memory" combines almost all my obsessions, all my priorities. We are committed to memory. I am, because of what I remember. If I do what I do, what I'm trying to do, it's again because I remember. And therefore "memory" is probably the key word in my vocabulary.

He was aptly described as a "Jewish guardian of memory" (Chmiel 2002: 61) and as "memory keeper of the Holocaust" (Langer 2016). But he was also widely characterized as "the conscience of humanity," or, in Obama's words, as "the conscience of the world" (*Times of Israel* 2016: 7), and in all fairness, it is important to point out that Wiesel's focus was not exclusively on those who were murdered in the Holocaust. In 1974 he stated:

> I don't think [the Jew] should become obsessed with only Jewishness. I think he should be obsessed with everything else as well. I am. I was obsessed by Biafra; I think I was among the first to fight for Biafra. I saw the children's pictures in the newspapers and I couldn't sleep.

Wiesel was an activist who passionately defended the victims of oppression in many parts of the world, but the works in which he depicted the Holocaust were specifically designed to keep alive the memory of Hitler's victims. He even made a point of never likening other atrocities to the Holocaust until 1976, when, in concern for the desperate situation of the Aché Indians who were being exterminated by the government of Paraguay, he wrote (Wiesel 1976: 165):

> Until now, I always forbade myself to compare the Holocaust of European Judaism to events foreign to it. Auschwitz was something else, and more, than the Vietnam War; the Warsaw Ghetto had no relation of substance with Harlem – deplorable and misplaced comparisons which often reveal the ignorance, the arrogance of those who formulate them. I found these offensive, revolting. The Universe of concentration camps, by its dimensions and its design, lies outside, if not beyond, history. Its vocabulary belongs to it alone.

This quotation is sometimes used without the opening words "Until now." When this is done, the reader is led to believe that Wiesel *never* likened other atrocities to the Holocaust.

Resnais, on the other hand, saw *Night and Fog* not as a commemoration of those who were murdered in the death-camps, but rather as a wake-up call. Both he and Jean Cayrol, who would write the spoken narration, were convinced that the stage was being set for a new wave of racism in connection with the Algerian war for independence and it was largely in order to warn their compatriots against the creation of new concentration camps that Resnais and Cayrol agreed to make *Night and Fog* (Raskin 1987: 51, 137). It is for this reason that the film encourages viewers to search their own souls for tell-tale signs of the racist contagion, while other representations of the Holocaust generally position audiences in a self-exempting stance of righteous indignation.

The final scene is particularly significant to this perspective. As the camera moves over the terrain and relics of what was once a concentration camp, we are cautioned that this abandoned village is still heavy with peril and that new executioners, with faces like our own, may soon be among us. The final words are then spoken:

> And here we are, earnestly looking at these ruins as though the old monster of the camps lay dead beneath the rubble,
>   we who pretend to regain hope before this image that recedes into the distance, as if one could ever be cured of the plague of the camps,
>   we who pretend to believe that it is all confined to a single epoch and a single country and who don't think of looking around ourselves, and who don't hear that people are crying out without end.

It is largely thanks to this positioning of the viewer in a soul-searching stance that *Night and Fog* was shown on six French TV channels at midnight on May 14, 1990, as a symbolic response to the desecration of the Jewish cemetery at Carpentras (*Le Monde* 1990: 11).

This simultaneous broadcast of the film on numerous channels was an unprecedented event in the history of television, and a confirmation of the utterly unique status occupied by *Night and Fog* in contemporary culture.

In the light of the above discussion describing two major differences between Elie Wiesel's and Alain Resnais' understanding of the relationship between art and the Holocaust, and with all due respect for Elie Wiesel's extraordinary wisdom and moral leadership, I believe that Alain Resnais' approach is the more viable of the two.

# References

Benayoun, Robert (1980). *Alain Resnais, Arpenteur de l'imaginaire*. Paris: Stock/Cinéma.

Cavani, Liliana (1974). *The Night Porter / Il portiere di note*. Rome: Ital-Noleggio Cinematografico.

Chmiel, Mark (2002). "Elie Wiesel and the question of Palestine," *Tikkun*, vol. 17, no. 6, Nov/Dec, p. 61. https://www.questia.com/magazine/1P3-235974221/elie-wiesel-and-the-question-of-palestine Accessed 28 April 2017.

Chomsky, Marvin J. (1978). *Holocaust* [TV mini-series]. Titus Productions.

Heffner, Richard D. (2009). "The Mystic Chords of Memory," in *Conversations with Elie Wiesel*. Schocken. https://archive.org/details/openmind_ep1518 Accessed 28 April 2017.

Langer, Emily (2016). "Elie Wiesel, Nobel laureate and memory keeper of the Holocaust, dies at 87," *The Washington Post*, 2 July 2016. https://www.washingtonpost.com/national/elie-wiesel-nobel-laureate-and-memory-keeper-of-the-holocaust-dies-at-87/2016/07/02/4a2d2472-50b5-11e5-8c19-0b6825aa4a3a_story.html Accessed 28 April 2017.

Lanzmann, Claude. *Shoah* (1985). France and U.K.: BBC, Historia, Les Films Aleph, Ministére de la Culture de la République Francaise.

*Le Monde* (1990). "*Nuit et Brouillard* sur les six châines," 16 May 1990, p. 11.

Pakula, Alan J. (1983). *Sophie's Choice*. Keith Barish Productions.

Raskin, Richard (2014). "Art and the Holocaust: positioning *Seven Minutes in the Warsaw Ghetto*," *Short Film Studies*, vol. 4, no. 2, pp. 223-226.

Raskin, Richard (1987). *Nuit et Brouillard. On the Making, Reception and Functions of a Major Documentary Film*. Aarhus: Aarhus University Press.

Resnais, Alain. *Night and Fog* (*Nuit et brouillard*). France: Argos, 1956.

*The Times of Israel* (2016). "Obama: Elie Wiesel was 'the conscience of the world,'" 3 July 2016, p. 7. http://www.timesofisrael.com/obama-elie-wiesel-was-the-conscience-of-the-world/ Accessed 28 April 2017.

Wiesel, Elie (1976). "Now We Know," in Richard Arens (ed.), *Genocide in Paraguay*. Philadelphia: Temple University Press, pp. 165-167.

Wiesel, Elie (1977). "The Holocaust as Literary Inspiration," in *Dimensions of the Holocaust*. Annotated by Elliot Lefkovitz. Northwestern University Press.

Wiesel, Elie (1983a). Foreword to Annette Insdorf, *Indelible Shadows: Film and the Holocaust*. New York: Random House, p. xii.

Wiesel, Elie (1983b). "Does the Holocaust lie beyond the reach of art?" *New York Times*, 17 April 1983, section 2, p. 12. http://www.nytimes.com/1983/04/17/movies/does-the-holocaust-lie-beyond-the-reach-of-art.html?pagewanted=all Accessed 28 April 2017.

Wiesel, Elie (1986). Nobel Prize acceptance speech. https://www.nobelprize.org/mediaplayer/index.php?id=2028 Accessed 28 April 2017.

Wiesel, Elie (1989). "Art and the Holocaust: Trivializing Memory," *New York Times*, 11 June 1989. http://www.nytimes.com/1989/06/11/movies/art-and-the-holocaust-trivializing-memory.html?pagewanted=all Accessed 28 April 2017.

# 8

# An Iconic Holocaust Photo in Context

## Introductory note

Widely considered the most iconic of all Holocaust photos, this picture was taken by a German propaganda photographer in the Warsaw Ghetto during the so-called "grand operation" (*Großaktion*), which began on April 10 and ended on May 16, 1943, and was intended to clear the ghetto of the remaining 60,000 Jews. More than 300,000 had already been put to death at Treblinka and other camps. This final clearing of the ghetto was expected to last three days, but because of fierce resistance on the part of Jewish fighting units within the ghetto, it took nearly an entire month to carry out the operation. This was the first major uprising against the Nazis in any of the occupied territories.

In charge of the "grand operation" was Jürgen Stroop, who was ordered to send daily dispatches to his immediate superior in Krakow, Wilhelm Friedrich Krüger, who in turn sent the communiqués on to SS Chief Heinrich Himmler in Berlin. After the crushing of the revolt, Stroop was ordered by Krüger to make a report, the bragging title of which was to be *Es gibt keinen jüdischen Wohnbezirk in Warschau mehr!* (*The Jewish Quarter in Warsaw Is No More!*), and which is generally referred to simply as the *Stroop Report*. It consisted of a list of German casualties, daily dispatches Stroop teletyped to Krüger during the operation, and a pictorial section (*Bildbericht*) containing photographs, including the one shown here.

Three leather-bound copies of the report were made – one for Himmler, one for Krüger and one for Stroop himself. And one unbound file copy (*das Konzept*) was kept at SS headquarters in Warsaw. One leather-bound specimen is now preserved in Warsaw at the Institute for National Remembrance, while the file copy is in Washington at the National Archives and Records Administration. The report played a prominent role in the Nuremberg trials.

Captured in Bavaria by American forces in May 1945, Stroop was eventually turned over to Polish authorities who had him share a prison cell with Kazimierz Moczarski, a Polish Home Army officer who had been active in the anti-Nazi resistance. Utterly unrepentant, Stroop candidly confided in his former enemy, who took copious notes that would eventually be published in English as *Conversations with an Executioner* (1981).

## Preliminaries

Previous attempts to describe the photograph in its original context have focused, for example in Lucy L. Davidowicz's words (1975: 166), on the Germans' delusional perception of *themselves* as "innocent and aggrieved victims," while every Jewish man, woman and child – such as those appearing specifically in this photograph – was "a supercunning and all-powerful antagonist," a "warrior of a vast Satanic fighting machine" bent on destroying the German people. Seen from this perspective, the S.S. men in the picture would be the defenders of innocence, while the Jewish women and children would be the shameless aggressors.

Other writers, including Herman Rapaport (1997), have found it useful to invoke the concept of a "murderous gaze" in discussing this photograph. For Rapaport, what appealed to the compilers of the *Stroop Report* was the utter inevitability of the death awaiting the child with raised hands – "a being-toward-death [that] is as fated to occur as a stone is fated to fall down a steep mountain slope" (197). Taking two levels of meaning into account, Rapaport suggested that "the camera has been used obscenely to document not only the child's destruction but also the gazer's pleasure, which emanates from the secure sovereignty of the viewer, a sovereignty we are being tempted to share" (203). In this way, the contemporary viewer as well as the 1943 photographer are both encompassed by the concept of the gazer.

Largely in agreement with Rapaport, and also citing Sybil Milton's contention that "photography was a routine part of the extermination process in Nazi Germany," Marianne Hirsch (2003) focused on the "conflation between camera and weapon" (24), suggesting that photographer and executioner played parallel roles in the same murderous process, shooting the victims first in one way and then another (25).

> The soldier pointing his gun at the boy, with his characteristic helmet and uniform, is an embodiment of genocidal intent. The camera gaze mirrors the machine gun, and announces the gas chamber.

Also considering two levels of meaning, Marianne Hirsch found that this photograph "is evidence not only of the perpetrator's deed but also of the desire to flaunt and advertise the evidence of that deed" (25). Aptly designating the photograph as a "perpetrator image," Hirsch also pointed out that "the photographer, the perpetrator and the spectator share the same space of looking," originally defined by the photo as positioning "the genocidal gaze of the Nazi death machine" (24).

All of these commentaries are invaluable contributions to an understanding of the photograph in its original context, and should be kept in mind.

I will however propose a somewhat different approach, more concretely grounded in specific structures of S.S. thought, in an attempt to understand what this photograph may have meant to Jürgen Stroop and to the two SS dignitaries to whom he sent it in his report.

## Possible meanings and functions of the photo for Stroop, Krüger and Himmler

It is in more than one way that this photograph is likely to have given an "us and them" experience to the three S.S. men for whom the *Stroop Report* was made.

The obvious sense of course is in the playing off of the Jewish prisoners, embodying defeat and surrender, against the SS soldiers embodying power in the photo – soldiers carrying out orders issued by the SS hierarchy and therefore literally acting as agents of Stroop, Krüger and Himmler.

But far more interesting than the all too evident "us and them" dichotomy is an implicit one that played a major role in the SS mentality with respect to the routine slaughter of Jewish women and children. And this other dichotomy, which will eventually lead us into the very heart (or heartlessness) of the picture, concerns a distinction between two ways of being in relation to the killing of helpless victims.

As a starting point for considering these two ways of being, we will look at several revealing statements made by Stroop himself in conversation with Kazimierz Moczarski, his post-war Warsaw cell-mate, beginning with a bizarre comment on Christianity. This is what Stroop told his cell-mate on that subject (Moczarski 1981: 58):

> Christ [...] was half-Nordic, of course. His mother, who served in the Temple under the protection of an important priest, became pregnant by a blond German, a soldier from one of the Germanic tribes that reached Asia Minor from the Carpathians. That's why the Christ was fair-haired and thought differently from the Jews who doctored his teachings and spread them around the world to further their own aims – the weakening and debasement of man through guilt.

What this implies, among other things, is that for Stroop, to experience guilt is to allow oneself to be infected by a Jewish poison. In this delusional perspective, guilt is simply written off as an unacceptable Jewish invention, and regardless of what one may or may not do, to feel guilty would be to betray one's Aryan nature and to succumb to the Judaic plot.

Stroop was just as adamant with regard to the question of pity, as can be seen in relation to two separate incidents.

One concerned an Askari, a member of an auxiliary unit assigned to the ghetto and comprised of Ukrainian, Latvian and Lithuanian solders. The story begins this way (Moczarski 1981: 118):

> As I was leaving the Ghetto that afternoon, I heard a shot on the Aryan side of the wall. I rushed toward the culprit, a young Askari in a black coat, and gave that Latvian hell! 'But it's so boring here sir,' he insisted. 'When will we

begin firing at the animals in this Jewish zoo?' I slapped his blond head with my glove (he was an Aryan), then slipped him a Reichsmark. Fine fellows, those Askaris, or so I thought at the time.

At a later point in his conversations with Moczarski (138), Stroop returned to the story of this Askari once again, this time bringing it to completion:

There was fire everywhere. Walls crumbled, balconies, masonry, and timber crashed into the street. The smoke made it impossible to breathe. The SS watched from a distance. I stood behind them, protected by my bodyguard unit. I had stopped using those Askaris, who turned out to be a real disappointment. In fact I'd assigned half of them to the Schutzpolizei for other less responsible work. Do you remember that Askari I told you about earlier – the one who couldn't wait to fight the Jews? Well, that Latvian turned out to be a total idiot. I ran into him in the Ghetto one day, and can you believe it, he was crying. A Nordic, with blue eyes, who spoke half-decent German, an anti-Semite, and he was crying. He mumbled something about he couldn't ... the blood ... the corpses ... the children ... I completely lost my head and gave him a punch in the nose. Then I had him thrown out of the Ghetto area along with a hundred and fifty or so of his lily-livered pals.

What was contemptible in Stroop's eyes was the Askari's attack of pity for the victims. Stroop would tolerate no such feelings on the part of men serving under his command.

The other incident concerns women of the *HeChalutz* movement, whom Stroop called *Haluzzenmädeln* and whose ferocity as fighters had made a great impression on him. Here is the story as Stroop told it to Moczarski (132):

Stroop expressed his admiration of the *Haluzzenmädeln* on a number of occasions. "I sometimes think that they were super-beings – demons or Amazons," he reflected. "Nerves like steel and the dexterity of circus performers. They often fired two pistols simultaneously, one in each hand. They were fighters to the end and extremely dangerous at close quarters. I remember *Haluzzenmädeln* we cornered who blinked at us like frightened rabbits. But when our men began to move in, they'd pull grenades from their skirts or trousers and hurl them at us, shrieking curses that made our hair stand on end! They caused us so many losses that I ordered them cut down from a distance, instead of taken alive."

I gasped. "You mean you felt no pity for their youth and womanhood?"

There was a long silence during which Stroop methodically kneaded the area surrounding his heart. Finally, he looked up, smoothed back his hair, and said in clipped tones:

"Anyone attempting to be a true man – that is a strong one – would have been forced to act like me. *'Gelobt sei was hart macht'.*"

Moczarski explains that *Praise be to what hardens one* is "a quote from Nietzsche used as a Nazi slogan."

Here, as was the case with the Askari incident, manhood is categorically defined by Stroop as incompatible with pity.

But this stigmatization of guilt and pity is still only a small part of the overall picture, which will now be further illustrated from a broader S.S. perspective.

In her book on Eichmann and the banality of evil, Hannah Arendt (1994: 105-106) mentions the ways in which Himmler solved problems of conscience by coining slogans or other one-liners in his speeches to the commanders of the *Einsatzgruppen* and the Higher S.S. and Police Leaders, such as: "The order to solve the Jewish question, this was the most frightening order an organization could ever receive." Or: "We realize that what we are expecting from you is 'superhuman,' to be 'superhumanly inhuman.'"

Further developing her analysis of the ways in which Himmler conceptually packaged the slaughter of women and children for those serving under him, Arendt puts her finger on a specific mechanism whereby the perpetrator turned the killing of innocent victims into a heavy burden he himself had to bear (106):

> ... the problem [for the murderers] was how to overcome not so much their conscience as the animal pity by which all normal men are affected in the presence of physical suffering. The trick used by Himmler – who apparently was rather strongly afflicted with these instinctive reactions himself – was very simple and probably very effective; it consisted in turning these instincts around, as it were, in directing them toward the self. So that instead of saying: What horrible things I did to people!, the murderers would be able to say: What horrible things I had to watch in the pursuance of my duties, how heavily the task weighed upon my shoulders!

This analysis is certainly borne out by the description given by Rudolf Höss, commandant of Auschwitz, of the ways in which he managed and experienced his own role in the murder of Jewish women and children. It is only fair to mention that the following quotation from Höss' autobiography may be upsetting and might best be skipped by readers who don't wish to know more than they already do about this particular subject (1959: 165, 169-172):

> The smaller children usually cried because of the strangeness of being undressed in this fashion, but when their mothers or members of the Special Detachment [*Sonderkommando*, consisting of prisoners (RR)] comforted them, they became calm and entered the gas chambers, playing or joking with one another and carrying their toys.
> I noticed that women who either guessed or knew what awaited them nevertheless found the courage to joke with the children to encourage them, despite the mortal terror visible in their own eyes.
> One woman approached me as she walked past and, pointing to her four children who were manfully helping the smallest ones over the rough ground, she whispered:
> "How can you bring yourself to kill such beautiful, darling children? Have you no heart at all?" […]
> This mass extermination, with all its attendant circumstances, did not, as I know, fail to affect those who took a part in it. With very few exceptions, nearly all of those detailed to do this monstrous "work," this "service," and who, like myself, have given sufficient thought to the matter, have been deeply marked by these events.
> Many of the men approached me as I went my rounds through the extermination buildings, and poured out their anxieties and impressions to me, in the hope that I could allay them.
> Again and again during these confidential conversations I was asked: is it necessary that we do all this? Is it necessary that hundreds of thousands of women and children be destroyed? And I, who in my innermost being had on countless occasions asked myself exactly this question, could only fob them off and attempt to console them by repeating that it was done on Hitler's order. I had to tell them that this extermination of Jewry had to be, so that Germany and our posterity might be freed forever from their relentless adversaries.
> There was no doubt in the mind of any of us that Hitler's order had to be obeyed regardless, and that it was the duty of the SS to carry it out. Nevertheless we were all tormented by secret doubts.

I myself dared not admit to such doubts. In order to make my subordinates carry on with their task, it was psychologically essential that I myself appear convinced of the necessity for this gruesomely harsh order.

Everyone watched me. They observed the impression produced upon me by the kind of scenes that I have described above and my reactions. Every word I said on the subject was discussed. I had to exercise intense self-control in order to prevent my innermost doubts and feelings of oppression from becoming apparent.

I had to appear cold and indifferent to events that must have wrung the heart of anyone possessed of human feelings. I might not even look away when afraid lest my natural emotions got the upper hand. I had to watch coldly, while the mothers with laughing or crying children went into the gas chambers.

On one occasion two small children were so absorbed in some game that they quite refused to let their mother tear them away from it. Even the Jews of the Special Detachment were reluctant to pick the children up. The imploring look in the eyes of the mother, who certainly knew what was happening, is something I shall never forget. The people were already in the gas chamber and becoming restive, and I had to act. Everyone was looking at me. I nodded to the junior noncommissioned officer on duty and he picked up the screaming, struggling children in his arms and carried them into the gas chamber, accompanied by their mother who was weeping in the most heart-rending fashion. My pity was so great that I longed to vanish from the scene; yet I might not show the slightest trace of emotion.

I had to see everything. I had to watch hour after hour, by day and by night, the removal and the burning of the bodies, the extraction of the teeth, the cutting of the hair, the whole grisly, interminable business. I had to stand for hours on end in the ghastly stench, while the mass graves were being opened and the bodies dragged out and burned.

I had to look through the peephole of the gas chambers and watch the process of death itself, because the doctors wanted me to see it.

I had to do all this because I was the one to whom everyone looked, because I had to show them all that I did not merely issue the orders and make the regulations but was also prepared myself to be present at whatever task I had assigned my subordinates.

The *Reichsführer* SS sent various high-ranking Party leaders and SS officers to Auschwitz so that they might see for themselves the process of extermination of the Jews. They were all deeply impressed by what they saw. Some who had previously spoken most loudly about the necessity for this extermination fell silent once they had actually seen the "final solution of the Jewish question." I was repeatedly asked how I and my men could go on watching these operations, and how we were able to stand it.

My invariable answer was that the iron determination with which we must carry out Hitler's orders could only be obtained by a stifling of all human emotions. Each of these gentlemen declared that he was glad the job had not been given to him.

Even Mildner and Eichmann, who were certainly tough enough, had no wish to change places with me. This was one job which nobody envied me.

I had many detailed discussions with Eichmann concerning all matters connected with the "final solution of the Jewish question," but without ever disclosing my inner anxieties. I tried in every way to discover Eichmann's innermost and real convictions about this "solution."

Yes, every way. Yet even when we were quite alone together and the drink had been flowing freely so that he was in his most expansive mood, he showed that he was completely obsessed with the idea of destroying every single Jew that he could lay his hands on. Without pity and in cold blood we must complete this extermination as rapidly as possible. Any compromise, even the slightest, would have to be paid for bitterly at a later date.

In the face of such grim determination I was forced to bury all my human considerations as deeply as possible.

Indeed, I must freely confess that after these conversations with Eichmann I almost came to regard such emotions as a betrayal of the Führer.

There was no escape for me from this dilemma.

I had to go on with this process of extermination. I had to continue this mass murder and coldly to watch it, without regard for the doubts that were seething deep inside me.

As Höss narratively framed these events and shaped his own experience of them, he turned himself into a kind of tragic figure, whose job it was to carry out these monstrous tasks, sacrificing his own inner peace in the process and having to stifle all natural and instinctive reactions to the suffering of his victims. In his own telling of this story, it is he, even more than the women and children he murdered, who truly deserved compassion. Yet at the same time, Höss implicitly took pride in his ability to carry out a heavy duty that even Eichmann might not have been able to execute.

Something of this same "martyrdom of the executioner" was incisively depicted by Jorge Luis Borges in a short story he wrote in 1949 entitled "*Deutsches Requiem*," told in the first person by a man who was made subdirector of the Tarnowitz concentration camp. The fictional speaker of this tale describes his overcoming of compassion in dealing with a well-known Jewish poet, David Jerusalem, who had turned up as a prisoner at the camp (Borges 1998: 231-232).

> Nazism is intrinsically a moral act, a stripping away of the old man, which is corrupt and depraved, in order to put on the new. In battle, amid the captains' outcries and the shouting, such a transformation is common; it is not common in a crude dungeon, where insidious compassion tempts us with ancient acts of tenderness. I do not write that word "compassion" lightly: compassion on the part of the superior man is Zarathustra's ultimate sin. I myself (I confess) almost committed it when the famous poet David Jerusalem was sent to us from Breslau. [...] I was severe with him; I let neither compassion nor his fame make me soft. [...] In late 1942, Jerusalem went insane; on March 1, 1943, he succeeded in killing himself.
>
> I do not know whether Jerusalem understood that if I destroyed him, it was in order to destroy my own compassion. In my eyes, he was not a man, not even a Jew; he had become a symbol of a detested region of my soul. I suffered with him, I died with him, I somehow have been lost with him; that was why I was implacable.

Here, we rejoin Stroop's view of guilt and pity as Jewish poisons and of the necessity of ridding oneself of them. What Borges makes explicit is that for the Nazi, the killing of the Jewish victim and the amputation of one's own compassion are one and the same act – and that it is through the one that the other is achieved. Here again, the overcoming of pity is both a burden requiring the sacrifice of one's humanity, and also implicitly a matter of exhilarating pride in the accomplishment of becoming a "new man" in place of the old one who could still be tempted to perform "ancient acts of tenderness."

Returning now to the photograph, I would suggest that this particular picture – the only one in the *Stroop Report* showing women and children at close quarters – was in a sense the most daring image in that document. In sending this picture to Krüger and Himmler, Stroop was in effect saying to them: "While *others* may not be able to rise to this historic occasion, because pity and other archaic forms of weakness hold them back, *we* are able to carry out our mission of killing even women and children without batting an eye." This is the underlying "us and them" dichotomy implied by the photograph for people like Stroop, Krüger and Himmler, and for them it was just as palpable as the more obvious "Jew versus Nazi" dichotomy portrayed in the picture.

The message this photograph communicated from its sender to its recipients was a complicitous one, shared by the three "new men." It is precisely because the little boy with his hands raised looks so utterly helpless and vulnerable, and appeals so forcefully to whatever protective instincts the spectator may harbor, that only those who had shed all vestiges of pity and compassion could applaud the photo and see it as a trophy. Had the photo been less potentially moving, it would not have had this demonstrative value for those who had trained others to become "superhumanly inhuman," in Himmler's words.

The message it sent was also self-congratulatory – "*We can do this!*" – and at the same time, expressive of a burden or responsibility: "We *have* to do this!" As an obligation carried out unflinchingly, for the sake of future generations who would not have to do such things, this arrest and imminent *Vernichtung* of Jewish women and children was seen by the S.S. elite as deserving of gratitude and admiration, a difficult task well done. This too could be shared by Stroop, Krüger and Himmler.

In their eyes, what the picture told was not the story of the victims but that of the S.S., faithfully discharging their duties and utterly unmoved by a powerful spectacle that would reduce lesser men – like Stroop's Askari – to tears.

For men who felt they had to set an example, as Höss claimed he was obliged to do at Auschwitz when subordinates looked to his demeanor as mothers and babies were gassed, the photo appeared *to be* that example: an ultimate celebration of the heartlessness necessary for exterminating every last Jewish man, woman and child.

# References

Arendt, Hannah (1994). *Eichmann in Jerusalem. A Report on the Banality of Evil.* New York: Penguin Books. Orig. pub. 1963.

Dawidowicz, Lucy S. (1990). *The War Against the Jews: 1933-1945.* New York: Bantam, 1975.

Hirsch, Marianne (2003). "Nazi Photographs in Post-Holocaust Art: Gender as an Idiom of Memorialization," in Alex Hughes and Andrea Noble, eds, *Phototextualities. Intersections of Photography and Narrative.* Albuquerque: University of New Mexico Press, pp. 19-40.

Hoess, Rudolf (1959). *Commandant of Auschwitz. The Autobiography of Rudolf Hoess*. Cleveland and New York: World Publishing Co.

Moczarski, Kazimierz (1981). *Conversations with an Executioner*, ed. Mariana Fitzpatrick. Englewood Cliffs: Prentice-Hall. Orig. pub. in Polish 1977.

Rapaport, Herman (1997). "The Eye and the Law," in *Is There Truth in Art?* Ithaca: Cornell University Press, pp. 196-217.

Raskin, Richard (2004). *A Child at Gunpoint. A Case Study in the Life of a Photo*. Aarhus: Aarhus University Press.

Raskin, Richard (2013). *Seven Minutes in the Warsaw Ghetto and With Raised Hands. A film ebook*. Aarhus: Aarhus University Press.

# 9

# *Bad Day at Black Rock* and the Overcoming of Evil

*John Macreedy (Spencer Tracy) about to be attacked by one of the town's racist bullies: Coley Trimble (Ernest Borgnine)*

## Preliminaries

Though it is one of the most meaningful Hollywood productions of the 1950s, *Bad Day at Black Rock* is not widely known by younger audiences today. With that in mind, and for the sake of readers who have not yet had the opportunity to see this remarkable film, I am providing screenwriter Millard Kaufman's own thumbnail summary of the plot (2008: 76):

> [The story] centered on an army officer, John Macreedy, who after leading a unit of Nisei (Japanese-American) infantry, returns to the States with a paralyzed arm that keeps his war experience more than just an unpleasant memory. He seeks out the father of a young soldier who had died saving Macreedy's life, to hand over the medal the boy had won posthumously.

He finds that the man, a Japanese-American farmer, had been the victim of a racist murder, and now the killers are intent on liquidating Macreedy before he uncovers the crime.

*Bad Day at Black Rock* was produced at MGM by Dore Schary, for whom the making of this particular film was so important that he threatened to resign as the studio's production chief if MGM's president, Nicholas Schenck, had his way and canceled its production (Schary 1979: 277). To play Macreedy, Schary chose Spencer Tracy, who went on to win an Oscar nomination for this performance, while the three arch villains were played by Robert Ryan (Reno Smith), Ernest Borgnine (Coley Trimble) and Lee Marvin (Hector David). To write the screenplay, Schary selected Millard Kaufman, who had served in the Marine Corps during World War II and would have the kind of toughness the producer wanted in the writing.

The film's U.S. release was on January 7, 1955.

## 1. From short story to film and getting Spencer Tracy on board

American Magazine: January, 1947, p.40

*Bad Day at Black Rock* was based on a short story called "Bad Time at Honda," written by Howard Breslin and published in the January 1947 issue of *American Magazine* (pp. 40-43, 136-138). To the left is the title page, which should put to rest any further speculation as to the correct spelling of the place-name in Breslin's story. Many commentators, including Rob Nixon (n.d.), incorrectly cite the place-name as "Hondo," and some express doubt as to which spelling is correct or even whether it is possible to ascertain which is correct (Streamas 2003: 110-111). In managing the transition from short story to screenplay, Millard

Kaufman changed "Bad Time" to "Bad Day" and "Honda" to "Black Rock," because he "wanted the tell the story within the span of one day and the confines of one location," thereby respecting the Aristotelian unities of time and place; and because the place-name "Hondo" – dangerously close to "Honda" – had already been taken as the title of a John Wayne film that would be released in November 1953 (Kaufman 2008: 75).

However, the most striking difference between the short story and the film concerns the physical condition of the protagonist: in the short story, he has no handicap of any kind, while the Macreedy of the film has a paralyzed left arm. The reasons for this dramatic change concern primarily the need to bring Spencer Tracy on board as the star of the film, after extremely inauspicious preliminaries. As has been frequently noted, when Dore Schary first gave the notoriously volatile actor the short story to read, Tracy reportedly replied after reading it: "How dare you give me this kind of shit. I'm supposed to be the best male actor in America and you can jam this up your ass" (Davidson 1987: 113-114).

Given this initial attitude on the actor's part, and after some intermediate steps not worth detailing here, the question then became: what needed to be done in order to change Spencer Tracy's mind about starring in the film? And in this connection, we have two accounts, one by Dore Schary and the other by Millard Kaufman, both of whom agree that giving Macreedy a disability genuinely improved the story. But in Kaufman's version (2008: 76), Schary saw the paralyzed arm as primarily a ploy to win Tracy over: "Dore was convinced that no actor could resist playing a character with an impairment [...] He was still pursuing Tracy to play the part and thought the defect would help land him." In Schary's own account, the idea of the paralyzed arm emerged, not as a producer's tactic for landing a temperamental actor, but as a way of solving a very real storytelling problem that bothered Tracy when he saw the first version of Kaufman's screenplay (Shary 1979: 278):

> Tracy said he liked it but the guy who came to Black Rock had no real character.
> Listening to Tracy was always a pleasure. This time I learned something about the script. He was right – the character of McCreedy [sic] needed a personal story, an inside problem, a subtext. I promised we would find one. Millard [Kaufman] and I spent a night wrestling for something that would fill out the space. I remembered that years before, when I was with Selznick, I had worked on a story for Joe Cotton, Ingrid Bergman, and Eric von Stro-

heim that fell apart before it went into screenplay. But the character that Joe was to have played was a war veteran who had had a crippling injury to one hand. I tried that notion on Millard. It pulled things together. It made Tracy's reluctance to fight more credible, his desire to bring the medal to the father of the Nisei who had saved his life in combat more understandable, and when there was no way out except to resist and strike back, it gave Tracy's character a new confidence that he could prevail even without the use of one hand. Millard and I worked it all out in that one night and Millard rushed home and went to work on rewriting the screenplay.

The next morning I called Tracy, told him I had good news. He came in a few hours later. I laid out the new character line and he smiled and said, "That's it," and wanted to know when we'd get started.

Both accounts are of course of little more than anecdotal interest. However, at a later point in the present essay, I will return to the ways in which Macreedy's paralyzed arm contributes to the *meaning* of the film in relation to the viewer's experience of its political agenda.

## 2. Racism

Macreedy and Joe Komoko – as Tracy pronounces the surname in the film, though it is spelled 'Komako' in Millard Kaufman's script – had presumably served in Italy in the legendary 442nd Regimental Combat Team, formed in 1943 with Japanese-American volunteers – the most decorated unit in US military history for its size and length of service, and best known for having rescued a "lost battalion" of Texas infantrymen trapped behind German lines in the Vosges Mountains. This combat team was the subject of a film Dore Schary produced in 1951, *Go for Broke!*, directed by Robert Parish. The epigraph with which the film opens is a statement made by Franklin D. Roosevelt:

> The proposal of the War Department to organize a combat team consisting of loyal American citizens of Japanese descent has my full approval. The principle on which this country was founded and by which it has always been governed is that Americanism is a matter of the mind and the heart; Americanism is not, and never was, a matter of race or ancestry.

The protagonist is a Lieutenant Grayson played by Van Johnson, and his journey in this film is a gradual overcoming of his own racial prejudice toward the Nisei volunteers he leads. Along the way, and as an indicator of the path on which he is irreversibly embarked, he reads to himself the following sentence from a military manual called *Pocket Guide to Italy*: "Racial prejudice is abhorrent to our American concept of democracy."

According to Schary's own account, the making of this film began with his suggestion to Robert Parish that they tell a story about the Nisei detention centers that had sprung up just after the attack on Pearl Harbor (Schary 1979: 226-227).

> To have rushed Japanese, who were American citizens, into those faraway areas – treeless, barren, lonely, surrounded by vistas of flat, scrubby plains – was unconscionable. The Nisei were not guilty of anything but became victims of terror and panic, losing their homes, farms, equipment and security. That crime against them we wished to report.

But as the project evolved, Schary and Parish decided instead to tell the story of the 442$^{nd}$ Infantry Battalion, whose heroism stood in sharp contrast to the mistrust, insults and physical abuse to which the volunteers and their Stateside families were subjected. One such incident is described in a letter received by an enlisted man, Sam, played by Lane Nakano; back home in the States, Sam's brother had been "beaten to a pulp" along with a couple of his buddies on the farm where they were working. The brother was told by his aggressors that "they'd lynch him if he ever came back." When questioned by a fellow enlisted man, Sam explains that this happened "because they've got slant eyes," and muses: "We're good enough to carry their rifles but not good enough to pick sugarbeets." And although, as John Streamas pertinently points out (2003: 99), not a single Nisei character is actually seen in *Bad Day at Black Rock*, the same racism evoked in *Go for Broke!* is depicted in this film as well, where it results in the murder of the farmer Komoko – father of the soldier who died saving Macreedy's life in Italy. Macreedy's search for the farmer in order to deliver the son's posthumous medal to him meets resistance, intimidation, threats and eventually attempts on his life from the time Macreedy steps off the train in Black Rock and announces to the telegraphist Hastings (Russel Collins) that he wants to go to Adobe Flat. Once there, at the site of Komoko's burned out home, Macreedy discovers wild flowers growing on a patch of ground that could only be an unmarked grave. From that point on, he knows that Komoko is dead and Macreedy's quest is to identify the Nisei farmer's killer and bring him to justice.

Reno Smith is the primary embodiment of racism in this film. At one point he admits to Macreedy that the Japanese made him mad, "After that sneak attack on Pearl Harbor, Bataan." Macreedy leads him on by saying "Komoko made you mad," to which Smith replies: "The same thing. Loyal Japanese-Americans, that's a laugh. They're all mad dogs. What about Corregidor, the death march!" When Macreedy asks him what Komoko had to do with Corregidor, Smith replies: "He was a Jap, wasn't he? Look, Mr. Macreedy, there's a law in this county against shooting dogs. But when I see a mad dog, I don't wait for him to bite me." (Cited dialogue is a transcription of what the actors actually say in the film, which is rarely identical to the lines as they appear in scripts available online.)

It turns out of course that Reno Smith, accompanied by four other drunken "patriots," murdered Komoko, as is finally disclosed to Macreedy by the hotel clerk, Pete Wirth (John Ericson), with the help of Doc Viele (Walter Brennen):

### DOC VIELE
Smith owns Adobe Flat. He leased it to Komoko. He figured he'd cheated him because you gotta have water to raise anything. There never was any water on Adobe Flat. Komoko dug a well. He must have gone down sixty feet.

### PETE WIRTH
He got plenty of water. That made Smith pretty sore. He didn't like Japs anyway. Day after Pearl Harbor, Smith went to Sand City.

### MACREEDY
Yeah, he got turned down. Tried to enlist.

### PETE
When he got back he was pretty sore again. Around ten o'clock we all started drinking.

### MACREEDY
Ten in the morning.

#### PETE

Yeah. Smith, Coley, Sam, Hector and … me. We were all drunk – patriotic drunk. We wanted to go out to scare the Jap a little. Have a little fun. But when we got there, he heard us comin' and he locked the doors. Smith started a fire. And the Jap he came running out. His clothes were all burning. Smith shot him. I didn't even know he had a gun.

Though only the five men involved in the killing of Komoko knew for sure what had happened at Adobe Flat, the entire town was well aware that these five men had a guilty secret to hide and that anyone who pried or in any way failed to protect their secret would face the wrath of Reno Smith and his henchmen, Coley Trimble and Hector David. For that reason, the townspeople did not dare discuss or even want to know about Komoko's fate; nor would they offer any help to Macreedy. And the townspeople's loyal acquiescence to Reno Smith's bullying and intimidation amounted to what might be called "a community arrangement" of a kind that is reminiscent of the situation depicted in a news item with that title, appearing in the *Time Magazine* issue of June 11, 1945:

> Walking home at dusk from an afternoon's jack rabbit-shooting in the flat, dusty San Joaquin Valley, Levi Multanen, 33, thought of his nephew, long missing in the South Pacific. That reminded him how much he hated Japs. Passing the home of Nisei Charles Iwasaki, a raisin-grape grower, Rancher Multanen paused. He knew who lived there—a Jap. Impulsively he leveled his shotgun, fired four times. He walked home, feeling better. The Iwasakis, scared but unwounded, did nothing.
>
> In the past month there had been seven cases of violence against Nisei in the San Joaquin Valley. It seemed time for at least a gesture of law & order. Rancher Multanen was arrested, charged with "rude and threatening" use of his gun.
>
> Two score Parlier Township ranchers showed up for the trial. Before the trial started they talked with Justice of the Peace L. B. Crosby, 65. Mounting the bench, Justice Crosby said: "I guess we know how we feel about this. What shall we do?" He did not wait for an answer. He sentenced Multanen to six months in jail, [then] promptly suspended sentence.
>
> In Washington, Interior Secretary Harold Ickes, whose War Relocation Authority had heckled Valley authorities for their tolerance of terrorism, sputtered with rage: "A disgrace to the bench …." Justice Crosby sputtered right back. His decision, he said, was "a community arrangement." Observed

one Parlier resident: if the judge had been any tougher, he would have been run out of town.

## 3. McCarthyism

Many commentators have suggested that *Bad Day at Black Rock* is not only an indictment of racism but also "a thinly veiled attack on McCarthy's Hollywood blacklisting" (Wheeler 1989: 16) or an "indictment of those who both spearheaded, and submissively accepted, the House Un-American Activities Committee's actions" (Shager 2005).

This is an interesting but potentially confusing issue since the investigator role in this film is filled by Macreedy, not by a villain. It is therefore appropriate to proceed with caution and to avoid overstating the case when considering possible parallels between *Bad Day at Black Rock* and the anti-Communist hysteria of the 1940s and 1950s.

Reno Smith's bullying, intimidating and threatening relationship to the people of Black Rock can be seen as analogous to HUAC's crippling treatment of the Hollywood film community or to Senator Joseph McCarthy's reign of terror in other areas of American life. Smith's abusive wielding of power is perhaps most evident in his humiliating responses to Sheriff Tim Horn (Dean Jagger), who makes two brave but feeble attempts to fulfill his duties, having spent the past four years – since the time he failed to investigate Komoko's mysterious disappearance – drinking himself into a stupor. The first conversation between Reno Smith and the sheriff takes place in the jail, where Smith forces Tim Horn to back down from trying to find out what happened to Komoko before Macreedy does. Smith tells the sheriff: "Macreedy'll do nothing. And neither will you." When Tim then asks: "Suppose I decide to try?" the result is an insult and a thinly disguised threat that brings the sheriff back to the submissive mode to which he had become accustomed:

**SMITH**
That might be dangerous. Tim, you got the body of a hippo,
but the brain of a rabbit. Now don't overtax it.

**TIM**
Yes, Mr. Smith.

Their second confrontation is set in the hotel lobby, when the telegraphist Hastings commits a federal offense by giving to Reno Smith the telegram Macreedy had asked him to send to the State Police. In response to Macreedy's suggestion – "Maybe you'd better do something about this, Sheriff." – Tim Horn decides to stand up to Smith, telling him that there is a law against divulging information. When Smith tells Horn that he is pathetic, Horn replies: "Well maybe so but … I'm still Sheriff." The dialogue then takes a turn that reveals the power relationships in this community:

> **SMITH**
> That's the point. You're not Sheriff any more.
> You're so pathetic you just lost a job.

*Smith tears the badge from Tim's chest and jabs it onto Hector's vest.*

> **SMITH**
> (*to Hector*)
> Okay, Sheriff. Take over.

> **DOC**
> You can't do that!

> **SMITH**
> I can't? Well I put him in the job and now I'm taking him out.

As Paul Simpson rightly suggests (2011), "Dean Jagger's alcoholic sheriff symbolizes the ineffectual response of many American political institutions when McCarthy was at his most powerful." Simpson evokes a "community ruled by fear of a charismatic bully with a populist touch – McCarthy in real life, Reno Smith (Robert Ryan) in the movie" and he goes so far as to suggest that Hector David is Reno Smith's Roy Cohn, "enthusiastically acting on his boss' behalf and sometimes – as Cohn did – exceeding his brief" (Simpson, 2011). While the Hector David/Roy Cohn parallel is somewhat tenuous, the Reno Smith/Joseph McCarthy connection would be accepted by many commentators, and as John Streamas points out, relating the Wisconsin senator's alcoholism to the murder at Adobe Flat: "the parallel between Smith and McCarthy is assured in the idea of 'patriotic drunk'" (2003: 108).

That other townspeople are unresponsive to Macreedy's requests for information and pleas for help is also a function of the "community arrangement" mentioned earlier. This can be seen in a key exchange with Liz Wirth at the garage she runs. When Macreedy asks "What's wrong with this town of yours, Miss Wirth?" and is told "Nothing is wrong with this town, Mr. Macreedy. It's none of your concern," he goes on to remind her that people here are trying to kill him, to which she replies "I don't want to get involved." She explains: "Whatever happens, I've got to go on living in this town. These people are my neighbors, my friends." When Macreedy asks why she doesn't leave Black Rock and she answers that she is staying for her brother's sake, Macreedy continues probing and she replies: "What do you care? What do you care about Black Rock?"

### MACREEDY
I don't care anything about Black Rock. Only it just seems to me there aren't many towns like this in America. But one town like it is enough. And because I think something kind of bad happened here, Miss Wirth. Something I can't quite seem to find the handle to …

### LIZ
You don't know what you're talking about.

### MACREEDY
Well I know this much: the rule of law has left here. The gorillas have taken over.

Similarly, when Macreedy asks Doc Viele to help prevent Smith and his men from murdering him, Viele replies: "I feel for you, but I'm consumed with apathy. Why should I mix in?" In response to Macreedy's reply "To save a life," Viele explains:

> I got enough trouble saving my own. Look, I try to live right and drink my milk every day. But mostly I try to mind my own business …

As Simpson points out concerning Viele's position: "He knows what is happening is wrong but is reluctant to take a risk and stop it – this attitude was especially prevalent in Hollywood which was reeling from accusations that it had been infiltrated by Communist sympathizers and had spread subversive messages" (Simpson 2011). Similarly, Liz Worth's "I don't want to get involved" was an attitude adopted by many in Hollywood who declined to stand up to the witch-hunting politicians when actors, screenwriters and other film workers were threatened with blacklisting or prison.

## 4. Turnabout: Macreedy's victory and the town's redemption

When Macreedy first encounters the villains' efforts to intimidate him, he responds by yielding to them rather than standing his ground. This happens when Hector David takes over Macreedy's hotel room, which Macreedy then vacates, and again when Coley Trimble rams the jeep Macreedy is driving and forces him off the road. When subsequently scolded by Trimble for hogging the road, Macreedy apologizes for the mishap and offers to pay for the damage to Trimble's car. Similarly, in the restaurant scene, when Trimble wants the stool on which Macreedy is seated, Macreedy moves to another one, and when Trimble empties a bottle of ketchup onto Macreedy's food, Macreedy once again refuses to be provoked into fighting back. It is only when Trimble has worked himself up to the point of laying a hand on Macreedy that the latter's submissiveness finally gives way to a totally unexpected turn of events: Macreedy's sudden and explosive use of his one good arm to inflict on Trimble a series of karate chops and other martial arts moves that reduce the infuriated bully to a bloody heap on the floor. And while dealing these punishing blows, Macreedy remains perfectly collected, with his suit jacket neatly buttoned and his hat in place. His complete control and calmness throughout this scene, as the uncomprehending Trimble goes reeling and staggering under Macreedy's blows, helps to make this one of most thrilling turnabouts ever staged in a Hollywood film.

As the reader will recall, when Schary decided that Macreedy should be given a disabled arm, Kaufman thought the real reason for this was to land Tracy in the role. However, Kaufman agreed that the handicap was also "a shrewd ploy to squeeze empathy from the audience and direct it toward our protagonist; all of us are wounded in one way or another" (Kaufman 2008: 76). It also serves as a constant reminder to the viewer that Macreedy is a war veteran who had been seriously wounded in battle. And as Martin F. Norden suggested (1994: 198), in "turning Breslin's explicitly able-bodied veteran into one with a missing arm […], the filmmakers presumably wanted to increase the movie's tensions by stacking near-insurmountable odds against their courageous lead character, who in effect becomes 'remasculinized' through his heroic deeds."

This meshes with the villains' taunting denial of Macreedy's manhood, for example when Hector David repeatedly and pointedly addresses him as "boy" in the hotel room scene and later in the hotel lobby. And when Macreedy declines Reno Smith's invitation to go hunting with him, Smith implicitly denigrates Macreedy by referring to someone else who had lost an arm but who hunted all the time and who (in that respect) was "quite a man."

During the earlier scenes when Macreedy yielded to those who bullied him rather than standing his ground, perhaps he wasn't strategically biding his time but rather, as suggested by his own later statements, he may have been too full of self-pity to fight back – too afraid he couldn't function any longer. The threat to his life forced him to overcome that fear, and to turn the tables on Smith and his thugs. The ultimate showdown is of course the one in which Smith, armed with a rifle and having drawn Macreedy into a trap outside of town with Liz Wirth's help, is unexpectedly attacked by the fast-thinking Macreedy who manages to put together a Molotov cocktail on the spot and to seriously injure his assailant. Macreedy then drives the burned and subdued Smith back into town and delivers him to an astonished Tim Horn, who once again has become the sheriff, and no longer in name only.

Earlier in this essay, I proposed returning to the issue of Macreedy's disability in relation to the social or political meaning of the film. I can finally do so now by taking Norden's observations concerning "remasculinization" one step further and suggesting that, in showing a one-armed man successfully defeating a gang of ruthless villains, the makers of this film invite the viewer to regard the fight against the scourges of racism and McCarthyism as one that can be won despite what appear to be most unfavorable odds. In other words, if with one disabled arm Macreedy can defeat a powerful bully, then even so formidable an enemy as HUAC is by implication vulnerable to defeat by people who are seemingly at a serious disadvantage on a far from level playing field. In this respect, and without suggesting that the victory is by any means an easy one, the film offers a more optimistic message regarding the possibilities of overcoming apparently unstoppable social or political evils than it would have done had Macreedy been as physically intact as his adversaries.

Macreedy's triumph over his own fear and over Reno Smith paves the way for the possibility of a parallel turnabout in the life of Black Rock, the deplorable moral condition of which Doc Viele had previously described in these terms:

Four years ago something terrible happened here. We did nothing about it. Nothing. The whole town fell into a sort of settled melancholy, and all the people in it closed their eyes and held their tongues and failed the test with a whimper.

Now, as the story draws to an end, the posthumous medal takes on its full meaning. There had been no mention of a medal in the short story, where Macreedy's purpose for coming to Black Rock was simply to look in on the dead soldier's father. In the short story, Macreedy explains (Wheeler 1989: 30):

> I came here to find Old Man Kamotka. […] There was a kid named Jimmy Kamotka. He left here years ago. He never wrote his father. The old man couldn't read. I met Jimmy in the army. In Italy. He asked me to look in here … Jimmy Kamotka was killed in Italy. I think maybe this town should know that. And remember it.

In the film, Macreedy states: "This Komoko boy died trying to save my life. They gave him a medal. I came here to give it to his old man, I figured that was the least I could do was give him one day out of my life." In adding the medal to the narrative, the screenwriter invested Macreedy's visit with a more concrete and specific focus. And although John Streamas suggests that the medal "has little significance except as a plot device by which Macreedy is brought to Black Rock" (2003: 108), it is no mere McGuffin or at least no longer one once we arrive at the final scene, just before Macreedy boards the train:

> DOC
> … about that medal. Can we have it?
>
> MACREEDY
> Who's "we"?
>
> DOC
> We. Us.
>
> MACREEDY
> Why?

DOC

Maybe we need it. It would give us something to build on.

This town is wrecked, just as though it was bombed out. Maybe it can come back...

MACREEDY

Some towns do and some towns don't. It depends on the people.

[…]

DOC

That medal would help.

*Macreedy takes the box containing the medal from his pocket and hands it to Doc Viele.*

DOC

Thanks, Mr. Macreedy. Thanks for everything.

In this way, the medal comes to symbolize for the town the overcoming of its own racism and of its fearful acquiescence to the tyranny of a vicious bully. Black Rock – and indirectly Hollywood as well – may now be on its way to redemption.

# References

Breslin, Howard (1947). "Bad Time at Honda," *American Magazine,* January, pp. 40-43, 136-138.

Davidson, Bill (1987). *Spencer Tracy. Tragic Idol.* London: Sedgwick & Jackson.

Kaufman, Millard (2008). "A Vehicle for Tracy: The Road to Black Rock," *The Hopkins Review,* vol. 1, no. 1, Winter (New Series), pp. 70-88.

Kaufman, Millard (1955). *Bad Day at Black Rock.* Screenplay by Don McGuire and Millard Kaufman. Based on the story "Bad Day at Hondo" [sic] by Howard Breslin. Shooting Draft, http://sfy.ru/?script=bad_day_at_black_rock_1955 and http://www.weeklyscript.com/Bad%20Day%20At%20Black%20Rock.txt

Both accessed 5 May 2017.

Niall, Michael [Howard Breslin] (1954). *Bad Day at Black Rock.* New York: Fawcett Publications.

Nichikawa, Lane (2006). *Only the Brave*. San Diego: Mission from Budda Productions.

Nixon, Rob (n.d.). "The Big Idea Behind Bad Day at Black Rock," Turner Classic Movies Film Article http://www.tcm.com/this-month/article/288079%7C296103/The-Big-Idea-Bad-Day-at-Black-Rock.html Accessed 5 May 2017.

Norden, Martin F. (1994). *The cinema of isolation: a history of physical disability in the movies*. Rutgers University Press.

Pirosh, Robert (1951). *Go for Broke!* Los Angeles: produced at MGM by Dore Schary. http://www.archive.org/details/go_for_broke_ACM Accessed 5 May 2017.

Schary, Dore (1979). *HEYDAY. An Autobiography*. Boston: Little, Brown and Co.

Shager, Nick (2005). "Bad Day at Black Rock," *Slant Magazine*, 19 May. http://www.slantmagazine.com/film/review/bad-day-at-black-rock/1520 Accessed 5 May 2017.

Simpson, Paul (2006). *The Rough Guide to Westerns*. London and New York: Rough Guides.

Simpson, Paul (2011). Personal email communication on McCarthyism and *Bad Day at Black Rock*, 29 July.

Streamas, John (2003). "'Patriotic Drunk': To be Yellow, Brave, and Disappeared in *Bad Day at Black Rock*," *American Studies*, vol. 44, nos. 1-2 (Spring/Summer), pp. 99-114.

Sturges, John (1955). *Bad Day at Black Rock*. Los Angeles: produced at MGM by Dore Schary.

Wheeler, David (ed.) (1989). *No, But I Saw the Movie, The Best Short Stories Ever Made to Film*. Harmondsworth: Penguin Books.

Unsigned (1945). "Community Arrangement," *Time Magazine*, 11 June. http://www.time.com/time/magazine/article/0,9171,775804,00.html Accessed 5 May 2017.

# 10

# The Moth in *Merry Christmas, Mr. Lawrence*

## Introduction

> It's always nice of course to do movies like this, which cause people to think a bit...
> *Tom Conti (1983)*

Fortunate accidents are not a rarity in filmmaking but the one that occurred during the filming of David Bowie's final shot in *Merry Christmas, Mr. Lawrence* (1982) is in a class of its own.

In this shot, a moth has alighted on the hair of Major Jack Celliers (David Bowie), who has finally expired after days of being buried up to his neck in sand and helplessly baking in the sun. The entire scene, which concludes with this extraordinary shot, appears as follows in an unpublished post-production script dated February 3, 1983, kindly provided by Karin Padgham at Recorded Picture Company:

101. EXT: GROUNDS BEFORE THE PIT (THE ASSEMBLY AREA)
It is late in the evening. YONOI, in uniform but without his weapons, appears at the pit. He waves the guards away, and comes up behind CELLIERS for a moment. He takes a small knife, from his pocket. He cuts off a lock of CELLIERS' hair. He stands with his eyes closed for a few moments, lost in thought. YONOI opens his eyes, walks around to CELLIERS' face, bows low, and turns and walks away. CELLIERS is dead, and on his hair is a beautiful white moth.

In reading the literature on *Merry Christmas, Mr. Lawrence*, I came across the following passage in a review by Karen Jaehne (1984: 47):

> [Captain Yonoi] cuts a lock of Celliers' hair and then steps back to salute the unconscious head, or perhaps the "winged spirit" implied by the moth. (The symbolic value of the moth, it turns out, was not part of the original conception but rather an addition suggested by Bowie when the moth made its unerring way into the shot.)

Since Jaehne gives no source for her reference to the moth as an unplanned element in the shot, and I was unable to find any corroboration in other commentaries on the film or in consultation with Oshima expert Maureen Turim (2007), I contacted the producer, Jeremy Thomas, who was present when the shot was made and who assured me that the moth was "completely coincidental, just the random quality of art" (2007). Further confirmation that there was no mention of a moth in the original script was provided by its co-author, Paul Mayersberg (2007), who added that at the time of the shoot, Oshima called the moth "a wonderful accident."

There had been no mention, of course, of a moth in the corresponding passage of *The Seed and the Sower*, Laurens van der Post's largely autobiographical account on which the screenplay was based. In this text, after Yonoi bows to Celliers and departs with what the reader will subsequently learn is a lock of Celliers' hair, the narrator simply states: "By morning, Celliers was dead" (Van de Post 1963: 176).

While the intrusion of the moth into the filming of the shot was fortuitous, the choice to use it in the film was just that: a deliberate choice, doubtlessly made because the director, reportedly complying with David Bowie's wishes, was convinced that the moth belonged, and added something precious to the story at that crucial moment.

What then did it add, and how might its meaning be understood?

Before addressing these questions, I would like to set the shot in context by reminding the reader of the following:

Jack Celliers (David Bowie) was buried up to his neck in sand as a punishment for humiliating Captain Yonoi (Ryuichi Sakamoto), the camp's commandant, by kissing him demonstrably on both cheeks in full view of the Japanese troops and their Allied prisoners on the camp's parade ground, in order to prevent the immanent beheading of a fellow British officer, Group Captain Hicksley (Jack Thompson). The fair-haired Celliers knew that Yonoi was irresistibly attracted to him, and would therefore be incapable of warding off the mortifying kiss. Celliers was also well aware of the fatal consequences the kiss would entail for him, and he undertook this act of self-sacrifice as a way of redeeming himself for not having protected his younger, equally fair-haired and slightly deformed brother from a devastating experience during their childhood. It is after Celliers has endured this "living grave" punishment for several days, and imagined (flash-back fashion) a momentary reunion with the brother he had wronged, that Captain Yonoi visits his silently agonizing captive and cuts off a lock of his golden hair.

Later, in the film's post-war coda, Colonel John Lawrence (Tom Conti) tells Sergeant Gengo Hara (Takeshi Kitano): "Captain Yonoi gave me a lock of Jack Celliers' hair and asked me to take it to his village in Japan and dedicate it in his shrine." In this final scene, Lawrence also shares with Hara, soon to be executed for war-crimes as had been Yonoi: "It was as if Celliers by his death sowed a seed in Yonoi that we might all share by its growth."

## What the moth contributes to the shot

Considering for a moment how the moth enriches the shot in primarily visual terms, several forms of contrast are worth mentioning.

Had the shot been made as originally planned, it would have been quite static, showing only the scorched and lifeless head of Celliers rooted in the sand. With the moth in the shot, a contrast is introduced between the movement of the insect and the stillness of the corpse; and also between the *freedom* of movement now displayed by the moth and the absolute immobility that had been suffered by Celliers for days on end.

Similarly, as the shot turned out, it earned a place among examples that have been cited of the striking visual qualities of *Merry Christmas, Mr. Lawrence,* in that "[t]he white glow of a moth breaks the dark night as it lands on a condemned man's head" (Bergen-Aurand 2004: 179). Without the moth, the differentials between the brightest and darkest shades in the shot would have been far more limited.

However, in addition to enhancing the visual properties of the shot, the presence of the moth also invites the viewer to consider the possible meanings it suggests in relation to Celliers' death. Here are three surprisingly varied interpretive options to be taken into account.

## 1. CELLIERS' SOUL

Appearing immediately after Celliers' death, the moth could be understood as representing the soul of the deceased, finally released from his literally earthbound mortal remains and able to take flight. This would be consistent with the transformational history of the moth, in that a larva crawling on the ground metamorphoses into an ethereal creature capable of flight. This interpretation of the moth's role in the shot was a possibility suggested by screenwriter Paul Mayersberg (2007). The same symbolism is in play in the poem "The White Moth" by Sir Arthur Quiller-Couch (1863-1944, best known as the inventor of the concept "kill your darlings"), which contains the verses:

> And twice and thrice there buffeted
> On the black pane a white-winged moth:
> 'T was Annie's soul that beat outside
> And "Open, open, open!" cried.

While this is clearly the most obvious interpretation of the moth as symbol in the shot, one could also argue that from this perspective, it might have made more sense if the moth were shown flying away from Bowie's head, after or instead of apparently lingering on his hair.

## 2. POLLINATION/GERMINATION IMAGERY

The very title of the book on which the film is based – *The Seed and the Sower* – indicates the governing metaphor at the heart of the story, and which is made explicit in the film, as already shown, when Colonel Lawrence says to Sergeant Hara in the latter's prison cell: "It was as if Celliers by his death sowed a seed in Yonoi that we might all share by its growth."

In the book, the metaphor is unfolded more fully and given a geographical scope as well, particularly in this passage, which begins with a reference to the England of the Celliers brothers' childhood, continues with an evocation of the "living grave" in Java and concludes with an allusion to the lock of Celliers' hair that ended up in Yonoi's shrine in Japan (180):

> 'You see,' Lawrence said to me now, his voice low with feeling: 'the seed sown by brother in brother in that far-off homeland was planted in many places. It was planted that day in your prison in Java. Yes, even in the manner they killed Celliers his enemies acted out their unwitting recognition of the seed of his deed, for they did not only bury him alive but planted him upright like a new young growth in the earth. Even the manner of their denial of the deed was confirmation of what was rejected. He was planted again by Yonoi on the hills and spirit of his native country, and here again the seed is alive and growing in you and me.'

In the film, that central metaphor, evoked when Colonel Lawrence speaks of the sowing of a seed, can also be related – though only retrospectively – to the moth, in that it alights on Celliers' hair the way it might have landed on a flower, as part of its role in the natural cycle of pollination and germination.

## 3. YONOI'S DESIRE

In an interesting analysis of *Merry Christmas, Mr. Lawrence,* the distinguished French critic Pascal Bonitzer saw a decidedly negative meaning in the moth: "There remains on the blackened forehead of the dying man a nocturnal moth that is white and malevolent, like the very sign of Yonoi's desire" (1983: 20, my translation from the French). In this interpretation, the moth's presence in this shot might refer in part to the notion that Yonoi was attracted to Celliers – perhaps even more specifically to Celliers' golden hair – like a moth to a flame, and that the moth's resting place on Celliers' hair is related to Yonoi's having earlier in the same scene cut off a lock of that hair to be preserved as a relic.

However, while Bonitzer makes a somewhat convincing case when describing the film as a whole – for example in suggesting that its "true subject is the perverse fascination of the blondness that Major Celliers displays like a challenge, and to which [Captain] Yonoi suffers a fatal attraction" (Bonitzer 1983: 19) – his assertion regarding the moth's malevolent role in this context is as purely conjectural as it is intriguing.

# Conclusion

When asked about his own view of the moth's symbolic meaning in the shot, screenwriter Paul Mayersberg's first response was: "you have to invent it yourself" (2007). The three interpretive options discussed above – the moth as representing Celliers' soul, seed imagery or Yonoi's desire – are widely divergent, and not one of them is a perfect and self-evident fit.

This openness to a variety of interpretations is not the usual fare in mainstream cinema. But in a film that requires some effort on the part of the viewer and that is designed to make people think, the moth image's resistance to simple and unambiguous decoding is an asset. This is in the spirit of Oshima's cinema, not only regarding the viewer's experience but even in connection with the very making of the film. As Tom Conti recounts in *The Oshima Gang* (1983/2005):

> Someone asked Oshima why he didn't give his first assistant more information. And he said, "I don't like to give too much information because then people will stop thinking."

And as is made clear in this 'making of' film, it is in the same spirit that Oshima almost always followed suggestions made by his actors during the shooting of *Merry Christmas, Mr. Lawrence,* including of course David Bowie's request that the take with the moth be used as his final shot.

Perhaps Oshima's openness to the providential possibilities of random occurrences during a shoot – of which the moth is undoubtedly the ultimate example – is related to his overall conception of art as expressed in the following statement (Oshima 1995: 64):

> A work of art is made without any kind of certainty. It is produced in fear, apprehension and doubt. It isn't a purposeful, deliberate undertaking that knows exactly where it is going.

# References

Bergen-Aurand, Brian K. (2004). *Seeing and the Seen: Post-phenomenological Ethics and the Cinema*. Doctoral dissertation, University of Maryland. http://drum.lib.umd.edu/bitstream/handle/1903/1950/umi-umd-1899.pdf;jsessionid=C5836F9E6B48B2DFE2D823B39259C5CD?sequence=1 Accessed 22 April 2017.

Bonitzer, Pascal (1983). "La bosse et la voix," *Cahiers du Cinéma*, nos. 348-349, June/July, pp. 18-21.

Jaehne, Karen (1984). "Merry Christmas, Mr. Lawrence," *Film Quarterly*, vol. 37, no. 3, pp. 43-47.

Mayersberg, Paul (2007). Telephone interview, 15 August.

Oshima, Nagisa (1995). Interviewed by Nahal Tadjadod and Jean-Claude Carrière, *A Century of Cinema, UNESCO Courier*, July-August 1995, pp. 60-64. http://unesdoc.unesco.org/images/0010/001005/100576eo.pdf#nameddest=100566 Accessed 22 April 2017.

Quiller-Couch, Sir Arthur (n.d.). "The White Moth" http://mypoeticside.com/show-classic-poem-22993 Accessed 22 April 2017.

*The Oshima Gang. The Making of 'Merry Christmas, Mr. Lawrence'* (1983; released 2005). No directorial credit listed. 30 min. U.K.: Palace Pictures.

Thomas, Jeremy (2007). Email to author, 1 August, and telephone interview, 14 August.

Turim, Maureen (1998). *The Films of Oshima Nagisa. Images of a Japanese Iconoclast*. Berkeley: University of California Press.

Turim, Maureen (2007). Email to the author, 12 August.

Van der Post, Laurens (1963). *The Seed and the Sower*. London: Hogarth Press.

# 11

# The Role of the Birds in *Seven Minutes in the Warsaw Ghetto*

NB. *Readers wishing to see the film can find it at https://vimeo.com/43785060 using 'Samek' as the password.*

*Shots referred to by number can be found in the shot-by-shot breakdown provided as an Appendix to this essay.*

## Introduction

Given the vital role birds play in *Seven Minutes in the Warsaw Ghetto* (Oettinger 2012), anyone seeing the film might naturally assume that birds must have been an integral part of the story from the earliest phase of its development. That is far from the case, however. In fact there is no mention of birds in the initial screenplay, "The Carrot" (Raskin 2003a), nor had birds appeared in the brief account of the actual incident that inspired this film (Grynberg 2002: 41-42):

One day a small Jewish boy was killed on Biala Street as he attempted to pull a carrot lying in the gutter on the Aryan side through a hole in the fence. A German spotted him, inserted his gun in the hole, and killed the boy with one well-aimed shot.

It was not until I wrote the second draft of the screenplay, "Four Minutes in the Warsaw Ghetto" (Raskin 2003b), that birds were included for the first time in the story and their presence was expanded in the film itself, where they appear at three key moments:

1) in the pre-title sequence, in which a carrion crow pecks at a desiccated carrot lying on the ground outside the ghetto wall, then flies over the wall, finally landing in a courtyard within the enclosure (Shots 1-3);

2) in the scene in which eight-year-old Samek sees a bird while drawing Hitler's face and adds the bird to his drawing, with a copious stream of bird-droppings landing on the Führer's head (Shots 9-17);

3) at the end of the film, when birds startled by the sound of gunshot fly upward from the ghetto wall (Shot 47) and, with the S.S. men looking up at them (Shot 48), swirl in the sky, circling repeatedly over the scene of the killing just witnessed (Final sequence).

What follows is an attempt to pinpoint some of the purposes the birds might be seen as fulfilling in *Seven Minutes in the Warsaw Ghetto*.

## Symbolic functions

One of the many improvements Johan Oettinger and Emil Brahe made in progressing from my screenplay to their puppet film was to change the pigeons in the screenplay to carrion crows. As pigeons – inspired in part by the doves in the Swedish film, *Brothers Lionheart* (Helbom 1977) – the birds would have had more neutral connotations, with no ambiguity whatsoever.

As carrion crows, they can still be seen in a positive light as allies of the child, first by virtue of a black feather that Samek picks up when it lands on his drawing. He tenderly brushes his cheek with it, closing his eyes in pleasure and finally tucking it in his pocket (Shots 9-11). At a later point, he will pull it out of his pocket and let it float down to the stones, pinecones and other little treasures he has collected, bringing them to life as it touches them, making them spin and glow and levitate (Shots 30-34). These lyrical shots, not present in the screenplay, were fortunately added by the filmmakers for whom this film was not just a Holocaust narrative, but above all a story about the magic and radiance of childhood (Oettinger 2012c). And as just shown, the feather is what brings that magic into play. These uplifting shots add an extra dimension to the film and balance its darker moments; without them the film would have been merely one-dimensional, lacking in a broader range of moods. These remarkable shots also lengthen the film and are largely responsible for the change of the title from *Four* to *Seven Minutes in the Warsaw Ghetto*. That the feather with its magical properties belonged to one of the crows is indisputable; when the crow that Samek sees when he is drawing cleans its inner wing with its beak, it loosens a feather that the camera follows as it floats downward (Shots 12-13), thus making clear what the source of any found black feathers must be.

It is also as an inspiration assimilated into Samek's drawing that the crow enables the boy to express his contempt for Hitler (Shot 17), in a manner already described. Furthermore the crow in the pre-title sequence and Samek are also linked by the image of the carrot, since the crow is seen pecking at a carrot (Shot 2) and the boy plays with one in Shots 21-22, and ultimately loses his life by trying to pull a carrot through the hole in the ghetto wall – possibly the same one the crow was pecking at in Shot 2. As Johan Oettinger wrote (2012b): "We also gave the birds more space and meaning [than in the screenplay] in order to create parallels between the animal's and the child's simple mindset."

It is the crows that react to the sound of the shot that kills the child (Shot 47). They circle overhead, their swirling over the spot where he was killed constituting a kind of living marker, bearing witness to his death. That the S.S. men are last seen watching the swirling birds (Shot 48) might even suggest that they feel somehow addressed by that spectacle.

But of course as scavengers, and by virtue of their blackness, the birds can also be seen in this context as emblems of death, and even their circling overhead in the final sequence as vulture-like. And the very ambiguity of the birds – perceivable either as allies of the child or as harbingers of death – makes them far more interesting than they would have been as purely positive figures.

Another inspiration I had for adding the birds to the screenplay was the song "*Donna Donna*," originally called "*Dos Kelbl*" ("The Calf"), written by Aaron Zeitlin for a Yiddish stage production performed in New York in

1940-1941. Here are portions of the lyrics in the English translation written by Arthur Kevess and Teddi Schwartz in the mid 1950s, and popularized in 1960 by Joan Baez:

On a wagon bound for market
There's a calf with a mournful eye.
High above him there's a swallow,
Winging swiftly through the sky.

"Stop complaining!" said the farmer,
Who told you a calf to be?
Why don't you have wings to fly with,
Like the swallow so proud and free?"

Calves are easily bound and slaughtered,
Never knowing the reason why.
But whoever treasures freedom,
Like the swallow has learned to fly.

In this song, which indirectly refers to the situation of the Jewish populations in Europe at the time, captivity and slaughter are embodied by the calf while freedom and survival are linked to the ability to fly like swallows. In *Seven Minutes in the Warsaw Ghetto*, the crows are able to fly over the ghetto walls, unlike Samek and his family who are captives within them. By virtue of their ability to fly the crows in this film embody a freedom that is denied to the Jewish inhabitants of the ghetto and in that respect, something of the captivity vs freedom or slaughter vs survival polarities of the song are carried over into the film, thanks to the inclusion of the birds in the story.

## Closural issues

Roman Polanski's award-winning film *The Pianist* (2002) repeatedly confronts the viewer with disturbing Holocaust scenes. A wheelchair-bound elderly man is thrown to his death from a third-story balcony and his family shot down in the street when ordered to run away moments later. Some civilians are instructed by an NCO to gather their belongings and when a woman asks the soldier where they are being taken, she is summarily shot in the head. Seven men are selected at random from a column of prisoners and told by a young S.S. man to lie down on the ground where they are perfunctorily shot, one by one, with the final victim getting a moment's reprieve while the executioner dispassionately changes the clip in his pistol before putting a bullet in the seventh man's head. The unflinching ruthlessness of these and other scenes has a powerful and upsetting impact on the viewer.

But as the film draws to a close when the war has ended, life returns to normal and Szpilman (played by Adrian Brody), the main character who had become an unwashed figure in ragged clothes as the conditions in the Warsaw Ghetto grew progressively more desperate, resumes his prewar elegance; in the final scene he is clad in tuxedo and white tie as he performs Chopin once again as a concert pianist. In this way, the final moments of the film are reassuring and leave the viewer feeling relieved, in stark contrast to earlier portions of the film that are exceptionally disturbing.

*Seven Minutes in the Warsaw Ghetto* breaks with this pattern of ending on a reassuring note, for reasons indicated in a "Writer's note of intentions" written when the film was still expected to run a total of four minutes (Raskin 2003c):

> Feature films portraying the Holocaust tend either to conceal the true horror (*Life Is Beautiful*) or to show glimpses of that horror but concluding nevertheless with a reassuring ending (*Schindler's List, The Pianist*). In either case, the filmmaker's intention is a noble one: to keep the memory of the Holocaust alive, and to inscribe that memory in a life-affirming story. And in either case, the viewer is left feeling good at the end, even if the filmic journey included unbearable moments.
>
> "Four Minutes in the Warsaw Ghetto" violates a major convention of Holocaust cinema [...] by *not* offering the viewer a feeling of relief at the end. This is not a gratuitous defiance of conventions. Well aware of the risks involved, I want the viewer to experience a striking image of the Holocaust that leaves him or her with an undiluted sense of loss and despair. The final moments of this film are *deliberately* left unbearable.

Instead of offering a feel-good ending, *Seven Minutes in the Warsaw Ghetto* concludes with a final sequence – a series of shots already briefly commented upon in which the crows fly in circles above the scene of Samek's murder – the very repetitiveness of which, both visually and with respect to Emil Brahe's haunting music, affords viewers a chance: a) to digest what they have just witnessed; b) to experience a moment of reflection and perhaps even of grieving; c) to accept that nothing more will happen in this film, that it is now winding down and has no miraculous surprises up its sleeve; and d) to let go of the narrative. These processes, along with the symbolism briefly described above, provide a sense of closure that offers no narrative pleasure to the viewer but that helps the viewer to accept an unbearable ending.

## Summary and conclusions

I have suggested that birds, not present in the earliest versions of the narrative, were given an important role to play in the film because of specific ways in which they enrich the storytelling. Their very ambiguity is interesting. They can be seen both in a positive light, as Samek's allies (thanks for example to the magical powers their feathers give him, to their enlistment in his drawing and to their bearing witness to his death by circling over the scene of his murder) and in a negative light as emblems or harbingers of death. Their ability to fly over the ghetto walls also helps to sharpen our sense of the prisoners' captivity within those walls. And I have tried to describe some of the ways in which the visual and auditory representation of the birds in the final sequence can help the viewer to accept an unbearable ending by offering a form of closure that differs radically from that of the reassuring endings common in other Holocaust films.

## References

Benigni, Roberto (1997). *La vita è bella / Life IsBella.* Italy: Melampo Cinematografica et al.
Grynberg, Michal (ed.) (2002). *Words to Outlive Us. Voices from the Warsaw Ghetto.* Translated by Philip Boehm. New York: Metropolitan Books, pp. 41-42. Orig. pub. in Poland, 1988.
Helbom, Ole (1977). *Bröderne Lejonhjärte / Brothers Lionheart.* Sweden/Iceland: Artfilm, Svensk Filmindustri.
Oettinger, Johan (2012). *Seven Minutes in the Warsaw Ghetto.* Denmark: Basmati Film, Wired Fly.
Oettinger, Johan (2013a). "Director's Note of Intentions," in Richard Raskin, *Seven Minutes in the Warsaw Ghetto* and *With Raised Hands. A film ebook*, p. 31.

Oettinger, Johan (2013b). "Johan Oettinger on the making of Seven Minutes in the Warsaw Ghetto," in Richard Raskin, *Seven Minutes in the Warsaw Ghetto* and *With Raised Hands. A film ebook*, pp. 32-33.

Polanski, Roman (2002). *The Pianist*. France/Poland/Germany/U.K.: R.P. Productions, Heritage Films, Studio Babelsberg et al.

Raskin, Richard (2003a). "The Carrot," unpublished handwritten manuscript dated 25 January 2003.

Raskin, Richard (2003b). "Four Minutes in the Warsaw Ghetto," in *Seven Minutes in the Warsaw Ghetto* and *With Raised Hands. A film ebook*, p. 28.

Raskin, Richard (2003c). "Writer's note of intentions," in *Seven Minutes in the Warsaw Ghetto* and *With Raised Hands. A film ebook*, p. 27.

Raskin, Richard (2013). *Seven Minutes in the Warsaw Ghetto* and *With Raised Hands. A film ebook*. Aarhus: Aarhus University Press.

Spielberg, Steven (1993). *Schindler's List*. USA: Universal Pictures, Amblin Entertainment et al.

# Film Credits

Director: Johan Oettinger
Concept Development: Emil Brahe and Johan Oettinger
Screenplay: Richard Raskin
Producer: Ellen Riis
Storyboard: Anders Bøge Henriksen
Composer: Emil Brahe
Audio Design and Sound Mix: Jess Wolfsberg
Design: Johan Oettinger, Emil Brahe, Anders Bøge Henriksen
Actors/eyes: Vibe Lilmoes, Ene Øster Bendtsen, Sanne Løwe, Jonas Bjarnøe, Jonas Bregnhøj Nielsen
Animation: Johan Oettinger, Rie Nymand
Photography: Johan Oettinger
Editor: Johan Oettinger
Puppet Builders: Hanna Habermann and Henni Tomczak
Assistant Puppet Builder: Else M. Rasmussen
Scenography and Props: Johan Strandgaard, Steffen Kastrup, Tore Abbednæs
Costumes: Ann Juel Nielsen
Eye-Compositing: Jakob Eriksen
Production: Basmati Film, Wired Fly, with funding from New Danish Screen, Den Vestdanske Filmpulje, ANIS and Open Workshop
Release: 2012 Run time: 7 min. 48 sec.

# APPENDIX

**A shot-by-shot breakdown of *Seven Minutes in the Warsaw Ghetto***
This material first appeared in my publication *Seven Minutes in the Warsaw Ghetto* and *With Raised Hands. A film ebook* (2013) and is reprinted here with the kind permission of Aarhus University Press and Johan Oettinger.

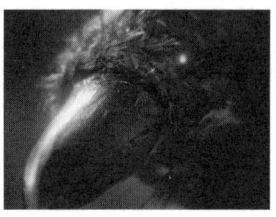  

**Shot 1** (6 sec)
A carrion crow looks around.

**Shot 2** (9 sec)
The bird pecks at a dried-up carrot lying on the ground, then flies upward along a wall, past warning signs in German and Polish, and over the barbed wire covering the top of the ghetto wall.

 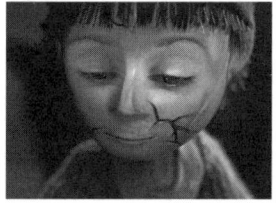 

**Shot 3** (17 sec)
The bird descends within a courtyard inside the ghetto wall. The title, visible as the shot begins, is partially obscured as the bird crosses in front of it. After the bird lands on the ground, the title is faded out in waves.

**Shot 4** (10 sec)
Samek, an eight-year-old boy, is lying on the floor of a sparsely furnished apartment, drawing a picture.

**Shot 5** (9 sec)
As he continues drawing, we see his mother, Yetta, and grandmother in the background, preparing food. Yetta turns to look toward Samek, then resumes her work.

**Shot 6** (4 sec)
Steam rises from a pot on the stove (off camera) where she is working.

**Shot 7** (6 sec)
As both women continue preparing food, the grandmother reaches into a bowl and pulls out …

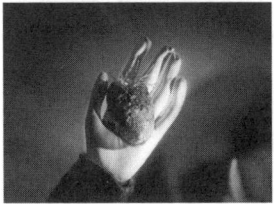  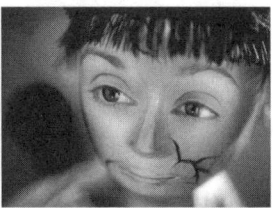

**Shot 8** (4 sec)
… a damaged potato. She tries to cut away the spoiled portions.

**Shot 9** (4 sec)
We now see that Samek is drawing Hitler, as a black feather lands on his paper. He picks up the feather …

**Shot 10** (5 sec)
… and tenderly brushes his cheek with it, closing his eyes in pleasure …

 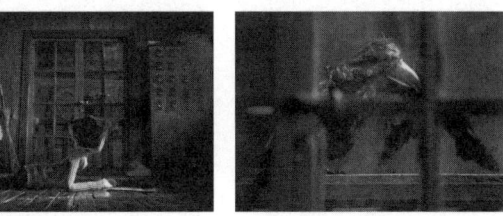

**Shot 11** (8 sec)
… and then tucks it in his pocket. A bird (like the one in the opening shots) can be seen through nearby French doors as it lands on a balcony and Samek turns to look at it.

**Shot 12** (4 sec)
The bird squawks and cleans its inner wing with its beak. A feather is loosened and falls.

THE ROLE OF THE BIRDS IN SEVEN MINUTES IN THE WARSAW GHETTO

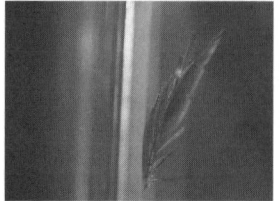 

**Shot 13** (7 sec)
The feather continues falling, then the camera rises to show the bird once again.

**Shot 14** (5 sec)
The reflection of the bird in the window pane shows that it now appears to be looking squarely at Samek.

**Shot 14** (cont.)
A focus pull shows Samek looking back at the bird. He then returns to his picture …

**Shot 15** (8 sec)
… drawing a bird perched above Hitler's head.

**Shot 16** (6 sec)
The bird flies away, and Samek notices the bird's departure, then returns to his picture.

**Shot 16** (cont.)
He looks toward the window again, where the bird is no longer in sight, and returns once again to his picture …

**Shot 17** (5 sec)
… drawing copious amounts of bird-shit dropping onto the Führer's head.

**Shot 18** (11 sec)
Yetta, visible in the background, puts down her work and turns toward Samek.

 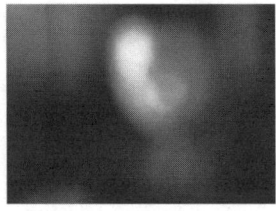

**Shot 18** (cont.)
She begins walking toward her son.

**Shot 19** (13 sec)
Out of focus at first, Yetta approaches Samek and looks down at his drawing.

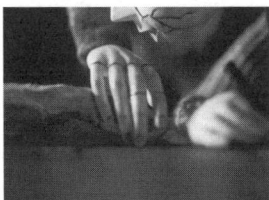  

**Shot 19** (cont.)
She swoops down and snatches up the drawing, then walks back to the kitchen, with Samek watching her from his position on the floor.

**Shot 20** (10 sec)
On returning to the kitchen, Yetta shows the drawing to her own mother, who shrugs. Yetta then crumples up the drawing and kneels down toward the oven.

**Shot 21** (5 sec)
She opens the oven door and as she throws the drawing into the fire, Samek's arm reaches into a nearby bowl and pulls out a carrot.

**Shot 22** (3 sec)
Samek waves the carrot in the air, flying it like a plane, and Yetta snatches it from his hand.

**Shot 22** (cont.)    **Shot 23** (4 sec)    **Shot 24** (4 sec)
Samek, empty handed and having been rebuked, looks toward his grandmother.

 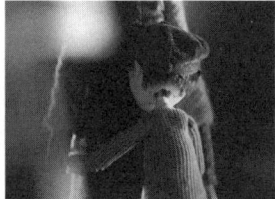 

**Shot 25** (10 se)
Samek buries his face in his grandmother's bosom for comfort. She kisses his face.

**Shot 26** (3 sec.)
After she finishes kissing him, he wipes away the kiss from his face.

**Shot 27** (13 sec)
Samek heads for the door and leaves the apartment.

 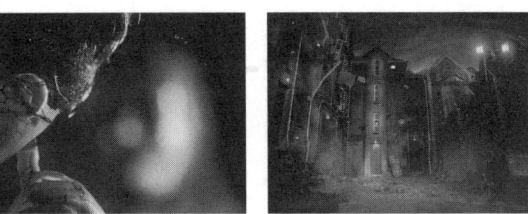

**Shot 27** (cont.)
The grandmother watches Samek leave then puts an affectionate hand on Yetta's shoulder. Yetta touches her mother's hand.

**Shot 28** (17 sec)
Samek makes his way down the stairway inside the apartment building.

**Shot 28** (cont.)
He enters the courtyard and begins crossing it.

**Shot 29** (13 sec)
Carefully making sure he is not being observed, he removes a metal sheet concealing his cache of little treasures and a hole in the ghetto wall.

**Shot 30** (15 sec)
Samek opens a box that had been hidden behind the metal sheet, and removes his collection of stones, pine cones and other objects. He reaches for the feather he had saved in his pocket.

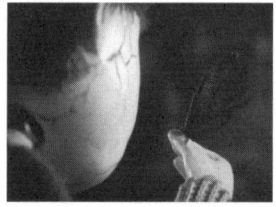

**Shot 31** (13 sec)
Samek holds the feather, then lets go of it. It floats down to the stones and other objects, making them spin …

**Shots 32, 33, 34** (22 sec)
… and glow.

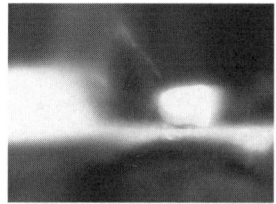 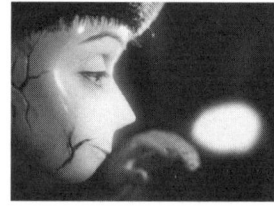 

**Shots 32, 33, 34 cont.**
The magic continues, as the feather makes a glowing stone rise in the air, just in front of Samek's face.

**Shot 35** (5 sec)
Samek touches the stone, which once again obeys the law of gravity, falling to the ground. He pushes it aside, clearing the way to a small hole in the ghetto wall through which he begins to peer.

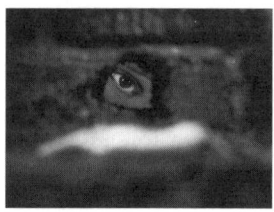  

**Shot 36** (5 sec)
Samek's eye seen through the hole from outside the ghetto wall, where a carrot is lying on the ground.

**Shot 37** (10 sec)
Samek pulls a piece of wire from his treasure chest and fashions one end of it into a loop, which he inserts in the hole.

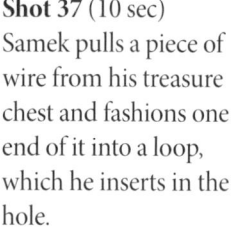

  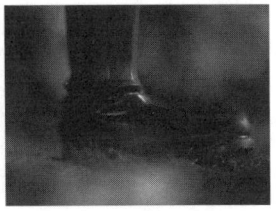

**Shot 38** (11 sec)
Samek guides the wire through the hole, trying to catch the carrot inside the loop. But just beside the carrot and just out of Samek's view are a pair of military boots, and as the camera tilts upward, we see that the boots belong to an S.S. man, Josef, smoking a cigarette and with another S.S. man, Karl, standing beside him.

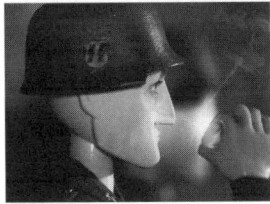 

**Shot 38** (cont.)

**Shot 39** (19 sec)
Josef takes several puffs on his cigarette, then throws the butt to the ground, where it lands near the wire loop and carrot.

**Shot 40** (5 sec)
The wire loop and carrot are just beside the still-smoking cigarette butt.

**Shot 41** (3 sec)
Judging from the direction in which he is facing, Josef has seen the wire and carrot and then turns to face Karl.

**Shot 42** (2 sec)
Karl looks inquisitively at Josef.

THE ROLE OF THE BIRDS IN SEVEN MINUTES IN THE WARSAW GHETTO

**Shot 43** (2 sec) Josef nods in the direction of the wire and carrot.

**Shot 44** (5 sec) Karl looks down, understands, and nods "yes" to Josef.

**Shot 45** (6 sec) Josef puts his index finger in front of his lips, making the 'ssshhhh' signal.

**Shot 46** (10 sec) As Samek continues trying to catch the carrot in the metal loop, Josef inserts his pistol into the hole and pulls the trigger.

  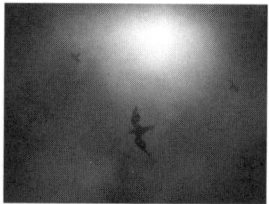

**Shot 47** (3 sec) Four birds react to the sound of the gunshot by flying up from the ghetto wall, on top of which they had been standing, amid the barbed wire.

**Shot 48** (11 sec) Josef reholsters his pistol, looks at Karl, and then looks upward, toward the birds.

**Final sequence** (1 min 24 sec) A series of shots in which birds swirl in the sky. The credits begin after about 30 seconds.

# 12

# 'Le Chant des Partisans': Functions of an Underground Song

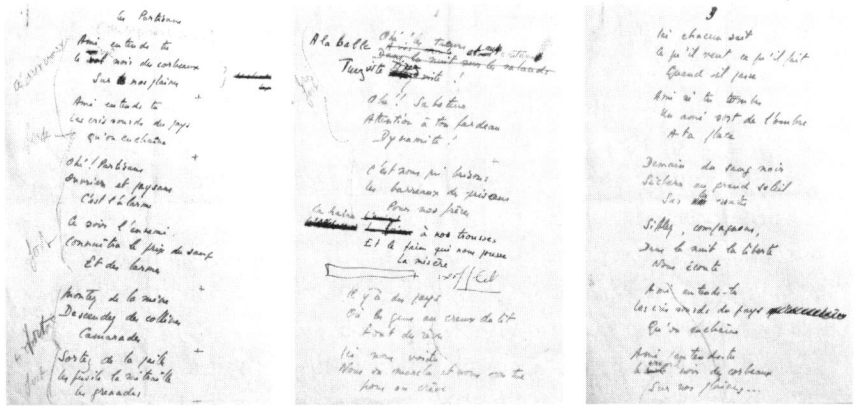

*The original manuscript for* Le Chant des Partisans. *Musée de la Légion d'honneur et des ordres de chevalerie.*

When France was defeated in June of 1940, the country was divided into an 'occupied zone' in the north, directly under German military control, and an 'unoccupied zone' in the south, administered from Vichy by French authorities who eagerly implemented most of the policies dictated by the occupying power.

In both zones, men and women who felt called upon to engage in active opposition to the Nazis and their collaborators formed small groups which were eventually linked up into networks. The French Resistance movement, comprising the totality of these groups and networks, was a microcosm of French society in the sense that all social classes and all shades of the political spectrum were represented, from conservative and Catholic to socialist and communist.

The members of a Resistance group might lead double lives: a 'normal' one, involving a job and home, and a secret life, in which illegal activities were carried out. Some found it necessary to leave their homes, to 'go underground,' which often meant going out into the countryside and joining groups of armed fighters – the *maquis* (literally, 'the bush'), referring to the countryside base of operations as well as to the partisan army, an individual member of which would be called a *maquisard*.

Among the activities carried out by the Resistance – at great personal risk – were: the creation of a clandestine press to counteract the propaganda disseminated by Germany and Vichy; the supplying of false identity papers to people who would otherwise be arrested or conscripted to obligatory labor by the Germans; the gathering and transmission of information to the Allies; and the carrying out of sabotage and rescue missions, often under orders from the Free French, who were based in London and operating under the leadership of de Gaulle.

Efforts were of course made to maintain a steady flow of information between the Free French in London and the Resistance within France. From the very beginning, the BBC made it possible for the Free French to make radio broadcasts that could be heard on the continent. And in 1943, the Free French were authorized to establish a radio station of their own, which they called *Honneur et Patrie* (Honour and Country). The importance of the broadcasts from London was incalculable.

As will be seen in the account which follows, the major song of the French Resistance – '*Le Chant des Partisans*' (a title its own writers translated as 'Underground Song') – was born in London, and under circumstances involving the new radio station just mentioned, as well as the visit of a key member of the French Resistance to the British capital.

After briefly outlining the extraordinary story behind the writing of this song and what is known of its dissemination in France, I will try to describe the major functions 'Underground Song' fulfilled for those who sang it in the *maquis* and in German prison camps in 1943-1944, as well as the functions it fulfilled for other groups and at other times.

|   | *LE CHANT DES PARTISANS* | UNDERGROUND SONG |
|---|---|---|
| 1 | *Ami, entends-tu*<br>*Le vol noir des corbeaux*<br>*Sur nos plaines?* | Friend, do you hear<br>The black flight of ravens<br>Over our plains? |
| 2 | *Ami, entends-tu*<br>*Les cris sourds du pays*<br>*Qu'on enchaîne?* | Friend, do you hear<br>The muffled cries of the country<br>Put in chains? |
| 3 | *Ohé partisans,*<br>*Ouvriers et paysans*<br>*C'est l'alarme!* | Come on, partisans,<br>Workers and peasants<br>The alarm has sounded! |
| 4 | *Ce soir l'ennemi*<br>*Connaîtra le prix du sang*<br>*Et des larmes.* | Tonight the enemy<br>Will know the price of blood<br>And tears. |
| 5 | *Montez de la mine,*<br>*Descendez des collines*<br>*Camarades.* | Come up from the mines<br>Come down from the hills<br>Comrades. |
| 6 | *Sortez de la paille,*<br>*Les fusils, la mitraille,*<br>*Les grenades!* | Remove from the straw<br>The rifles, machine gun,<br>The grenades! |
| 7 | *Ohé les tueurs*<br>*À la balle et au couteau*<br>*Tuez vite!* | Come on, killers<br>With bullet and with knife<br>Kill swiftly! |
| 8 | *Ohé saboteur,*<br>*Attention à ton fardeau*<br>*Dynamite!* | Come on, saboteur,<br>Be careful with your load<br>Dynamite! |
| 9 | *C'est nous qui brisons*<br>*Les barreaux des prisons*<br>*Pour nos frères,* | We are the ones who break<br>The prison bars<br>For our brothers, |
| 10 | *La haine à nos trousses*<br>*Et la faim qui nous pousse,*<br>*La misère…* | Tracked by hatred,<br>Driven by hunger,<br>Hardship… |
| 11 | *Il y a des pays*<br>*Où les gens au creux du lit*<br>*Font des rêves.* | There are countries<br>Where people dream<br>In the comfort of their beds. |

| 12 | *Ici, nous, vois-tu,* <br> *Nous on marche, nous on tue,* <br> *Nous on crève.* | Here, you see, as for us, <br> We march, we kill, <br> We die like dogs. |
|---|---|---|
| 13 | *Ici chacun sait* <br> *Ce qu'il veut, ce qu'il fait* <br> *Quand il passe …* | Here, each man knows <br> What he wants, what he's doing <br> When he goes by … |
| 14 | *Ami, si tu tombes,* <br> *Un ami sort de l'ombre* <br> *À ta place.* | Friend, if you fall, <br> A friend emerges from the shadows <br> In your place. |
| 15 | *Demain, du sang noir* <br> *Sèchera au grand soleil* <br> *Sur les routes.* | Tomorrow, black blood <br> Will be drying in the sunshine <br> On the roads. |
| 16 | *Sifflez compagnons …* <br> *Dans la nuit, la liberté* <br> *Nous écoute.* | Whistle, companions … <br> In the night, freedom <br> Listens to us. |

*May 1943. Maurice Druon, Joseph Kessel, Anna Marly*

# THE GENESIS AND DISSEMINATION OF *'LE CHANT DES PARTISANS'*

In retelling the story of '*Le Chant des Partisans*', I hope to establish a factual framework within which subsequent discussion of the song's functions will be both realistic and fruitful. Unless other documentation is cited, the material in the following chronology is drawn from published accounts by Andre Gillois (1973: 325-329) and Maurice Druon (1973).

Winter 1942, LONDON: Anna Marly, a young singer-composer of Slavic origin, writes the melody and her own Russian text for '*Le Chant des Partisans*'.

13 May 1943: In search of a musical theme for the new Resistance station, *Honneur et Patrie*, scheduled to begin broadcasting on May 17, Andre Gillois visits Anna Marly, who plays six melodies for him on her guitar. Gillois selects two of the melodies for recording: '*Paris est à nous*' and '*Le Chant des Partisans*'.

14 May 1943: Andre Gillois and Anna Marly meet at a studio to record both melodies. Also present is Emmanuel d'Astier, on whose suggestion Gillois had approached Marly. (D'Astier, a leader of the Resistance movement, Libération, is in London on a mission, and soon to return to France.) Gillois and d'Astier whistle the opening bars of 'Le Chant des Partisans' in place of professional musicians, who whistled too well – "*pour donner l'impression de combattants clandestins sifflotant en marchant sur les routes.*"[1] The body of the song is then played by Anna Marly on her guitar, accompanied by other musicians.

16 May 1943: Andre Gillois listens to both recordings, and chooses Le Chant des Partisans as the musical theme for the Resistance broadcasts.

17 May 1943 to 2 May 1944: 'Le Chant des Partisans' is broadcast twice daily by Honneur et Patrie. The melody is whistled, without musical accompaniment or text, by Andre Gillois, Maurice Druon and Claude Dauphin.

30 May 1943: At the Ashdown Park Hotel, Surrey, frequented by the Free French, Joseph Kessel and Maurice Druon write the French text of 'Le Chant des Partisans', on a Sunday afternoon. When Anna Marly had previously played the melody of 'Le Chant' for Kessel – at Emmanuel d'Astier's request – Kessel remarked: "*Ah! cet air-là, je m'en souviendrai parce que c'est un air russe.*"[2] D'Astier had arranged this meeting, at the Club Français de Saint James, as part of an effort to convince Kessel to write a Resistance song. D'Astier had argued: "*On ne gagne les guerres qu'avec des chansons: La Marseillaise, La Madelon. Il faudrait un chant qui ait l'air de venir du maquis, comme l'indicatif du poste 'Honneur et Patrie.'*"[3] In addition to this encouragement from d'Astier, who was determined to return to France with the words and music of a Resistance song, a request for a song also came from Germaine Sablon, who had agreed to sing in a film Cavalcanti wished to make: *Three Songs of Resistance*, in the series, *Pourquoi nous combattons/ Why We Fight*. At noon on May 30, Kessel tells Germaine Sablon: "*On s'y met. Après tu me laisseras tranquille.*"[4] By late afternoon, the text is completed.

---

1 "to give the impression of underground fighters whistling while walking along the roads."
2 "Ah! That tune I'll remember because it's a Russian tune."
3 "Wars are only won with songs: *La Marseillaise, La Madelon*. We need a song that seems to have sprung from the *maquis*, like the theme for the *Honneur et Patrie* station."
4 "We're going to do it. Afterwards, you'll leave me in peace."

That same evening, Kessel, Druon, Anna Marly, Germaine Sablon and others assemble at d'Astier's, where '*Le Chant des Partisans*' is sung for the first time. In the course of the evening, Joseph Kessel – foreseeing the importance of the song – remarks to Maurice Druon: "*C'est peut-être tout ce qui restera de nous deux.*"[5]

31 May 1943: Germaine Sablon records '*Le Chant des Partisans*' at Ealing Studio. Its English title: 'Underground Song'.

Early June 1943: Germaine Sablon sings '*Le Chant des Partisans*' in Cavalcanti's film. She is seen standing on a hill with a vast sky as the background, and makes defiant gestures as she sings, with the wind blowing in her hair and unfurling her scarf. While the film may have been made "specifically to be parachuted to partisans" (Barnoux 1974: 149), I know of no evidence that the film was seen in France before the liberation of Paris.

Germaine Sablon and Anna Marly sing '*Le Chant des Partisans*' on numerous occasions for Free French audiences in London. Later, Germaine Sablon will sing the song for the 1st Division of the Free French and the 8th Army in the Libyan desert, and at the Opera of Algiers on the occasion of a visit by de Gaulle (Sablon 1980, Marly 1980).

25 September 1943, FRANCE: The text of the song is printed, under the title '*Les Partisans (Chant de la Libération)*', in Emmanuel d'Astier's clandestine review, *Cahiers de Libération*. Copies of the song may also have been sent into France in containers at about this time (Mercer 1980).

Late 1943 to Liberation, FRANCE: The song is known and sung by some Resistance groups – for example, the *maquis* of the Landes region (Druon 1980) – but will not be known by others until the Liberation (Fournier-Bocquet 1980). It is reportedly whistled as a 'coast-is-clear' signal, sung in prisons, notably in the Massif Central region, and before German firing squads (Fournier-Bocquet 1980). It is possible that the number of *maquisards* who knew the song before the Liberation was quite small, and that the song's real importance within France dates from the summer of 1944.

1944, RAVENSBRÜCK: '*Le Chant des Partisans*' is sung by some of the French women imprisoned at this camp (L'Herminier, Deranty 1980).

---

5   "This may be all that will ever be left of the two of us."

February 1944, LONDON: The text is read twice, as a poem, on the B.B.C.'s French Broadcasts (Crémieux-Brilhac 1975: Vol. 4, 177).

April 1944: 'Le Chant des Partisans' is broadcast on a single occasion by the B.B.C. as a song (Crémieux-Brilhac 1975: Vol. 4, 177).

6 June 1944: 'Le Chant des Partisans' follows de Gaulle's B.B.C. address, announcing the Allied debarkation.

19 August 1944, LONDON: 'Le Chant des Partisans' is broadcast as a song by the B.B.C. during the battle of Paris (Crémieux-Brilhac 1975: Vol. 4, 177).

21 (?) August, PARIS: *Le Chant des Partisans* precedes and follows Camus' reading of a *Combat* editorial over the air, on the newly liberated Parisian radio as part of Pierre Shaeffer's *Chronique sonore de Paris libéré*, as can be heard on a recording of the broadcast.

Autumn 1944, PARIS: 'Le Chant des Partisans' is sung at numerous galas celebrating the Resistance and Liberation, and enjoys immense popularity. Cavalcanti's film is shown in Paris and later in theatres throughout France (Sablon 1980).

Post-war period to present, FRANCE: 'Le Chant des Partisans' is played or sung on ceremonial occasions commemorating the Resistance. In 1962, the song is officially recognized by the French government as a national hymn.

# FUNCTIONS OF 'LE CHANT DES PARTISANS'
## 1. FOR GROUPS WHO SANG IT IN THE *MAQUIS*

In writing a French text to accompany Anna Marly's music, Joseph Kessel and Maurice Druon were fulfilling the Resistance movement's need for a song – a need concretized in Emmanuel d'Astier's direct appeal for a song he could take back to the French underground. 'Le Chant des Partisans' was written to be sung by Resistance groups and was deliberately designed to "*magnifier la lutte, soutenir les combattants, les unir*"[6] (Druon 1980). In this connection, Henri Michel wrote (1970: 154):

---

6  "to magnify the struggle, to sustain the fighters, to unite them."

> *même engagés dans la guérilla, les combattants volontaires n'en avaient pas moins besoin de raisons pour se battre, d'encouragements pour persévérer, et même de chansons pour s'émouvoir ensemble, d'un seul coeur. De ce dernier point de vue, il convient de rappeler la miraculeuse réussite que fut 'Le Chant des Partisans'...*[7]

### a. strengthening social cohesion

The very act of singing the song in chorus – *d'un seul coeur* – was both a symbolic affirmation of solidarity and a means for heightening both the individual's sense of integration into the group and the group's experience of itself as a unified body.

Furthermore, 'Le Chant des Partisans' defined relationships between members of the Resistance movement in the language of personal affection and loyalty. The word *ami* opens and sets the tone for the song, occurring a total of six times, and is accompanied by the variants *camarades, compagnons* and *frères*. *Ami* and its variants are presented as the appropriate forms of address when one member of the movement speaks to another: *Ami, entends-tu..., Ami, si tu tombes...*, and as the appropriate forms of reference to another member: *...un ami sort de l'ombre à ta place*. This language not only reflected but also helped to cultivate the movement's ethos of comradeship, and thereby contributed to the internal cohesion of the Resistance groups which sang the song.

### b. counteracting anxieties

As is well known, Resistance groups suffered extremely heavy losses. Joseph Kessel wrote in his novelized *Chronique de la Résistance – L'Armée des ombres* (1944: 159):

> *Louis H. calcule que sur les quatre cents membres qui au début formaient leur groupe, il en reste cinq qui sont en vie ou en liberté. Si chez nous la proportion des survivants est plus importante (question de chance... d'organisation,*

---

[7] "even when already engaged in guerilla warfare, those who had volunteered to fight still needed to draw upon their reasons for doing so; they also needed encouragement to persevere, and even songs to be moved by in unison, with shared emotion. In that last connection, it is fitting to recall the miraculous success of 'Underground Song'..."

*peut-être), le déchet est tout de même terrible. Et la Gestapo fauche sans cesse, plus serré, plus dru.*[8]

Some relief from the anguish caused by these losses was undoubtedly provided by the image in the song: *Ami, si tu tombes, un ami sort de l'ombre à ta place.*[9] Without holding out the hope of a mythic resurrection, as Resistance poetry sometimes did, for example (Masson 1943) –

*Nul d'entre vous n'est seul, nul d'entre vous ne meurt*
*Lorsqu'on tue vos corps, vous revivez dans les fleurs de l'été*[10]

– the image in 'Le Chant des Partisans' of *Ami, si tu tombes, un ami sort de l'ombre à ta place* better enabled individuals who were constantly risking their lives to see the *role* they occupied as immortal, if not their person. This simple and powerful image compensated to some degree, and without relying on wish-fulfilling myths, for the acute sense of mortality with which members of the Resistance lived day and night.

A second and equally important purpose served by this line of the song concerns anxieties over the movement's ability to survive the loss of members. In the continuation of the passage quoted above, Kessel affirmed that no amount of losses inflicted by the enemy could set the movement back for long: "*La Résistance a pris la forme de l'Hydre. Coupez-lui une tête, il en repousse dix, à chaque jet de sang.*"[11] Similarly, stanza 14 of the song implicitly promises that the movement will survive – with undiminished strength – despite the loss of individuals.

In these ways, the image – which is probably the most memorable one in the song – helped to counteract anxieties concerning individual death and group survival.

---

8 "Louis H. figures that of the four hundred members who originally formed their group, five are left alive or free. If for us the proportion of survivors is greater (a matter of chance ... possibly of organization), the loss is still terrible. And the Gestapo mows us down continually, more intensely, more thick and fast."
9 "Friend, if you fall, a friend emerges from the shadows in your place"
10 "None of you is alone, none of you dies. When your body is killed you come back to life in the summer flowers."
11 "The Resistance has taken the form of the Hydra. Cut off one head and ten more grow back with every spurt of blood."

### c. unburdening

The choice to participate in Resistance activities meant opting for a life of hardship and risk, as opposed to seeking the relative comfort and security of prudently coming to terms with the Occupation. *Maquisards* had to live with making sacrifices, and one of the functions of '*Le Chant des Partisans*' was to provide them with a shared and sanctioned form for unburdening themselves with regard to the hardships incurred by joining the Resistance:

*La haine à nos trousses*
*Et la faim qui nous pousse,*
*La misère ...*

*Il y a des pays*
*Où les gens au creux du lit*
*Font des rêves.*

*Ici, nous, vois-tu,*
*Nous on marche, nous on tue,*
*Nous on crève.*[12]

### d. promoting confidence, pride and a sense of purpose

Two verbs in the song are in the future tense, and both refer to losses about to be inflicted on the enemy: *Ce soir l'ennemi connaîtra le prix du sang et des larmes*[13] and *Demain du sang noir sèchera au grand soleil sur les routes.*[14] Singing lines such as these was a means for collectively affirming confidence in a successful outcome for whatever operations were to be carried out against the Germans.

Similarly, singing two other stanzas –

---

12 "Tracked by hatred, driven by hunger, hardship ... There are countries where people can dream
In the comfort of their beds. Here, you see, as for us, we march, we kill, we die like dogs."
13 "Tonight the enemy will know the price of blood and tears"
14 "Tomorrow, black blood will be drying in the sunshine on the roads."

> *C'est nous qui brisons*
> *Les barreaux des prisons*
> *Pour nos frères*[15]

and

> *Ici chacun sait*
> *Ce qu'il veut, ce qu'il fait*
> *Quand il passe…*[16]

– was a means whereby *maquisards* defined and presented themselves in terms which enabled them to take particular pride in their work and to share a sense that – though life may be easier and safer for other people and in other places – nowhere is it more purposeful.

Furthermore, the very fact of having a song of the quality of 'Le Chant des Partisans' to sing was in itself an enrichment of the Resistance culture, and contributed to a sense of the wholeness of the movement.

### e. legitimizing violence

In *L'Armée des ombres*, Joseph Kessel wrote (1944: 136):

> *Les Français n'étaient pas préparés à tuer. Leur tempérament, leur climat, leur pays, l'état de civilisation où ils étaient arrivés, les éloignaient du sang. Je me rappelle combien, dans les premiers temps de la Résistance, il nous était difficile d'envisager le meurtre à froid, l'embuscade, l'attentat médité. Et combien il était difficile de recruter des gens pour cela.*[17]

However, this reluctance to kill during the early days of the Resistance was overcome soon enough overcome. Referring to the present situation (in

---

15 "We are the ones who break the prison bars for our brothers"
16 "Here, each man knows what he wants, what he's doing when he goes by"
17 "Frenchmen were neither prepared nor predisposed for killing. Their temperament, their climate, their country, the level of civilization they had attained, estranged them from bloodshed. I remember how difficult it was for us, in the early days of the Resistance, to imagine cold-blooded murder, ambush, deliberate assassination. And how difficult it was to recruit people to carry that out."

1943), Kessel stated: "... *de notre côté, on tue, on tue, on tue [...] L'homme primitif est reparu chez les Français*" (136-137).[18]

Later in this novelized *chronique*, the character Felix tests the nerve of two new recruits to the movement by ordering each of them to shoot a German officer in cold blood. Felix is almost appalled by the ease with which his recruits pass the test, and remarks: "*On a bien changé les Français*" (156).[19]

Given this change which had already occurred by September 1943, it would be illogical to attribute a *disinhibiting* function to 'Le Chant des Partisans' with respect to the use of violence. But singing the song – with its reference to the blood that would soon be spilled (stanzas 4 and 15), and such prescriptions as "*Ohé les tueurs / À la balle et au couteau / Tuez vite!*"[20] – presumably reinforced the *maquisards*' shared sense of the absolute *legitimacy* of killing.

Another and perhaps more importance aspect of this problem will be discussed with regard to the song's orienting functions for outsiders to the movement.

Finally, in this connection, it is worth noting that 'Le Chant des Partisans' fits into a rich tradition of French political songs, some of which are quite bloody. The '*Marseillaise*', for example, contains the lines: "*Qu'un sang impur / Abreuve nos sillons!*"[21]

## 2. FOR PRISONERS WHO SANG IT

Two women who remember singing '*Le Chant des Partisans*' at the Ravensbrück concentration camp in 1944 attributed the following functions to the act of singing the song in those circumstances (L'Herminier and Deranty 1980):

a) "*Il évoquait l'opposition à l'Occupation.*"
b) "*Nous nous retrouvions un peu dans notre pays, au centre même de l'Allemagne nazie.*"
c) "*Il encourageait notre résistance intérieure.*"

---

18 "... on our side, people kill, kill, kill [...] Primitive man has reappeared among the French."
19 "The French have certainly been changed."
20 "Come on, killers/with bullet or with knife, kill swiftly."
21 "May an impure blood water our furrows."

d) *"Il renforçait notre sentiment de solidarité, malgré les différences politiques, confessionnelles, sociales."*
e) *"Il nous aidait à garder la foi, l'espoir dans la libération, à conserver le courage de vivre."*[22]

Another former prisoner at Ravensbrück, who did not know 'Le Chant des Partisans' at the time (but who now always carries a copy of the song with her, wherever she goes), told me: "*Les Allemands voulaient nous faire chanter Hei li hei lo – nous chantions la Madelon. Si nous avions connu Le Chant des Partisans, c'est ce que nous aurions chanté.*"[23]

Anna Marly (1980) was told of two prisoners forced to dig their own grave before being shot by the Germans "and singing my song to keep courage. Another one dying asked his comrade to sing it to him." And Maurice Druon stated (1980):

> *Je sais aussi, par des témoignages de combattants, que le Chant circula dans diverses prisons, notamment du Massif Central. Il m'a même était dit qu'un groupe de condamnés l'avaient chanté devant le peloton d'exécution ... C'était bien devenu le Chant de la Résistance.*[24]

Singing 'Le Chant des Partisans' in all of these desperate situations was both a means for gaining some measure of relief and strength, and the seizing of an opportunity to symbolically enact defiance despite one's utter helplessness, and to embody the spirit of the Resistance in one's own and the enemy's eyes.

---

22 a) "It evoked opposition to the Occupation"; b) "It was as though we were back in our own country for a moment, while in the middle of Nazi Germany"; c) "It encouraged our inner resistance"; d) "It strengthened our feeling of solidarity despite political, religious and social differences"; e) "It helped us to keep our faith, the hope of liberation, to hold on to the courage to live."
23 "The Germans wanted us to sing *Hei li hei lo* – we sang *la Madelon*. If we had known *Le Chant des Partisans*, that's what we would have sung."
24 "I also know, through the testimony of combattants, that *Le Chant* circulated in prisons, notably in the Massif Central. I've even been told that a group of men condemned to death sang it in front of the execution squad... It had truly become the Song of the Resistance."

## 3. SIGNAL FUNCTIONS

As the musical theme for the radio station, *Honneur et Patrie*, broadcasted from London, 'Le Chant des Partisans' – whistled unprofessionally enough "to give the impression of fighters whistling as they walk along the roads" (Gillois 1973: 326) – informed the listener that he or she was tuned in to a Resistance broadcast. And Camus' *Combat* editorial, read over the air on *Radio Libre* during the battle of Paris, was 'framed' by 'Le Chant des Partisans', as if to signal unequivocally to the listener that the broadcast was made under the aegis of the Resistance.

Another kind of signal function fulfilled by the melody was pointed out by Maurice Druon (1980): "*Je sais que les passeurs alsaciens, qui faisait franchir aux résistants ou au pilotes alliés abattus, la frontière de la zone interdite, sifflaient le Chant des Partisans pour signaler que la voie était libre.*"[25]

## 4. ORIENTING FUNCTIONS FOR OUTSIDERS TO THE MOVEMENT

The German and Vichy authorities attempted to turn French public opinion against underground activities by characterizing them as terrorist and by taking heavy reprisals against the civilian population whenever a German officer was assassinated. In a journal he kept during the occupation, Jean Ghéhenno referred to a text he was shown by members of a Resistance group seeking to defend themselves against Vichy propaganda. The text they had written, but never published, was described by Ghéhenno as follows in a journal entry dated March 1944 (1947: 465-466):

> ... *une protestation contre l'ignoble propagande qui les dénonce comme des terroristes et des bandits, et qui, par comble, n'est pas sans toucher l'opinion. Ils étaient partis pensant n'être que l'avant-garde des armées de libération, et voici qu'ils doivent constater que la masse de la nation, réservée et méfiante, ne les suit pas. Ils expliquent très bien eux-mêmes que ce pays de logiciens et de juristes est mal disposé à comprendre que 'l'ordre n'est pas nécessairement*

---

25 "I know that the men in Alsace who organized the passage of Resistance fighters or of allied pilots who had been shot down, across the fontiers of the forbidden zone, use to whistle *Le Chant des Partisans* as a signal that the road was clear."

*identique à la légalité.' Il a suffi à un Darnand d'appeler ses troupes d'assassins les 'forces du maintien de l'ordre', pour que les petits bourgeois se grattent la tête et se méfient en effet de ces 'bandits' qui sont leurs fils et leurs frères, et nous en sommes là que ces jeunes 'volontaires' qui sauvent l'honneur de tous, doivent se justifier et faire la preuve de leur simple honnêteté.*[26]

Another burden weighing on the *maquisards* Ghéhenno quoted was a failure to distinguish between the difficult road they had chosen and the efforts of so-called '*réfractaires*' (i.e. men trying to avoid forced labor for the Germans) to take the easy way out (1947: 468): "*Les maquisards ne veulent surtout pas qu'on les confonde avec les petits bourgeois 'planqués', qui par leur travail, ont cherché un abri à la campagne 'chez une tante ou dans une ferme de papa.*"[27]

Commentators have written: "One of the functions of the clandestine press was to impose and to keep alive the heroic image of the underground in the face of the adversary's stigmatization of their acts and the reprisals they drew" (Brée and Bernauer 1970: 199). The same can be said of '*Le Chant de Partisans*', almost every line of which served either directly or indirectly to legitimize underground activities and to invest with prestige those men and women who carried them out. The strategies for contributing to a climate of greater acceptance and support for the Resistance included: a) presenting the partisans as responding to the country's cry for help (*les cris sourds du pays qu'on enchaîne, l'alarme*); b) portraying the partisans as essentially liberators (*C'est nous qui brisons les barreaux des prisons pour nos frères*); c) evoking the hardships they endure in carrying out their tasks (Stanzas

---

26 "… a protest against the vile propaganda denouncing them as terrorists and bandits, and which – to crown it all is not entirely ineffective in shaping public opinion. They had set out thinking that they would merely be the avant-garde of the armies of liberation, and here they are, forced to recognize that the bulk of the nation, reserved and mistrustful, will not follow their lead. They themselves are capable of explaining that this country of logicians and lawyers is poorly equipped to understand that 'order is not necessarily the same as legality.' A Darnand [head of the collaborationist Milice] had only to call his troops of assassins the 'forces for the maintenance of order' for our petits bourgeois to scratch their heads and adopt a mistrustful attitude toward these 'bandits' who are their own sons and brothers; and we have now reached the point where these young 'volunteers' who are saving everyone's honour, have to justify themselves, to argue in their own defence and provide evidence of their simple honesty."

27 "Resistance fighters do not under any circumstances want to be confused with those *petits bourgeois* in hiding, who – out of an aversion for work – have sought a refuge in the country 'at the home of an aunt or at a farm owned by daddy.'"

10 and 12); d) presenting the act of killing the enemy as a natural part of the *maquisard*'s prescribed role (*Ohé les tuers à la balle et au couteau, tuez vite!*); e) and implicitly defining the Resistance as a popular-based movement (*ouvriers et paysans*).

In these respects, '*Le Chant des Partisans*' was a means of attempting to reshape the French public's mental image of the *maquisard*, and to promote the values and goals of the Resistance within a public subjected to massive German and Vichy propaganda.

An entirely different orienting function – and one of which I had no suspicion until Germaine Sablon called it to my attention – conerns the Free French in London. In response to my question as to why it was satisfying for her to sing '*Le Chant des Partisans*' in London, Germaine Sablon replied (1980): "*Les Français de Londres avaient l'air de mépriser ceux qui restaient en France et je voulais avec mes moyens essayer de faire comprendre la vérité*."[28] She wanted them to grasp that many Frenchmen remaining on the continent were fighting against the Germans and deserved to be respected by the Free French. In this way, '*Le Chant des Partisans*' was a means for evoking a positive image of the *maquisard* in the minds of the Free French, as well as for the general public within France.

## 5. CELEBRATION AND SYMBOLIC ENROLMENT (August 1944-1945)

In 'A Plea for France,' appearing in *Life Magazine* on November 6, 1944, Vercors described his country as undergoing a process of rebirth and an emergence from four years of shame and helplessness. What France retrospectively had to be proud of during those dark years was the Resistance, and when the nightmare finally came to an end, it is not surprising that '*Le Chant des Partisans*' should have enjoyed "*une popularité immédiate*" (Crémieux-Brilhac 1975: vol 4, 177). Celebrating the Resistance movement through its song was a means for a generalized symbolic enrolment of the French public in that movement, for expressing gratitude toward those who had kept alive the honour of the nation and whose sacrifices had not always been sufficiently appreciated (Ghéhenno 1947: 465-466) and for dispelling some of the lingering shame Vercors described. For those who

---

28 "The French in London seemed to look down on those who remained in France and I wanted to use whatever means I had to try and make them understand the truth."

had been active in the Resistance, the song was a celebration of their own recent struggle, and the popularity of '*Le Chant*' one of the many forms of public recognition accorded to them.

## 6. COMMEMORATION AND TRANSMISSION (post-war period to the present)

In an article published in *Résistance Unie* shortly before the 25th anniversary of the Allied victory, a commentator wrote (1960: No. 4, 12):

> ... *ce chant de lutte et d'espoir que l'on ne peut entendre sans ressentir un frisson d'angoisse, va retentir en des milliers d'endroits: devant les 'crématoires' des anciens camps de la mort, au bord des routes jalonnées de modestes plaques rappelant la lutte et le sacrifice des maquisards* ...[29]

In some respects, '*Le Chant des Partisans*' has apparently fulfilled the functions of a secular 'mourner's prayer' – a *kaddish* – commemorating the death of *maquisards* and of other victims of Nazism.

Furthermore, both on ceremonial occasions and through such recordings as Yves Montand's in *Chansons Populaires de France* (1991), the song has been a means for transmitting to successive generations a particular image of the *maquisards*, and a possibility for vicariously experiencing – and for symbolically enrolling oneself in – the French Resistance.

---

29 "... this song of battle and of hope that we cannot listen to without feeling a shudder of anguish will resound at a thousand places: in front of the crematoria of the former death camps, at roadsides interspersed with modest plaques that commemorate the struggle and the sacrifice of Resistance fighters ..."

# SCHEMATIC OVERVIEW OF FUNCTIONS FULFILLED BY *LE CHANT DES PARTISANS*

| SUMMER 1943 to SUMMER 1944 | 1. for *maquisards* | a) strengthening social cohesion within and between Resistance groups, partly through the song's contribution to the movement's ethos of comradeship<br>b) counteracting anxieties over individual death and the movement's ability to survive the loss of members, by depicting the role of the maquisard as immortal<br>c) unburdening, with regard to hardships and sacrifices<br>d) promoting confidence, pride and a sense of purpose<br>e) legitimizing the use of violence |
|---|---|---|
| | 2. for prisoners | a) providing a means for symbolic enactment of defiance<br>b) helping to sustain courage and hope and to give some measure of relief<br>c) contributing to social cohesion |
| | 3. signal functions | a) informing a radio listener that he or she is tuned in to a Resistance broadcast<br>b) a 'coast-is-clear' signal, whistled in the course of operations |
| | 4. orienting functions for outsiders to the movement | a) reshaping the French public's mental image of the *maquisard, maligned by* German and Vichy propaganda, and promoting the values and goals of the Resistance<br>b) in London: evoking a positive image of the maquisard, to undercut the condescending attitude of held by some of the Free French with regard to those who had remained on the continent |

| | | | |
|---|---|---|---|
| 1944-1945 | 5. celebration and symbolic enrolment | a) generalized symbolic enrolment of the French public in the Resistance movement<br>b) means for expressing gratitude toward the Resistance<br>c) means for dispelling shame<br>d) for members of Resistance: celebration of their own recent struggle | |
| POST-WAR PERIOD TO PRESENT | 6. commemoration and transmission | a) serving as a secular 'mourner's prayer' to commemorate the dead<br>b) a means for transmitting to successive generations a particular image of the maquisard, and a possibility for vicariously experiencing and celebrating the values of the French Resistance | |

# References and other works consulted

Barnow, Erik (1974). *Documentary – A History of the Non-Fiction Film*. New York: Oxford University Press.
Crémieux-Brilhac, Jean-Louis (1975). *Ici Londres 1940-1944 – Les Voix de la Liberté*. Paris: La Documentation Française, vol. 4.
Deranty, Germaine (1980). Interviewed by the author, 25 February.
Druon, Maurice (n.d). "Comment fut écrit 'Le Chant des Partisans,'" unpublished typewritten pages.
Druon, Maurice (1973). "Le jour où fut écrit 'Le Chant des Partisans,'" in *Au pas de la vie, I, Oeuvres complètes*, vol. 8, pp. 98-101.
Druon, Maurice (1980). Interviewed by the author, 24 April.
Fournier-Brilhac, C. (1980). Interviewed by the author, 26 February.
Frenay, Henri (1973). *La Nuit finira – Mémoires de la Résistance 1940-1945*. Paris: Robert Laffont.
Gillois, André (1973). *Histoire secrète des Français à Londres*. Paris: Tallandier.
Kessel, Joseph (1944). *L'Armée des ombres – Chronique de la Résistance*. New York: Pantheon.
L'Herminier, Jeanette (1980). Interviewed by the author, 25 February.
Marly, Anna (1980). Personal communication, 8 April.
Mercier, Odette (1980). Personal communication, 12 May.
Michel, Henri (1970). *La Guerre de l'ombre – La Résistance en Europe*. Paris: Grasset.
Sablon, Germaine (1980). Personal communication, 11 March.

# APPENDIX

## MAURICE DRUON'S REPLY TO MY QUESTIONS CONCERNING '*LE CHANT DES PARTISANS*'

## 24 APRIL 1980

*RR: Aviez-vous en composant* Le Chant des Partisans *une idée plus ou moins précise des fonctions que le chant devait remplir? Ou des besoins auxquels le chant devait répondre?*

MD: Assurément, et fort précise. On n'écrit pas un chant de guerre sans savoir pourquoi. Il est destiné à remplir une fonction évidente: magnifier la lutte, soutenir les combattants, les unir. Dans le cas d'un combat clandestin particulièrement, un chant est signe de ralliement, un lien invisible mais fort; et c'est bien dans ce dessein que les mouvements de résistance souhaitaient avoir *leur* chant.

*RR: Aviez-vous consciemment l'intention de rendre le mouvement mieux armé contre la propagande de Vichy, qui cherchait à imposer au public français une image négative des résistants, comme terroristes ou bandits?*

MD: Mieux armé contre la propagande, mieux armé contre les polices, mieux armé contre l'ennemi. Ce n'est pas la première fois dans l'histoire qu'un chant est une arme morale. Toutes les armées du monde, nationales ou révolutionnaires, et depuis le début des âges, ont chanté.

*RR: A propos du vers: "Ohé les tueurs, à la balle et au couteau, tuez vite!" qui remplace un autre vers figurant dans le premier brouillon: "Ohé cheminots à vos postes sur le rail, allez vite." Avez-vous voulu catalyser une plus grande acceptation de la violence contre l'ennemi, chez le public français en dehors du mouvement?*

MD: Ne tenez pas trop compte des brouillons. Quand on commence une chanson, on jette des mots, on note des idées comme elles viennent à l'esprit; on les remplace par d'autres qui semblent plus appropriés, ou dont la sonorité convient mieux. Ce qui compte c'est le texte définitif.

RR: A propos du vers: "Ami, si tu tombes un ami sort de l'ombre à ta place." Aviez-vous pensée aux effets de cette image? Y avait-il une intention particulière qui guidait l'élaboration de cette image?

MD: Une image ne s'élabore pas, elle s'impose, intuitivement. Et celle-là était dictée par la réalité même de la Résistance.

RR: "Le cri sourd du hibou" (dans le brouillon) devient "Le vol noir des corbeaux" (dans le texte définitif). Pourquoi des oiseaux pour symboliser l'ennemi?

MD: En cherchant un point de départ pour le chant, j'avais pensé aux "résistances" du passé, dans l'histoire nationale, aux armées clandestines, et plus particulièrement aux Chouans, dont le signe de ralliement, la nuit, était le hululement de la chouette ou du hibou. Par le glissement naturel, nous sommes passés du hibou au corbeau, plus sinistre, et du cri au vol noir symbolique de l'occupant.

RR: Je sais que déjà, le 14 mai 1943, l'enregistrement de la mélodie sifflée (par d'Astier, Gillois et vous) avait eu lieu. Est-ce que le sifflement était déjà évocateur de la Résistance, ou est-ce grâce au Chant des Partisans que le sifflement s'est intégré à notre image du résistant?

MD: Le sifflement est signal naturel pour les combattants de l'ombre et de la lutte secrète. Il se peut que Le Chant des Partisans ait contribué à faire entrer le sifflement comme l'un des éléments classiques et représentatifs du résistant.

RR: Le texte fait par Anna Marly – était-il écrit en français, en russe, les deux langues? Aviez-vous retenu centaines images de son texte, ou êtes-vous plutôt repartis de zéro? Savez-vous par hasard vers quelle époque elle a fait la mélodie et son texte à elle?

MD: Anna Marly m'a dit qu'elle avait initialement composé quelques paroles, en russe, sur sa musique, une ébauche de texte; mais je n'en ai jamais eu connaissance. Je ne sais pas si Kessel les avaient entendues; en tout cas, il n'en avait rien retenu. Nous ne sommes partis que de nos souvenirs et de ceux de nos amis de la Résistance, en prenant appui sur la mélodie. Mais quel bon appui! Je pense qu'Anna Marly avait composé quelques semaines auparavant cette musique forte et très rythmée, qui n'était pas d'ailleurs sans quelque réminiscence des chants soviétiques de la même époque. Les chants de guerre, plus que tous autres, sont des synthèses.

*RR: J'aimerais pouvoir documenter que* Le Chant des Partisans *a été chanté par des groups de résistants, mais jusqu'ici je n'ai rien trouvé de très concret. Est-ce que des combattants vous ont affirmé avoir chanté* Le Chant des Partisans *avant la Libération? Et comment expliquer la popularité du* Chant *au lendemain de la Libération?*

MD: Les résistants n'avaient pas coutume de tenir leur journal; et moi-même, après la Libération, je n'ai pas pris soin de consigner qui m'avait dit avoir chanté *Le Chant des Partisans* et en quelles circonstances. Il a commencé de se répandre en France, grâce à la B.B.C. et au poste "Honneur et Patrie" dans les derniers mois de 1943.

Je sais que les passeurs alsaciens, qui faisaient franchir au résistants, ou au pilotes alliés abattus, la frontière de la zone interdite, sifflaient *Le Chant des Partisans* pour signaler que la voie était libre.

L'écrivain Frison-Roche m'a dit l'avoir chanté, avec ses compagnons de maquis, la nuit de Noël 1943. L'actuel Ministre des Anciens Combattants, Monsieur Maurice Plantier, lui-même grand résistant qui appartenait au réseau Buckmaster puis à l'OCM (Organisation Civile et Militaire), se rappelait que l'on connaissait *Le Chant des Partisans* dès la fin 1943 dans le maquis des Landes et qu'il l'entendît chanter la nuit du 1er janvier 1944.

Je sais aussi, par des témoignages de combattants, que *Le Chant* circula dans diverses prisons, notamment du Massif Central. Il m'a même été dit qu'un groupe de condamnés l'avaient chanté devant le peloton d'exécution … C'était bien devenu *Le Chant de la Résistance*.

Quant à sa popularité immédiate, dès la Libération, elle s'explique par le fait précisément que *Le Chant* était déjà connu, et s'était répandu à travers la France.

## MAURICE DRUON'S REPLY TO MY QUESTIONS CONCERNING 'LE CHANT DES PARTISANS'

24 APRIL 1980

*RR: When composing* 'Le Chant des Partisans', *did you have a fairly definite idea as to the functions the song was to fulfill or of the needs it was to satisfy?*

MD: Certainly, a most precise idea. No one writes a war song without knowing why. It is intended to fulfill an obvious function: to celebrate the struggle, to sustain and unite the fighters. Particularly in the case of an underground struggle, a song serves to rally the combatants, as a bond that is invisible but strong; and it was for this reason that the Resistance movements wanted a song of their own.

RR: *Were you specifically concerned with making the movement better armed against Vichy propaganda that sought to impose on the French public a negative image of Resistance fighters as terrorists or bandits?*

MD: Better armed against propaganda, better armed against the police, better armed against the enemy. This wasn't the first time in history that a song served as a moral weapon. Since the dawn of time, all the armies of the world – both national and revolutionary – have sung.

RR: *Concerning the line, 'Come on, killers, with bullet and with knife, kill swiftly,' which replaced another line that appeared in the first draft: 'Come on, railway men, take up your positions on the tracks, go there swiftly,' did you wish to make the French public, outside of the movement, more willing to accept the use of violence against the enemy?*

MD: Don't attach too much importance to first drafts. When you begin writing a song, you put some words down on paper, you jot down ideas as they occur to you: you replace them with others which seem more appropriate or which have a better sound. What matters is the definitive text.

RR: *Concerning the line: 'Friend, if you fall, a friend emerges from the shadows to take your place.' Had you thought about the effects of this image? Did a particular intention guide you in the elaboration of this image?*

MD: An image is not elaborated, it imposes itself intuitively. And that one was dictated by the very reality of the Resistance.

RR: *'The muffled cry of the owl' (in the first draft) becomes 'The black flight of ravens' (in the final text). Why use birds to symbolize the enemy?*

MD: In looking for a starting point for the song, I had thought about the resistance movements of the past in our nation's history, about secret armies, and more specifically about the 'Chouans' (royalist insurgents in Normandy and Brittany during the Revolution), whose nocturnal rallying sign was the hooting of an owl. Through a natural process of association, we moved on from the owl to the more sinister raven, and from the cry to the black flight symbolic of the occupying forces.

*RR: I know that as early as May 14, 1943, a recording of the melody whistled by d'Astier, Gillois and yourself had already been made. Had whistling already become evocative of the Resistance, or was it through 'Le Chant des Partisans' that whistling became an integral part of our image of the resistance fighter?*

MD: It is natural for those who take part in a secret struggle in the shadows to use whistling as a signal. It is possible that *'Le Chant des Partisans'* contributed to making this one of the classical representative elements of the resistance fighter.

*RR: Was Anna Marly's text written in French, Russian or both languages? Did you keep any of the imagery from her text, or did you begin entirely from scratch? And do you happen to know roughly when it was that she composed the melody and her own lyrics?*

MD: Anna Marly told me that she had initially written some lyrics in Russian to accompany her melody, a first outline of a text: but I never knew anything about it. I don't know whether Kessel had ever heard these lyrics; in any event, he didn't recall any of them. We based our work entirely on our own recollections and on those of our friends in the Resistance, letting the melody guide us. And what a marvelous support it was! I think it was several weeks earlier that Marly had composed this powerful and rhythmic melody, which is somewhat reminiscent of Soviet songs from that period. War songs, more than any other kind, are syntheses.

*RR: I should like to be able to document the fact that 'Le Chant des Partisans' was sung by groups of resistance fighters, but until now I have not been able to find very much concrete evidence for this. To your knowledge, have combatants confirmed that they sang the song before the Liberation? And how would you explain the popularity of the song in the wake of the Liberation?*

MD: Resistance fighters were not in the habit of keeping a diary; and for my part, after the Liberation, I hardly took note of who had told me he or she had sung '*Le Chant des Partisans*' and under what circumstances. It spread through France thanks to the B.B.C. and the station *Honour and Country* in the final months of 1943. I know that 'Underground Song' was whistled to signal that the coast was clear, when Resistance fighters or allied pilots who had been shot down were smuggled over the Alsatian border of the 'Prohibited Zone.' The author, Frison-Roche, told me that he and his companions in the underground sang it on Christmas Eve in 1943. The present Minister of Former Combatants, Monsieur Maurice Plantier, was himself a distinguished Resistance fighter belonging to the Buckmaster underground and later attached to the OCM (Organisation Civile et Militaire); he remembers that the song circulated in the underground of the Landes region (near Bayonne) from the end of 1943 and that he heard it sung on New Year's Eve, 1944. A number of combatants have also informed me that the song circulated in various prisons, particularly in the Massif Central region. It has even been stated that a group of prisoners who had been sentenced to death sang it before the firing squad ... It had in point of fact become the Song of the Resistance.

As far as its popularity immediately after the Liberation is concerned, the explanation for that is that the song was already known and had been spread throughout France.

# 13

# On Barbara's Need to Write the Song *'Göttingen'*

Link to a video of Barbara singing Göttingen *with French and English subtitles: https://www.youtube.com/watch?v=2beYoAxxC8A*

## Introduction

*'Göttingen'* was written in 1964 by Barbara, as Monique Serf called herself from about 1950 on. Much of the attention that has been focused on this song concerns: a) the unusual circumstances of its creation, beginning with the singer/songwriter's initial refusal and eventual agreement to perform in Germany; b) the role played by the song in helping the French and Germans to overcome the lingering animosity left by the Second World War; and c) such expressions of gratitude toward Barbara as the Medal of Merit (*Bundesverdienstkreuz*) awarded to her in 1988 by Chancellor Gerhard Schröder on behalf of the German Federal Republic for her heartfelt contribution to German-French understanding, and the naming of a street in Göttingen after her in 2002, five years after her death.

What makes these events especially poignant is the fact that Barbara was

Jewish and that during the German occupation of France, when she was 10 to 14 years old, she and her family were in hiding from the Gestapo, often moving from one place to another and constantly worrying about denunciations. She wrote in her memoirs (1998: 34):

> I have retained from this period a taste for travel, for the clandestine, for the precarious, for playing cards hidden from view in a back room, for hasty getaways, for the sound of knocking at the door, of 'It's the Gestapo,' [...] and for a tendency to provoke, to be aggressive as a result of fear. Even to this day, if someone knocks or rings, I am startled and sometimes run and hide.[1]

During those years, she was very much aware that she looked Jewish. She referred to her "physical difference" and stated: "I was neither ashamed nor especially proud of being Jewish but being able to 'read' my singularity in the way others looked at me made me aggressive" (Barbara 1998: 35-36).[2]

**'*Göttingen*', lyrics by Barbara**
©Editions Métropolitaines
My literal translations (RR)

| | | |
|---|---|---|
| 1 | Bien sûr, ce n'est pas la Seine<br>Ce n'est pas le bois de Vincennes<br>Mais c'est bien joli tout de même<br>À Göttingen, à Göttingen | Of course it's not the Seine<br>Nor the woods of Vincennes<br>But it's quite pretty all the same<br>In Göttingen, in Göttingen |
| 2 | Pas de quais et pas de rengaines<br>Qui se lamentent et qui se traînent.<br>Mais l'amour y fleurit quand même<br>À Göttingen, à Göttingen | No quays and no old tunes<br>That moan and drag on<br>But love still blossoms there<br>In Göttingen, in Göttingen |

---

1 "J'ai gardé de cette époque le goût du voyage, de la clandestinité, du précaire, des parties de cartes à l'abri dans la chambre du fond, des départs à la sauvette, du bruit des coups dans la porte, des "Y a la Gestapo" [...] et une certaine tendance à la provocation, à une agressivité inspiré par la peur. Aujourd'hui encore, si l'on frappe ou l'on sonne, je sursaute et il m'arrive de courir me cacher."

2 "cette différence physique [...] Je n'avais ni honte ni fierté particulière d'être juive, mais le fait de lire ma singularité dans le regard des autres me rendait aggressive."

| | | |
|---|---|---|
| 3 | Ils savent mieux que nous, je pense<br>L'histoire de nos rois de France<br>Herman, Peter, Helga et Hans<br>À Göttingen, à Göttingen | I think they know better than we do<br>The history of our French kings<br>Herman, Peter, Helga and Hans<br>In Göttingen, in Göttingen |
| 4 | Et que personne ne s'offense,<br>Mais les contes de notre enfance<br>"Il était une fois" commencent<br>À Göttingen, à Göttingen | And may no one be offended<br>But the tales from our childhood<br>"Once upon a time" began<br>In Göttingen, in Göttingen |
| 5 | Bien sûr nous, nous avons la Seine<br>Et puis notre bois de Vincennes<br>Mais Dieu que les roses sont belles<br>À Göttingen, à Göttingen | Of course we have the Seine<br>And our woods of Vincennes<br>But God the roses are beautiful<br>In Göttingen, in Göttingen |
| 6 | Nous, nous avons nos matins blêmes<br>Et l'âme grise de Verlaine<br>Eux, c'est la mélancolie même<br>À Göttingen, à Göttingen | As for us, we have our pale mornings<br>And Verlaine's grey [or tipsy] soul<br>Them, they are melancholy itself<br>In Göttingen, in Göttingen |
| 7 | Quand ils ne savent rien nous dire,<br>Ils restent là à nous sourire<br>Mais nous les comprenons quand même,<br>Les enfants blonds de Göttingen | When they don't know what to say to us,<br>They just stand there and smile at us<br>But we understand them all the same<br>The blond children of Göttingen |
| 8 | Et tant pis pour ceux qui s'étonnent<br>Et que les autres me pardonnent<br>Mais les enfants ce sont les mêmes<br>À Paris ou à Göttingen | And too bad for those who are surprised<br>And may the others pardon me<br>But children are the same<br>In Paris or in Göttingen |
| 9 | Ô faites que jamais ne revienne<br>Le temps du sang et de la haine<br>Car il y a des gens que j'aime<br>À Göttingen, à Göttingen | Oh, may it never return<br>The time of blood and hatred<br>For there are people I love<br>In Göttingen, in Göttingen. |
| 10 | Et lorsque sonnerait l'alarme<br>S'il fallait reprendre les armes<br>Mon coeur verserait une larme<br>Pour Göttingen, pour Göttingen | And if the alarm should sound<br>And arms have to be taken up again<br>My heart would shed a tear<br>For Göttingen, for Göttingen |

Barbara's Jewish background is of course kept in mind by everyone writing about 'Göttingen'. In what is unquestionably the finest study of the song to date, Joël July (2015) has pointed out that for Barbara, the song was an expression of love for the city rather than a deliberate attempt to change the attitudes of the French and Germans toward one another. As stated in a 1970 interview July quotes, Barbara didn't think songs could change the world and in her view, "*Göttingen* is a love song."[3] In his study, which includes an admirably subtle and precise textual analysis of the lyrics, July suggests that it was largely in the 1980s, when Franco-German reconciliation was an important item on the agenda of major politicians, that the song was perceived in a way that had not been purposefully intended when Barbara wrote it.

## Several changes of heart

While singing at the Left-Bank Paris night club, L'Écluse, in early 1964, Barbara was visited by the young director of the Jungen Theater in Göttingen, Gunther Klein, who had come to Paris to invite her to perform at his theater. At first the Jewish singer/songwriter refused: "Out of the question to go sing in Germany … I don't wish to go to Germany"[4] (Barbara 1998: 162). In one of her final interviews, she confided: "Germany for me was like a claw" (cited by Lehoux 2007: 316).[5]

However, Klein was unwilling to take no for an answer and when he persisted, Barbara agreed to think about it. The next day she told him that she would accept his invitation after all, on the condition that a baby grand piano be provided for her performance, so that she could see her audience while playing. Klein agreed and a date was set.

On the appointed date, July 4, 1964, when she arrived in Göttingen by train, Barbara's attitude had changed once again, since she was "already angry about having agreed to go sing in Germany" (Barbara 1998: 165).[6] Gunther met her at the station and offered to show her around but she was uninterested in touring the city and preferred to go straight to the venue

---

3 "*Göttingen*, c'est une chanson d'amour." The entire excerpt cited by July of the 1970 radio interview can be found at https://www.francemusique.fr/emissions/les-greniers-de-la-memoire/barbara-18072 from 52 min. 49 sec. to 53 min. 22 sec.
4 "Pas question d'aller chanter en Allemagne … Je ne souhaite pas aller en Allemagne."
5 "L'Allemagne était pour moi comme une griffe." Jean Luc Hess, "Synergie," *France Inter*, 27 December 1996.
6 "déja en colère d'avoir accepté d'aller chanter en Allemagne."

where she was scheduled to perform at 8:15 that evening. On arrival, she was "distant and showed signs of having extreme reservations," according to Horst Wattenberg, who had co-founded the Jungen Theater (Saint-Paul 2013)[7]. She immediately noticed that the upright piano at the theater would block her view of her audience and she angrily refused to perform unless a baby grand was provided as had been promised. On hearing Klein's excuse about a piano-mover's strike in the city, her anger faded but she was still adamant about refusing to perform.

A final change of heart began when a group of ten tall students took it upon themselves to accommodate Barbara's wishes by bringing a concert piano to the venue, borrowing it from an elderly woman they knew who had one. They arrived with it at 10 pm and the concert could finally begin. The public that had been waiting so patiently were wildly enthusiastic about her performance and Gunther extended the invitation for her to perform that entire week, which she now gladly accepted. The following day, students gave her the tour of Göttingen she had refused on her arrival, and this tour included seeing the house where the Brothers Grimm wrote the fairytales she had heard as a child. At her concerts that week, "Barbara was greatly impressed by the enthusiasm she encountered, by the thunderous applause every evening, by the welcoming of an entire city" (Wattenberg cited in Saint-Paul 2013).[8]

## Writing the song

On her last day in Göttingen, in a garden adjacent to the theater, Barbara scribbled some lyrics to a new song, '*Göttingen*'. At her final concert that night, she recited and sang some rudimentary verses with apologies for the incompleteness of the song. The audience went wild: "We were so touched by this gift and this gesture of reconciliation. My own engagement in favor of Franco-German friendship as well as that of the entire city, was immensely strengthened"[9] (Wattenberg cited in Saint-Paul 2013). She wrote

---

7   "En arrivant, elle était très distante et faisait preuve d'une retenue extrême."
8   "Barbara était très impressionnée par l'enthousiasme qui l'entourait, par les tonnerres d'applaudissements chaque soir, par l'accueil de toute une ville."
9   "Nous étions tous si touchés par ce cadeau et ce geste de réconciliation. Mon engagement en faveur de l'amitié franco-allemande, comme celui de toute la ville s'en est trouvé immensément renforcé."

in her memoirs that she felt she owed this song "to the stubborn insistence of Gunther Klein, to 10 students, to a sympathetic old lady [who provided the piano], to the blondness of the little children of Göttingen, to a profound desire for reconciliation but without forgetting. And as always I owe this song to the public, and in this case to the marvelous public of the Jungen Theater" (Barbara 1998: 168).[10] Later that summer, on her return to Paris, she finished the song and her manager, Claude Desjacques, decided it would be recorded on her next Philips album, *Le Mal de vivre* (released in mono in 1964, in stereo in 1965).

It is of course obvious that one of the purposes of the song was for Barbara to express her gratitude toward and love for the Göttingen audiences who had opened their heart to her.

But it was also a way for her to take control of her own story. Having vacillated as circumstances changed, sending her veering between positive and negative attitudes toward Germany, uncertain as to where she stood and unable to make sense of the conflicting feelings she held, she would now shape her own narrative by defining her relationship to the Germans once and for all in the form of a work of art that would also position her in the eyes of audiences as someone who had overcome her anti-German sentiments. Writing the song was her way of consolidating and owning what she had ultimately experienced in Göttingen and learned about herself in the process. Through the alchemy of creating the song she transformed the very blondness of German children from what in the past might have seemed to be a threatening negation of her own Semitic looks into a harmless difference with a natural charm of its own. And as can be seen in the handwritten page reproduced below, that blondness ("un enfant blond") was present in even her earliest notes for the song, which also contain a reference to very blue eyes ("les yeux de pervenche") – again the opposite of her own dark, Semitic eyes.

There is no need to repeat here what others – Joël July in particular – have already eloquently written about specific verses of the song, including those designed to parry foreseeable disapproval of this declaration of love, especially by co-religionists who had not yet overcome their own anti-German feelings:

---

10 "Je dois donc cette chanson à l'insistance têtue de Günther Klein, à dix étudiants, à une vieille dame compatissante, à la blondeur des petits enfants de Göttingen, à un profond désir de réconciliation, mais non d'oubli. Comme toujours je dois aussi cette chanson au public, en l'occurrence le merveilleux public du Jungen Theater."

Et que personne ne s'offense / And may no one be offended
Et tant pis pour ceux qui s'étonnent / And too bad for those who are surprised
Et que les autres me pardonnent / And may the others pardon me

I would only add that these observations in the literature on the song are well worth keeping in mind, also in relation to Barbara's fully taking charge of her own story in relation to Germany and in a way that could be ritually repeated, relived and admired at performances she gave for more than thirty years after her initial visit to Göttingen.

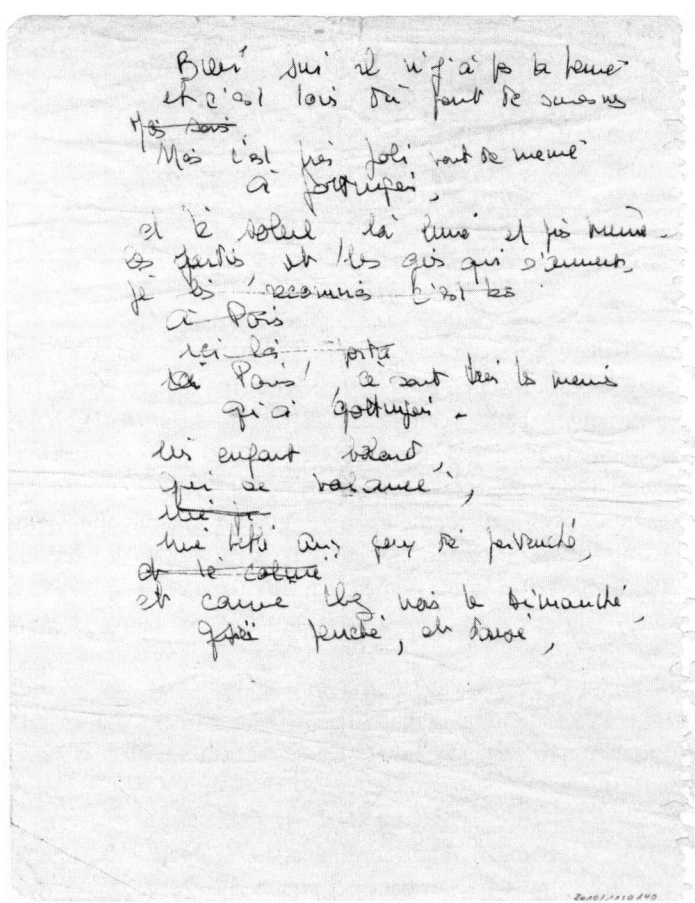

Haus der Geschichte, Bonn. A page of Barbara's earliest fragmentary notes for her new song, reproduced here with the kind permission of Bernard Serf. The following transcription is the result of guesswork and some help from my learned colleagues and friends, Zbigniew Sobkowicz, Hélène Cnops Rasmussen and Ole Wehner Rasmussen.

| | |
|---|---|
| Bien sûr il n'y pas la Seine | Of course there is no Seine |
| et c'est loin du Pont de Suresnes | and it's far from the Pont de Suresnes |
| Mais c'est très joli tout de même | But its very pretty all the same |
| À Göttingen. | In Göttingen |
| et le soleil, la lune et puis même | and the sun, the moon and even |
| les [jardins?] ah! les [gens?] qui s'aiment | the [gardens?] Ah! the [people?] in love |
| je les reconnais, c'est les | I recognize them, they are |
| à Paris ce sont bien les mêmes | In Paris they are the same |
| qu'à Göttingen | as in Göttingen |
| un enfant blond | A blond child |
| qui se balance | on a swing |
| une fille aux yeux de pervenche | a girl with very blue eyes |
| et comme chez nous le dimanche | and as we do on Sundays |
| [penché?], on danse | [leaning?], people dance, |

# References

Astro, Alan (2009). "Barbara (Monique Andrée Serf)." *Jewish Women: A Comprehensive Historical Encyclopedia*. 1 March 2009. Jewish Women's Archive. https://jwa.org/encyclopedia/article/barbara-monique-andree-serf Accessed 28 May 2017.

Barbara (1998). *Il était un piano noir… mémoires interrompus*. Paris: Fayard.

Bei der Kellen, Ralf and Susanne von Schenck (2013). "Barbara, Göttingen. Die Geschichte einer französisch-deutchen Annäherung," *Deutschlandradio Kultur*, 16 January 2013, http://www.deutschlandradiokultur.de/barbara-goettingen.984.de.html?dram:article_id=234452 Accessed 28 May 2017.

Belfond, Jean-Daniel (2000). *Barbara l'ensorceleuse*. Saint-Cyr-sur-Loire: Christian Pirot,

Chaix, Marie. *Barbara* (2013). Paris: Libela. Orig. pub. 2007.

Chouffan, Alain (2015). "Les mystères de Barbara," Harissa.com, 29 October 2015, http://www.harissa.com/news/article/les-mystères-de-barbara-par-alain-chouffan Accessed 28 May 2017.

Cyrulnik, Boris (2004). *Les villains petits canards*. Paris: Odile Jacob.

Evans, Sephan (2013). "Goettingen: The song that made history," B.B.C. News, Berlin, 22 January 2013, http://www.bbc.com/news/magazine-21126353 Accessed 28 May 2017.

Garcin, Jérôme (2013). *Barbara, Claire de nuit*. Paris: Gallimard/Collection Folio. Orig. pub. 1999.

Ivry, Benjamin (2014). Review of *The 110 Jewish Women Who Changed France* by Michèle Bitton, *The Forward*, 13 Sept 2014. http://forward.com/culture/205478/the-110-jewish-women-who-changed-france/ Accessed 28 May 2017.

July, Joël (2015). "Göttingen, de la réticence à l'évidence," in Phaeton, *L'Ire des marges*, pp. 231-241. https://hal.archives-ouvertes.fr/hal-01382627/ Accessed 28 May 2017.

Lebrecht, Norman (2011). "La belle dame sans publicité," *Standpoint*, December 2011. http://standpointmag.co.uk/node/4218/full Accessed 28 May 2017.

Lehoux, Valerie (2007). *Barbara: Portrait en clair-obscur*. Paris: Fayard/Chorus.

Levy, Elias (2016). "La musique française juive – Une grande énigme?," *Canadian Jewish News*, 14 March 2016. http://www.cjnews.com/en-francais/la-musique-francaise-juive-une-grande-enigme Accessed 28 May 2017.

Papenheim, Christoph (2015). "Stadt gedenkt französischer Sängerin, die Göttingen-Lied sang," 9 June 2015. https://www.hna.de/lokales/goettingen/goettingen-ort28741/rote-rosen-barbaras-grab-5081922.html Accessed 28 May 2017.

Saint-Paul, Patrick (2013). "À Göttingen, un trait d'union nommé Barbara," *Le Figaro*, 20 January 2013. http://www.lefigaro.fr/mon-figaro/2013/01/20/10001-20130120ARTFIG00179--gottingen-un-trait-d-union-nomme-barbara.php Accessed 28 May 2017.

Sasportas, Valerie (2017). "Barbara: *Göttingen*, le chant de la réconciliation," *Le Figaro*, 2 February 2017. http://www.lefigaro.fr/musique/2017/02/02/03006-20170202ARTFIG00019-barbara-gottingen-le-chant-de-la-reconciliation.php Accessed 28 May 2017.

Schröder, Gerhard (2003). "Rede von Bundeskanzler Schröder zum 40. Jahrestag der Unterzeichnung des Elysée-Vertrags", http://adrien.barbaresi.eu/corpora/speeches/BR/t/482.html Accessed 23 October 2017.

Wodrascka, Alain (2013). *Barbara: Une Vie Romanesque*. Paris: Cherche-Midi.

"Göttingen," *C'est une chanson* (2013). 13 November. http://www.cestunechanson.fr/les-chansons-se-racontent-gottingen-barbara_135/ Accessed 28 May 2017.

"Göttingen – Barbara," *Song of the Week* (2013). 23 January. https://songoftheweekblog.com/2013/01/23/song-of-the-week-35-gottingen-barbara/ Accessed 28 May 2017.

# 14

# Camus' Critiques of Existentialism

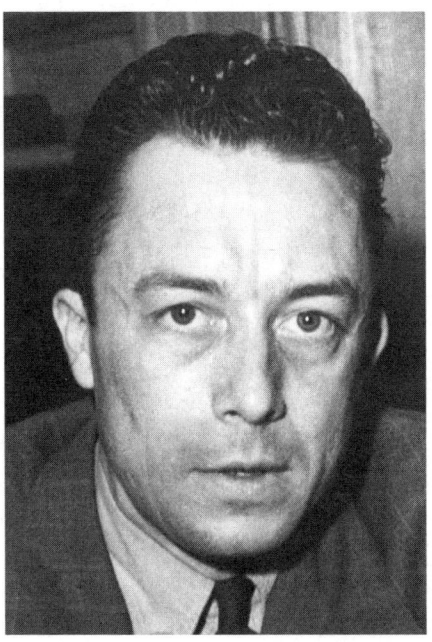

When Camus completed his novel *L'Étranger/The Stranger* in May 1940, he had already begun the writing phase of an essay on the absurd – a project mentioned in his *Carnets/Notebooks* four years earlier, and which would be completed in February 1941. This essay and novel, along with two plays – *Caligula* and *Le Malentendu/The Misunderstanding* – would constitute what Camus himself described as his series of the "absurd" or "negation," and although they were published between 1942 and 1945, Camus considered them expressions of his major concerns *before* the war.

It was only in the last months of writing his essay on the absurd, to be published in 1942, that Camus decided to call it *Le Mythe de Sisyphe/The Myth of Sisyphus*, thereby giving to the entire work the title of its final chapter.

Sisyphus was the figure from Greek mythology who the gods condemned to rolling a boulder up the side of a mountain to its summit, at which point the boulder would roll down again; Sisyphus would then descend the slope of the mountain and begin again his useless and never-ending task.

Early in this essay, Camus states that when comforting illusions are stripped away, life can be seen to be completely devoid of meaning. He asks whether that realization necessarily means that life is not worth living. The entire essay is an attempt to answer that question.

In developing the model on which his answer would be based, Camus argues that man desperately demands meaning and clarity of the world around him but finds himself confronting a universe that is irrational and meaningless. In the face of this negation of basic demands of the human spirit, the stance to assume, according to Camus, is one of defiance and revolt, even though the effort expended in that hopeless struggle is like that of Sisyphus rolling his rock up the mountainside. Despite that hopelessness, Camus argues that it is this very defiance and revolt in the face of a world without meaning that enable man to live life as fully and passionately as possible. Stating this conclusion in its most paradoxical form, Camus affirms: "*Il s'agissait précédemment de savoir si la vie devait avoir un sens pour être vécue. Il paraît ici au contraire qu'elle sera d'autant mieux vécue qu'elle n'aura pas de sens.*"[1] (*Essais*: 138). In this way, Camus maintains that what could easily be mistaken for grounds for suicide – a realization that life has no meaning – is in fact a basis for living life to the fullest. That, in a nutshell, is the point of the essay.

On several occasions in *Le Mythe de Sisyphe*, Camus makes it clear that he is arguing *against* what he sees as the existential position, which he characterizes as nothing less than "philosophical suicide" (*Essais*: 119). He states, for example (122):

> Or, pour m'en tenir aux philosophies existentielles, je vois que toutes, sans exception, me proposent l'évasion. Par un raisonnement singulier, partis de l'absurde sur les décombres de la raison, dans un univers fermé et limité à l'humain, ils divinisent ce qui les écrase et trouvent une raison d'espérer dans ce qui les démunit.[2]

---

1 "It was formerly a matter of knowing whether life had to have a meaning in order to be lived. It now appears to the contrary that it can be lived all the more fully if it has no meaning." Unless otherwise indicated, translations are my own.
2 "Restricting my discussion to existential philosophies, I see that every one of them, without exception, proposes evasion. By way of a unique kind of reasoning, they start

This clear condemnation of existentialism on his part was often missed by commentators. In an effort to dispel what had become and still is a common misconception, Camus stated in an interview in 1945 entitled "*Non, je ne suis pas existentialist*"/"No, I am not an existentialist": "*le seul livre d'idées que j'ai publié: le Mythe de Sisyphe, était dirigé contre les philosophes dits existentialistes*" (*Essais*: 1424).[3]

In his absurdist period, as shown above, Camus explicitly rejected existentialism. In the new and more mature philosophical position he developed in the works published just after the Second World War, Camus remained highly critical of existential thought, and though his rejection of existentialism was generally more implicit and indirect than it had been before, it was no less meaningful in relation to those issues that preoccupied him at the time.

It was in works such as *La Peste*/*The Plague* (1947), *L'Homme révolté*/*The Rebel* (1951) and the equally important editorials grouped under the title *Ni victimes ni bourreaux*/*Neither Victims Nor Executioners* (1946), that the somewhat abstract concepts merely outlined in the earlier period were for the first time given real substance. Here, in what Camus described as his "positive" series of "revolt," the absurd was no longer just a metaphysical category; now it had specific social forms as well, the most salient of which was murder. Likewise, revolt was now defined above all as a refusal to accept the loss of human lives and an insistence on viewing death as a scandal. Now in the framework of this second period of Camus' thought – consisting of works published between 1946 and 1951 – the characters who have taken over the role of Sisyphus are those who stubbornly fight to save human lives, no matter how hopeless that struggle may appear or how overpowering the murderous forces may seem; they are also characters who refuse to take part in the passing of death sentences or even in passively accepting that movements or institutions do so in their name.

This had not always been Camus' position. In fact, he adopted it as late as 1945 and its inception can be pinpointed to a decision he had to make

---

out from the absurd and move across the ruins of reason, in a universe that is closed and limited to the human; [there] they deify what crushes them and find a reason for pinning their hopes on what impoverishes them."

3  "the one philosophical book I have published, *The Myth of Sisyphus*, was written against philosophers called existentialists..." Yet on the back cover of the Vintage paperback translation of *The Myth of Sisyphus*, Camus' essay is, to this day, described as "a crucial exposition of existentialist thought."

concerning the execution of a convicted collaborator in the aftermath of the Liberation.

In October 1944, François Mauriac, writing in the conservative newspaper *Le Figaro*, accused the organizations of the Resistance of excesses in their condemnation of collaborators. In his own newspaper, *Combat* (originally founded as the clandestine organ of the Resistance movement of the same name, and on which Camus had worked since 1943), Camus argued that justice had to prevail over mercy if the soul of France was to be preserved and that certain crimes simply could not be forgiven. In one of the last editorials devoted to this issue, published on October 25, 1944, he added (*Essais*: 1536):

> Nous n'avons pas le goût du meurtre ... [Mais] la France porte en elle, comme un corps étranger, une minorité d'hommes qui ont fait hier son malheur et qui continueront de le faire. Ce sont des hommes de la trahison et de l'injustice. C'est leur existence même qui pose donc le problème de la justice puisqu'ils forment une part vivante de ce pays et que la question est de les détruire.[4]

Three months later, the writer Robert Brasillach was condemned to death for his crimes as a collaborator, and François Mauriac organized a campaign to obtain a pardon for him. On January 25, 1945, the writer Marcel Aymé – himself compromised for having worked for the collaborationist paper, *Je suis partout* – wrote to Camus, despite Camus' support for the death penalty in other cases, asking him to sign a petition to de Gaulle requesting that the death sentence not be carried out. Camus paced the floor of his apartment until dawn and finally decided to sign the petition, adding his name to those of Paul Valéry, Jean Anouilh, Jean-Louis Barrault, Jean Cocteau, Colette, Jean Paulhan, Gabriel Marcel and others, as well as Mauriac and Aymé (Lottman 1978: 363). (De Gaulle received Mauriac, read the dossier, and did nothing to prevent the execution of Brasillach in February 1945).

From that time on, a refusal to legitimize murder in any form became the very cornerstone of Camus' thought. And in "*L'Incroyant et les chrétiens*"/"The

---

[4] "We have no taste for murder ... [But] France carries within herself a kind of foreign body, a small number of men who recently caused her misfortune and who will continue to do so. They are men of treason and injustice. It is their very existence which is a problem for justice since they are a living part of this country and it is a question of destroying them."

Non-believer and the Christians," a speech he gave in 1948 at a Dominican monastery, he stated (*Essais*: 371-372):

> Il y a trois ans une controverse m'a opposé à François Mauriac. [...] j'en suis venu à reconnaître en moi-même, et publiquement ici, que, pour le fond, et sur le point précis de notre controverse, M. François Mauriac avait raison contre moi.[5]

How many public figures have the stature Camus showed on that occasion?

In virtually everything Camus published between 1946 and 1951, an opposition to murder was central. Of primary importance to Camus was the need to prevent murderers from killing their potential victims, without becoming a murderer in turn. This is the pivotal question Camus dealt with head-on in *L'Homme révolté/The Rebel*, and more obliquely in *La Peste/The Plague*, where the allegory has two distinct social meanings, since the team of doctors and volunteers fighting against the epidemic represent both the struggle of the Resistance movement against the Nazis *and* a post-war opposition to all ideologies which legitimize violence, including that of the Stalinists.

The character Tarrou, who had discovered that the revolutionary movement he had joined in his youth was ultimately as life-denying as the political system it sought to overthrow, states in a key passage: *"... j'ai décidé de refuser tout ce qui, de près ou de loin, pour de bonnes ou de mauvaises raisons, fait mourir ou justifie qu'on fasse mourir"*[6] (*Théâtre, Récits, Nouvelles*: 1425), thereby echoing the point of view Camus expressed in "*Ni victimes ni bourreaux*"/"Neither Victims Nor Executioners" when he wrote in 1946: *"... je ne saurais plus admettre, après l'expérience de ce deux dernières années, aucune vérité qui pût me mettre dans l'obligation, directe ou indirecte, de faire condamner un homme à mort"*[7] (*Essais*: 333)

Throughout this period (1946-1951), Camus distinguished between two types of thought: a destructive one, rooted only in History, absolute, messianic, reducing everything in its path to ideological abstractions; and a life-

---

[5] "Three years ago, I was engaged in a dispute with François Mauriac. [...] I have come to recognize for myself and now publicly that regarding the fundamental issue, and on the specific point of our dispute, Mr. François Mauriac was right and I was in the wrong."

[6] "... I have decided to refuse anything which, either immediately or remotely, and for good or for bad reasons, causes men to die or justifies causing them to die."

[7] "... I can no longer accept as true, after the experience of these past two years, anything which might require me, directly or indirectly, to have any man condemned to death."

affirming one, in which History and Nature balance one another, an outlook which is modest and respectful of limits. In "*La Pensée de Midi*" (sometimes translated as "Thought at the Meridian"), the final and most important chapter of *L'Homme révolté*, Camus identifies the life-affirming outlook with the sun-drenched cultures of the Mediterranean, and the destructive mode of thought with "*rêves allemands*"– "Germanic dreams" (*Essais*, 683-709).

Existentialism, for Camus in this period of revolt, was one of the forms taken by what he saw as a Germanic and life-denying mode of thought. For example, in an entry in his *Carnets/Notebooks* from 1946 (Camus 1964: 180), he wrote: "*L'existentialisme a gardé du hégelianisme son erreur fondamentale qui consiste à réduire l'homme à l'histoire*"[8] – a criticism Camus also made of Marxist ideology, when he wrote in "*Ni victimes ni bourreaux*" in 1946 (*Essais*: 332):

> Nous vivons dans la terreur [...] parce que l'homme a été livré tout entier à l'histoire et qu'il ne peut plus se tourner vers cette part de lui-même, aussi vraie que la part historique, et qu'il retrouve devant la beauté du monde et des visages.[9]

In another *Carnets* entry from the same period (174), Camus linked existentialism to what he saw as the excessive historicism of German thought, and identified his own outlook – rooted in nature – with that of the Greeks:

> Tout l'effort de la pensée allemande a été de substituer à la notion de nature humaine celle de situation humaine et donc l'histoire à Dieu et la tragédie moderne à l'équilibre ancien. L'existentialisme moderne pousse cet effort encore plus loin et introduit dans l'idée de situation la même incertitude que dans celle de nature. Il ne reste plus rien qu'un mouvement. Mais comme les Grecs je crois à la nature.[10]

---

8 "Existentialism has retained from Hegelian thought its fundamental error which consists of reducing man to history."
9 "We live in terror [...] because man has been entirely given over to history and can no longer turn toward that part of himself, just as real as the historical part, that he could find [in looking at] the beauty of the world and of faces."
10 "The whole effort of Germanic thought has been to substitute for the notion of human nature that of the human situation and therefore [to substitute] history for God and modern tragedy for the former equilibrium. Modern existentialism pushes this effort even further and introduces into the idea of situation the same uncertainty as in that of nature. All that is left is a movement. But like the Greeks, I believe in nature."

Camus identified existentialism with philosophical suicide in the series of the absurd, and with a reduction of human life to its historical dimension in the subsequent series of revolt. In each case, existentialism was seen as life-denying, and as such, as diametrically opposed to Camus' own life-affirming outlook.

In the years which followed the humiliating and paralyzing defeat Camus suffered in the wake of his public dispute with Sartre in 1952, Camus' objections to existentialism took on a more bitter and personal quality. In a 1954 entry in his notebooks (Camus 1989: 147), he wrote, for example: "*Existentialisme. Quand ils s'accusent on peut être sûr que c'est toujours pour accabler les autres. Des juges pénitents.*"[11] Here we have what would soon become the central concept *La Chute/The Fall* (1956), which is at least in part a mordant satire directed against Sartre and the philosophical position for which he stood (Nykrog 1989).

Despite Camus' lifelong opposition to existentialism, there are commentators who continue to classify him as an existentialist. Might this be a sign that Camus had more in common with the existential thinkers than he himself realized? Or is there another explanation, more respectful of Camus' understanding of his own work, yet also taking into account the intelligence and goodwill of those scholars who persist in calling him an existentialist?

The explanation I would propose consists of two postulates:

1) There is no one-word term – no "-ism" – which accurately identifies Camus' thought, with the result that a terminological vacuum has existed since the time Camus began his philosophical writings.

2) Commentators have tended to fill that vacuum by designating Camus as an existentialist, in order to anchor him firmly in his period and to ensure that he not be marginalized with respect to his contemporaries. Essentially the same process can be observed in other contexts as well, such as books on impressionist painting which include chapters on Manet and Cézanne, though their canvases bear neither the characteristic impressionist brushstroke nor the impressionist concern with capturing the play of light on objects. In such cases, movements are defined broadly, inclusively, and with surprisingly little regard for those specific characteristics that give them their distinctive quality.

---

11 "Existentialism. Whenever they accuse themselves, you can be sure it is invariably in order to assail others. Penitent judges."

If these postulates are correct, then those commentators who have described Camus as an existentialist had commendable reasons for doing so. The result, however, is nevertheless unfortunate, since it blurs important distinctions and obscures what is most specific to Camus' thought.

In calling attention to Camus' reasons for rejecting existential philosophy, the present article is an attempt to bring into sharper focus those aspects of Camus' thought that might otherwise be overlooked, or the importance of which might not be fully appreciated, by those who have come to regard him as an existentialist.

## References

Camus, Albert (1962). *Théâtre, Récits, Nouvelles*, ed. R. Quilliot. Paris: Gallimard (Pléiade).

Camus, Albert (1965). *Essais*, eds. R. Quilliot and L. Faucon. Paris: Gallimard (Pléiade).

Camus, Albert (1964). *Carnets*, vol. 2 (janvier 1942-mars 1951). Paris: Gallimard.

Camus, Albert (1964). *Carnets*, vol. 3 (mars 1951-décembre 1959). Paris: Gallimard.

Lottman, Herbert R. (1978). *Albert Camus*. Translated by Marianne Véron. Paris: Seuil.

Nykrog, Per (1989). "Sartre Penned by Camus, 1953-1955," *L'Esprit créateur*, vol. 29, no. 4, pp. 65-74.

# 15

# Five Explanations for the Naming of Malta's Gloster Gladiators 'Faith,' 'Hope' and 'Charity' in 1940-1941

*One of the Gloster Gladiators that defended Malta in the summer of 1940 (copyright: IWM)*

> *The origin of the Faith, Hope and Charity names is obscure.*
> Malta Aviation Museum, 20 May 2009

When Mussolini declared war on France and Great Britain on June 10, 1940, he immediately set his sights on Malta, the main base of the British Mediterranean Fleet. It was within convenient striking distance from his air bases in Sicily, of great strategic value, and thought to have no fighter aircraft to defend herself. Mussolini is said to have boasted that Malta would be conquered within a matter of days and that he would be in Valletta in two weeks (Oliver 1942: 11).

Shortly before 7 a.m. on June 11, the first Italian bombing raid of Malta began. Eight raids would be carried out that day, by waves of Savoia Marchetti 79s bombers escorted by Macchi 200 fighter planes.

When war first broke out in 1939, there was widespread agreement that Malta was indefensible (Cameron 1960: 15). Opponents of that view soon gained enough ground for the War Cabinet in London to earmark four fighter squadrons for the defense of Malta but in the Spring of 1940, no fighter aircraft had as yet been stationed on the island because they were now more desperately needed elsewhere and above all in the protection of Britain herself (Polmar 2006: 109). On May 28, 1940, the Cabinet came dangerously close to offering Malta as a concession to Italy for staying out of the war, but Churchill and the socialist members of the Cabinet prevailed over the conservatives, in a 3 to 2 vote (Spooner 2008: 19).

In March 1940, Malta's Commanding Air Officer, Air Commodore Foster Maynard, learned that eighteen Gloster Sea Gladiators belonging to the Navy were being stored in packing crates at the Air Repair Section at Kalafrana. They had been left behind by the aircraft carrier *H.M.S. Glorious* when she rejoined the Home Fleet to take part in operations in the Norwegian campaign. Eight of the crated Gladiators that were being held in reserve for her 802 Naval Air Squadron were now dispatched to the *Glorious*. And the remaining ten were soon in principle to be transferred to the *H.M.S. Eagle*. Maynard wanted a small number of these biplanes, since although they were obsolete, they could at least provide a rudimentary fighter defense. He asked the Mediterranean Fleet's Commander-in-Chief, Admiral Andrew Cunningham, whether the RAF might take over some of the Navy planes. Cunningham complied and obtained agreement from the Chief of Naval Staff, Rear-Admiral Willis, that the RAF could have four of the crated Gladiators. These planes – with serial numbers N5519, N5520, N5524 and N5531 – were unpacked, assembled and delivered to the Hal Far airport as the basis for a new Fighter Flight unit, established on April 23. Maynard now needed pilots who would train to fly the Gladiators, and eight volunteers – including Maynard's personal assistant, George Burges – began their basic training, though none of them had fighter experience. But a few days later, Maynard was informed that the ten Gladiators would now have to be transferred after all to the *Eagle*, and on April 29, the Malta Fighter Flight was dissolved and the four Gladiators taken apart and packed in their crates. Then reversing itself again, the Navy decided it only needed three of the planes after all and on May 4, the Malta Fighter Flight was reinstated and the four Gladiators reassembled and test flown. By the end of May, two more Gladiators were unpacked and assembled (N5523 and N5529) and one more was kept for spare parts (Holland 2009: 28; Shores and Cull 1987: 5-7).

Countless articles, books and websites have rightfully celebrated the exploits of a handful of obsolete Gloster Gladiators. These are the planes whose volunteer pilots defended Malta against the modern bombers and fighters of the Italian air force that raided the island for the first time on June 11, 1940. Though as already described, six Gladiators had been removed from packing crates and assembled at Kalafrana in April and May that year to constitute a fighter defense for the island, only three of the outmoded biplanes could be serviceable and airborne at any one time due to a shortage of engine parts and pilots. And whether the Gladiators that were engaged in dogfights with enemy planes over Valletta or Sliema were always the same three aircraft or three of a possible five or six is of no consequence. Nor is there anything mythical about the role they played in the conflict. During the first weeks of the bombing raids, for the Maltese watching the skies from rooftops and cheering on their defenders, there were three antiquated biplanes fearlessly engaging the bombers and fighter planes of the Regia Aeronautica. And those three defenders came to be known as Faith, Hope and Charity.

Most discussions of these events simply state that the planes were named, dubbed or christened Faith, Hope and Charity, with no indication as to who did the naming. But some commentators have either explained the origins of the names or have in passing expressed assumptions about those origins. Each of those commentators suggests one and only one possible explanation. The purpose of the present article is for the first time to provide an overview of five explanations that have appeared in the literature as to how the names Faith, Hope and Charity were given to Malta's legendary Gladiators.

## 1. Gladiator pilot John Waters

The single most detailed explanation for the christening of the Gladiators credits the pilot John Waters with the idea of giving them their names during the month after the bombing raids had begun (Cameron 1960: 42):

One quiet evening in early July, when there hadn't been a raid for several hours, the pilots were sitting on the grass at Hal Far, watching the three Gladiators being refueled.

"You know," Jock Martin said reflectively, "we ought to give them a name."

Someone suggested Pip, Squeak, and Wilfred; but this wasn't received with much enthusiasm. It was John Waters – quiet, good-looking, and technically the most brilliant pilot of the seven – who made the inspired suggestion.

"How about Faith, Hope and Charity?" he said.

The names caught on. They spread beyond Hal Far, beyond Valletta and the Three Cities, beyond the shore of Malta itself. Soon, every time the Gladiators took to the air, people would stop, point skyward, and cry:

"Look! There they go. *Faith*, *Hope* and *Charity*!"

To most Britishers on the Island the names brought no more than a wry, appreciative smile; but to the Maltese they brought something more. For the people of Malta are intensely religious, and it meant a great deal to them that the men and machines which were defending them so valiantly had been christened with the words of St. Paul. Now more than ever before, the three Gladiators came to epitomize the island's spirit of defiance; they became symbols of a cause which began to take on something like the sanctity of a crusade.

Two other commentators subscribe to the same explanation (Poolman 2004: 60-61; Wismayer 2007: 28).

However, attributing the naming of the planes to Gladiator pilots in July 1940 is inconsistent with the view expressed by the pilots' own Group Captain, George Burges (Spooner 2008: 19):

When asked about the famous names given to the Gladiators, George Burges is quite adamant that – in his day – and he was to remain on the Island for another year – the three planes were never called 'Faith, Hope and Charity.'

And Burges's view was shared by Malta's Commanding Air Officer, Air Commodore Foster Maynard, whose idea it had been to use the crated Gladiators in the first place, and who stated that "he first heard these names in connection with his Gladiators when he returned to the United Kingdom in 1941" (Mason 1964: 82). Furthermore, the earliest mention of the three names in the principal local newspaper, *The Times of Malta*, is on October 25, 1941 (3), in the transcription of a radio broadcast given the previous evening by Wing-Commander Grant-Ferris, M.P. and entitled "Malta's Air Defense". The opening sentence reads: "It does not seem so very long ago, and indeed it is little more than a year, since the days when the Fighter Defense of Malta depended upon the magnificent efforts of those three old Gladiators "Faith," "Hope" and "Charity" – when they took to the air and gave chase to swarms of Mussolini's Air Force."

In the light of these statements by Burges and Maynard, and considering the fact that no source is given for the reported conversation involving Martin, Waters and other Gladiator pilots, there are ample reasons for questioning the explanation offered by Cameron.

## 2. RAF Corporal Harry Kirk

Citing an article by Roy Nash entitled "The Unknown Air Ace" in *The Daily Star* from March 1958, but without indicating a specific date, Holland offers this as "the only explanation [he] was able to find for the naming of the Gladiators" (Holland 2009: 40, 402):

> On the first day [11 June 1940], an Italian plane pursued by one of the Gladiators was seen to dive, with smoke trailing behind it. It did, in fact, make it back to Sicily, but for those on the ground watching the dogfights above, this was the first victory to their gallant defenders, and the three planes they saw swooping and turning in the skies over Grand Harbour. Harry Kirk, an RAF pilot based at their headquarters in Scots Street, saw the Gladiators flying in tight formation and thought they looked rather like the three silver hearts on a brooch of his mother's. Each heart had a name – Faith, Hope and Charity. 'Look, there go Faith, Hope and Charity,' he told a fellow airman. The names stuck; soon everyone at HQ was calling them that.

Having tried unsuccessfully to obtain a copy of Nash's article without an exact date of publication, I have no way of assessing the reliability of this claim.

## 3. A Maltese newspaper

An anonymous author wrote about the three names in a footnote to a description of the Gladiators (h2g2 2006):

These names were not actually applied to the aircraft at the time; it was months later when a Maltese newspaper reported the air duels that the monikers stuck.

This claim would be more convincing if the name of the newspaper were provided as well as the title of the article in question, the name of its author and the date of its publication. In the absence of those details, there is no reason to treat the claim as anything but second- or third-hand hearsay. The same applies to another commentator's statement that contemporaries of John Waters attributed the Gladiators' names "to journalists at a later date" (Shores and Cull 1987: 370). Here again, a glaring lack of precision does not inspire confidence in the claim.

## 4. The people of Malta

A number of commentators attribute the naming of the three planes to "the Maltese," "the people of Malta" or "the locals." This makes the naming of the planes a collective act expressive of the profoundly religious nature of the Maltese people. And although one may be skeptical of any view attributing invention to a collective rather than an individual, this approach is especially interesting when it plays on a contrast between British and Maltese cultures. That is the case in this passage, which begins with sets of names for the planes that were inspired by British cartoon characters and that were soon forgotten (Hogan 1978: 27):

> [The planes] were known for a time as 'Pip', 'Squeak' and 'Wilfred', and as 'Freeman', 'Hardy' and 'Willis', like the cartoon characters or the 'shoebox' assemblies they at first might have seemed to be. But as they survived and prospered against odds, the Maltese called them almost naturally 'Faith', 'Hope' and 'Charity'. Which fitted them so well and signified the feelings of those who watched their tremendous efforts and hair-raising exploits.

This contrast between British and Maltese cultures is even more striking in a fictional work called *The Legend of Faith, Hope and Charity* (Royce 2014):

> "Do you know what the people of Malta call your planes?" Lucija asked.
> Robson was puzzled by the question. "They are Gloster Sea Gladiators mark ones. There's N-5-5-2-0, N-5-5-1-9. N-"

"No! What do you think we call your planes?" Lucija interrupted.

Still confused, Robson shrugged his shoulders and offered no answer.

"They are more to us than three planes, and definitely more than some silly numbers. We call them Faith, Hope and Charity. I know you have heard of Faith, Hope and Charity before?"

"They are the Christian virtues according to St Paul," Robson answered instantly, recalling many of the sermons he had attended with his mother.

"Marvik told me about your friendship with a Bishop, so I knew you would understand. The first morning of the war, I was horrified to see all those bombers attacking Valletta. But I also saw three small planes fly to meet them. The whole island saw it. And every time the bombers come, the same planes always fly to meet them. Your planes are symbols of our spirit. How can this island fall to the enemy when there are men willing to face such odds," Lucija explained, her voice was choked, and her eyes full of tears.

[...]

In the car, on the journey back to Hal Far, Robson voiced the names "Faith, Hope and Charity" aloud. He liked the resonance and he smiled as he contemplated their meaning.

There are other commentators who share the view that the Gladiators were christened Faith, Hope and Charity by the Maltese people (Oliver 1942:12; Grover and McGaffin 1942: 44; Wragg 2004: 117). And one commentator attributes the naming of the planes to "the Maltese personnel" (Kelly 1960: 7).

## 5. An Information Officer

In another work of fiction, an intriguing possibility is evoked as follows (Mills 2009: 15-17):

'So, tell me, what do you know about Malta?'

'I know about Faith, Hope and Charity.'

Everyone knew about Faith, Hope and Charity. The newspapers back home had made sure of that, enshrining the names of the three Gloster Gladiators in the popular imagination. The story had courage-in-the-face-of-adversity written all over it, just what the home readership had required back in the summer of 1940. While Hitler skipped across northern Europe as though it were his private playground, on a small island in the Mediterranean three obsolescent bi-planes were bravely pitting themselves against the full might of Italy's Regia Aeronautica, wrenched around the heavens by pilots highly qualified to fly them.

And so the myth was born. With a little assistance.

'Actually, there were six of them.'

'Six?'

'Gloster Gladiators. And a bunch more held back for spares.'

Pemberton frowned. 'I don't understand.'

'Three makes for a better story, and there were never more than three in the air at any one time· the others being unserviceable.'

The names had been coined and then quietly disseminated by Max's predecessor, their biblical source designed to chime with the fervent Catholicism of the Maltese.

'It's part of what we do at the Information Office.'

'You mean propaganda?'

'That's not a word we like to use.'

'I was told you were independent.'

'We are ostensibly.'

That censorship was a fact of life in Malta during the war should not be forgotten. R. Leslie Oliver writes in his foreword to his book (Oliver 1942: 3):

> My thanks go to Mr. R. Wingrave Tench, the Deputy Chief Censor of Malta, who has been most helpful and constructive in his criticisms and censored my book more promptly than I could have hoped.

And a great deal of the Gladiators' importance had to do with morale, as its most decorated pilot pointed out with admirable candor (Holland 2009: 40):

> 'People got the impression that our aircraft were shooting down enemy planes left, right and centre,' says George Burges. 'They did not, but morale was kept high.'

Given the realities of censorship and the need to give high priority to the morale of the local population, the creative license taken by novelist Mills with respect to the naming of the three Gladiators may not have been entirely off the mark.

On the other hand, it could be argued that at least during the period when Gladiators were the only fighters Malta had as a defense against the Italian air force – from June 11 to June 21/22, 1940, when first two and then six more Hurricanes arrived (Holland 2009: 41) – the last thing the censors would want known by the local population and by the enemy was that the island could muster no more that three obsolete aircraft at any one time in her defense. Once Hurricanes and eventually Spitfires were there to defend the island, no harm could be done by revealing the true extent of Malta's initial defenses when the bombing raids began. This may explain why in the daily accounts of the Gladiators' exploits in the local newspapers, the planes are invariably described as "British fighters," or "our fighters," or "our fighter aircraft," without a word about their being outdated or outnumbered or flown by volunteers with little or no experience as fighter pilots. In other words, the contemporary accounts describe what might be understood as a somewhat level playing field, with "our fighters" pitted against "their fighters," not our tiny number of Gloster Gladiators valiantly trying to hold back a modern air force. It is only when accounts of those exploits are made months or years later that the David-versus-Goliath aspect of the conflict in June 1940 is fully revealed.

Here are three representative samples, all excerpts from articles that appeared during the first week of bombings in *The Times of Malta*, illustrating how radically the contemporary accounts differ from the retrospective ones, not in their emphasis on the effectiveness of Malta's planes but in the omission of their outdatedness and maximum number:

> Following yesterday's report of the first day's eight air raids over Malta, it is now confirmed that two enemy machines were destroyed by anti-aircraft fire. Both fell into the sea. A third was damaged by our fighters which chased the enemy.
> "Two Enemy Planes Brought Down: Our Fighters Chase the Enemy," *The Times of Malta*, June 13, 1940, p. 6.

> But the raid: The leading formation of the enemy air raiders consisted of bombers and these machines were immediately attacked by our fighter-craft.
> Several bombs were dropped in the neighborhood of Kalafrana. There was no damage or casualties.
> The second formation of enemy bombers was also attacked by our fighters and quickly dispersed.
> The third formation of enemy aeroplanes were fighters, possibly "Macchi 200's," but these were also dispersed in an engagement with our own fighters.

> The fact that enemy bombers were yesterday accompanied by fighter-craft is obvious evidence of the healthy respect and even fear with which Italian pilots regard our fighters.
>
> "Two Sunday Raids," *The Times of Malta*, June 17, 1940, p. 2.

> A total of fifty-five bombs were dropped on Malta yesterday in three air raids by the enemy, all of short duration, thanks to our fighters and anti-aircraft. The first air raid was the earliest we have had so far – at 6.15 a.m. It ended at about 7 a.m., the raiders having been driven away by our fighters.
>
> "Italy's Attack on Malta," *The Times of Malta*, June 18, 1940, p. 1.

It is quite conceivable that an information officer encouraged withholding the fact that Malta's fighters were Gloster Gladiators. And in the unlikely event that in June 1940, the names Faith, Hope and Charity were in use, it might have been a strategic decision not to mention them, since they would have given away the number of Malta's airborne defenders.

These then are five explanations mentioned in the literature, attributing the idea for naming the three Gladiators Faith, Hope and Charity to:

- Gladiator Pilot John Waters
- RAF corporal Harry Keith
- A Maltese newspaper
- The people of Malta
- An information officer

While the present article has by no means settled any issues, it has at least charted the range of explanations that have been evoked to explain a particularly meaningful aspect of the Gladiators' role in Malta in the summer of 1940.

## References and other consulted material

Attard, Joseph (1994). *The Battle of Malta. An Epic True Story of Suffering and Bravery*. Valletta: Hamlyn.
Blouet, Brian (1997). *The Story of Malta*. Malta: Progress Press.
Boyd, Russel et al (2007). *Faith, Hope and Charity*. USA: Wingmen Productions. https://www.youtube.com/watch?v=KANP2dN2Ae8 Accessed 5 May 2017.
Bradford, Ernie (1987). *Siege: Malta 1940-1943*. Hammersmith: Penguin.

Cameron, Ian (1962). *Wings of the morning: the story of the Fleet Air Arm in the Second World War*. London: Hodder & Stoughton.

Cameron, Ian. *Red Duster, White Ensign*. London: White Lion, 1974. Expanded edition orig. pub. 1960.

Caruana, Richard J. (1999). *Malta George Cross. Victory in the Air*. Malta: Modelaid.

Castillo, Dennis Angelo (2006). *The Maltese Cross: A Strategic History of Malta*. Westport, Conn: Greenwood.

Cull, Brian and Frederick Galea (2008). *Gladiators Over Malta: the Story of Faith, Hope and Charity*. Rabat: Wise Owl Publications.

Cunningham, Andrew Browne (1951). *A Sailor's Odyssey. The Autobiography of Admiral of the Fleet Viscount Cunningham of Hyndhope*. London: Hutchinson.

Fleet Air Arm Archive (2000). "Gloster Sea Gladiator." Index of Naval Aircraft.

Gerard, Francis (1943). *Malta Magnificent*. New York: McGraw-Hill.

Gilchrist, Major R. T. (1945). *Malta Strikes Back – The Story of 231 Infantry Brigade*. Aldershot: Gale and Polden.

Gretch, Charles B. (1998). *Raiders Passed. Wartime recollections of a Maltese youngster*. Valletta: Midsea Books.

Grover, Preston L. and William McGaffin (1942). "Malta," *Life Magazine*, 4 May, pp. 43-44, 46,49-52, 54.

Gustavsson, Håkan (2011a). "Biplane Fighter Aces – Group Captain George Burges." http://surfcity.kund.dalnet.se/commonwealth_burges.htm Accessed 5 May 2017.

Gustavsson, Håkan (2011b). "Biplane Fighter Aces – Flight Lieutentant William Joseph 'Timber' Woods." http://surfcity.kund.dalnet.se/commonwealth_woods.htm Accessed 5 May 2017.

Gustavsson, Håkan (2013). "Biplane Fighter Aces – Squadron Leader John Lawrence Waters." http://surfcity.kund.dalnet.se/commonwealth_waters.htm Accessed 5 May 2017.

h2g2 (2006). "Gloster Gladiator – World War II Aircraft – Edited entry." https://h2g2.com/edited_entry/A10223885 Accessed 5 May 2017.

Hay, Ian (1943). *The Unconquered Isle. The Story of Malta. G.C.* London: Hodder & Stoughton.

Hogan, George (1978). *Malta: The Triumphant Years 1940-43*. London: Robert Hale.

Holland, James (2009). *Fortress Malta: An Island Under Siege 1940-1943*. London: W & N.

Kelly, G. A. (1960). "The Days of 'Faith,' 'Hope' and 'Charity,'" *The Times of Malta*, 26 August, p. 7.

Lucas, Laddie (1993). *Malta: The Thorn in Rommel's Side. Six Months that Turned the War*. Hammersworth: Penguin.

Mason, Francis K. (1964). *The Gloster Gladiator*. London: Macdonald & Co.

Micallef, Joseph (1981). *When Malta Stood Alone (1940-1943)*. Swindon: Interprint.

Mills, Mark (2009). *The Information Officer*. Hammersmith: HarperCollins.

Ministry of Information (1944). *The Air Battle of Malta. The Official Account of the R.A.F. in Malta, June 1940 to November 1942*. London: His Majesty's Stationery Office.

Neil, T. F. (1998). *Onward to Malta. Memoirs of a Hurricane pilot in Malta – 1941*. London: Corgi.

Oliver, R. Leslie (1942). *Malta at Bay. An Eye-Witness Account*. London: Hutchinson.

Polmar, Norman (2006). *Aircraft Carriers: A History of Carrier Aviation and Its Influence on World Events*, vol. 1, 1909-1945. Washington: Potomac.

Poolman, Kenneth (2004). *Faith, Hope & Charity. The Defence of Malta*. Bristol: Cerberus.

Raskin, Richard (2015). "Five explanations as to who named Malta's Gloster Gladiators Faith, Hope and Charity," *Journal of Maltese History*, vol. 4, no. 2. https://www.um.edu.mt/__data/assets/pdf_file/0003/269904/JMH-2015Raskincorrected1.pdf Accessed 5 May 2017.

Royce, D. (2014). *The Legend of Faith, Hope and Charity*. No publisher or place of publication listed. Kindle edition.

Shores, Christopher and Brian Cull (1987). *Malta: The Hurricane Years 1940-1941*. London: Grub Street.

Spooner, Tony (2008). *Faith, Hope and Malta GC. Ground and Air Heroes of the George Cross Island*. Manchester: Crécy. Orig. pub. 1992.

Sutherland, Jon and Diane Canwell (2009). *Air War Malta: June 1940 to November 1942*. Havertown, PA: Casemate. Wismayer, Capt. J. M. (2007). "Malta's involvement in World War II," *The Times of Malta*, 26 August, p. 28.

Wragg, David (2004). *Malta. The Last Great Siege 1940-1943*. Barnsley: Pen and Sword.

# 16

# Far from where? A Classic Jewish Refugee Joke

*Jewish Refugees, Tel Aviv, 1951. Copyright ©1981 Ruth Orkin. Used with permission.*

During and immediately after World War II, a number of Jewish refugee jokes began to appear in anthologies of humor. Three jokes in particular have become familiar landmarks in collections of Jewish humor published from the 1940's to the present. The first two, "Globe" and "Morning or afternoon?", broke into print in 1941 and 1943 respectively, and deal with thwarted efforts to escape from Europe. Both of these jokes end with a question that appears to disregard some basic reality at hand, and which sets in relief the hopelessness of the refugee's situation:

A Viennese Jew entered the office of a travel bureau and said to one of the clerks, "I want a steamship ticket."

"Where to?" asked the clerk.

"Where to? Yes, where to?" repeated the Jew meditatively. "I wish I could answer this question. Let me look at your globe, if you don't mind."

Thereupon the Jew turned the globe around several times, studying carefully countries and continents. After a few minutes, he raised his eyes to the clerk and said, "Pardon me, have you anything else to offer?" (Mendelsohn 1946: 135-136)

A harassed attache of the American Consulate at Lisbon told the story of a grey-faced little man who leaned over his desk one morning anxiously enquired: "Can you tell me if there is any possibility I could get entrance to your wonderful country?"

The attache pressed by thousands of such requests and haggard from sleepless nights, roughly replied: "Impossible now. Come back in another ten years."

The little refugee moved toward the door, stopped, turned and, with a wan smile, asked, "Morning or afternoon?" (Cerf 1943: 141)

The joke which completes this little triptych first appeared in print in 1948, and deals with the situation of the Jewish refugee in the aftermath of the Second World War. It too ends with a question:

> Three weary Jewish refugees stood before the Paris representative of the Jewish Joint Distribution Committee.
> "Where are you all going?" he asked them.
> "I'm on my way to Rome," said the first.
> "London is my destination," said the second.
> "My plan is to go to South Africa," said the third.
> "South Africa? Why so far?"
> "Far? Far from where?" wistfully countered the refugee.
> (Ausubel 1948: 25)

Unlike "Globe" and "Morning or afternoon?", the "Far from where?" joke can be understood in two different ways, and in this respect, is a richer and more interesting joke. In the remainder of this article, I will try to outline the two interpretations to which the joke lends itself.

One interpretation was proposed by Alan Dershowitz in his recent and immensely popular book, *Chutzpah*, in which he wrote (1991: 25):

> The concept of the "wandering Jew" gave rise to the old joke about the nineteenth-century Polish Jew from Warsaw, who tells his friend that he is moving to America. The friend exclaims: "But that's so far away." To which the rootless Jew responds: "From what?"

In suggesting that the joke was inspired by the concept of the "wandering Jew," Dershowitz emphasizes the timeless quality of the story as well as its connection to a body of folklore. And in characterizing the joke as expressive of rootlessness ("the rootless Jew responds"), Dershowitz further stresses that aspect of the joke which refers to the properties of the Jewish condition, rather than to anything situated outside of Jewish life. When the joke is interpreted in this way, it would also make sense to view the punch-line as spoken with quiet pathos, as is suggested by such expressions as "wistfully" (Ausubel 1948: 25) and "with a catch in his voice" (Spalding 1969: 179), or a look described as "*traurig*" [sad], (Muliar 1974: 91).

However, the joke can be understood in another way, particularly when it is told in a manner which reflects its original historical context, as is the case when the setting evoked is Paris in 1939 (Rosten 1970: 310), occupied France (Popeck 1978: 133) or post-war Paris (Ausubel 1948: 25), Berlin shortly after Hitler came to power (Landmann 1982: 235-236), Germany in the summer of 1939 (Hakel 1965: 87) or Austria when German troops marched in (Muliar 1974: 91). To whatever degree a national setting at the time of Nazi domination is an essential part of the story, the joke can be seen as in some sense a commentary on that setting. From this perspective, the "Far from where?" question could be understood as a reply to a given nation's indifference to the plight of the Jews, and would imply that the country in question *does not deserve* to be taken as a frame of reference of any kind. Perhaps this is why, in one of the versions (Adam 1966: 19), the question is spoken "*très bas*," so that no one else can hear it.

The Dershowitz interpretation focuses on the rootlessness of the Jewish people, and sees the joke as inspired by an ancient legend – in which case the tone of the punch-line would be essentially plaintive. According to the alternate reading I have sketched, it would be seen as inspired by the Holocaust, and the "Far from where?" punch-line as an indictment of a country in which Jews were offered little or no protection from the Nazis.

The two interpretations might be represented schematically as follows:

|  | interpretation 1 (Dershowitz) | interpretation 2 |
|---|---|---|
| primary focus | the rootlessness of the Jewish condition | the indifference of a nation to the plight of the Jews |
| inspiration | the concept of the "wandering Jew" | the Holocaust |
| spirit of the punch-line | plaintive | an indictment |

Both interpretations are valid and fully justified by the joke. When both are taken into account, they can be allowed to balance, complete and correct each other. In this respect, the "Far from where?" joke exhibits an interpretive quality found in a number of classic Jewish jokes, which leave us wondering how we are expected to understand the punch-line when two or more equally plausible options present themselves.

# References

Adam (1966). *L'humour juif*. Paris: Denoël.
Ausubel, Nathan (1948). *A Treasury of Jewish Folklore*. New York: Crown.
Cerf, Bennet (1943). *Pocket Book of War Humor*. New York: Pocket Books.
Dershowitz, Alan (1991). *Chutzpah*. Boston: Little, Brown & Co.
Hakel, Hermann (1965). *Oi, bin ich gescheit!* Munich: Südwest Verlag.
Landmann, Salcia (1982). *Jüdische Witze*. Munich: Deutscher Taschenbuch. Orig. pub. 1962.
Mendelsohn, S. Felix (1946). *Let Laughter Ring*. Philadelphia: Jewish Publication Society. Orig. pub. 1941.
Muliar, Fritz (1974), *Das Beste aus meiner jüdischen Witze- und Anekdotensammlung*. Munich: Wilhelm Heyne Verlag.
Popeck (1978). *Popeck raconte les meilleures histoires de l'humour juif*. Paris: Mengès.
Raskin, Richard (2015). *Life Is Like a Glass of Tea. Studies of Classic Jewish Jokes*, 2nd edition. New Orleans: Quid Pro Books.
Rosten, Leo (1970). *The Joys of Yiddish*. New York: Pocket Books.
Spalding, Henry D. (1969). *Encyclopedia of Jewish Humor*. New York: Jonathan David.

"Globe" appeared subsequently in Theodor Reik, *Jewish Wit* (New York: Gamut, 1961), p. 48; Hermann Hakel, *Der jüdische Witz* (Munich: Schuler, 1971), p. 63; Harry Golden, *The Golden Book of Jewish Humor* (New York: Putnam, 1972), p. 149; Alexander Drozdzynski, *Jiddische Witze und Schmonzes* (Dusseldorf: Droste Verlag,

1976), p. 31; *Popeck raconte les meilleures histoires de l'humour juif* (Paris: Mengès, 1978), pp. 230-231; William Novak and Moshe Waldoks, *The Big Book of Jewish Humor* (New York: Harper & Row, 1981), p. 61; Leo Rosten, *Hooray for Yiddish* (New York: Simon & Schuster, 1982), p. 354; and Ben Eliezer, *More of the World's Best Jewish Jokes* (London: Angus & Robertson, 1985), p. 22.

"Morning or afternoon?" appeared subsequently in S. Felix Mendelsohn, *Here's a Good One* (New York: Bloch, 1947), p. 13; Ausor Rajower, *Masses und Chochmes* (Zurich: Scheffelverlag, 1959), p. 26; Adam, *L'humour juif* (Denoël, 1966), pp. 49-50; Jan Meyerowitz, *Der echte jüdische Witz* (Berlin: Colloquium Verlag, 1971), pp. 87-88; Novak & Waldoks, *The Big Book of Jewish Humor* (New York: Harper & Row, 1981), p. 61; Ben Eliezer, *More of the World's Best Jewish Jokes* (London: Angus & Robertson, 1985), p. 22; Chaim Bermant, *What's the Joke?* (London: Weidenfeld & Nicolson, 1986), pp. 239-240.

## Publication History of "Far from where?"

NB. Numerous collections of Jewish jokes, published from about 1820 to the present, and written in English, German, French, Italian, Spanish, Danish and transliterated Yiddish, were consulted. No trace of this joke was found in any anthology published before 1948.

| Nathan Ausubel: A TREASURY OF JEWISH FOLK-LORE. New York: Crown, 1948; p. 25. | Three weary Jewish refugees stood before the Paris representative of the Jewish Joint Distribution Committee.<br>"Where are you all going?" he asked them.<br>"I'm on my way to Rome," said the first.<br>"London is my destination," said the second.<br>"My plan is to go to South Africa," said the third.<br>"South Africa? Why so far?"<br>"Far? Far from where?" wistfully countered the refugee. |
|---|---|
| Ausor Rajower: MASSES UND CHOCHMES. JÜDISCHE HUMOR. Zurich: Schefferverlag, 1959; pp. 26-27. | Drei Emigranten, in einem Zürcher Café, unterhalten sich.<br>"Heute habe ich das Visum nach Amerika bekommen," berichtet Kohn freudestrahlend.<br>"Und ich reise in einem Montat nach Kanada," sagt Schwarz.<br>"Und ich nach Chile," erklärt Weiß, der dritte.<br>"Nach Chile?!" ruft Kohn aus, "ist das nicht ein wenig weit weg?"<br>"Weit weg?" antwortet Weiß, "von wo?" |

| | |
|---|---|
| Salcia Landmann: JÜDISCHE WITZE. Munich: Deutscher Taschenbuch, 1982; pp. 235-236. Orig. pub. 1962. | Beim Auswanderungbureau in Berlin treffen sich kurz nach Hitlers Machtergreifung zwei Juden.<br>　"Moische," fragt der eine, "wohin willst du auswandern?"<br>　"Nach Schanghai."<br>　"Was! So weit?"<br>　"Weit, von wo?" |
| Hermann Hakel: OI, BIN ICH GESCHEIT! Munchen: Südwest Verlag, n.d. [1965]; p. 87. | Zwei Juden treffen einander im Sommer 1939. Sagt der eine:<br>　"Servus, wie geht's dir?"<br>　"Man lebt. Gestern hab' ich endlich meine Ausreise erledigt."<br>　"Du habst aber Glück! Und wohin wirst du auswandern?"<br>　"Nach Australien."<br>　"Geh, Australien –? Australien ist doch weit –"<br>　"Weit von wo?" |
| Adam: L'HUMOUR JUIF. Paris: Denoël, 1966; p. 19. | Deux amis se rencontrent:<br>　– Je pars demain, Moshé.<br>　– Où ça, Samuel?<br>　– Pour le Brézil.<br>　– Mais c'est loin!<br>Alors Samuel très bas:<br>　– Loin d'où? |
| Henry D. Spalding: ENCYCLOPEDIA OF JEWISH HUMOR. New York: Jonathan David, 1969; p. 179. | The following story may well elicit a sigh rather than a chuckle for those Jews who still remember Czarist oppression and the pathos of a people without a home.<br>　Three weary Jews were caught as they attempted to sneak across the Russian boundary.<br>　"Where were you three going?" asked the magistrate sternly.<br>　"I was hoping to get to Palestine," said the first.<br>　"My destination was Rome," said the second.<br>　"My plan was to go to Australia," said the third.<br>　"Australia!" exclaimed the surprised judge. "Why so far?"<br>　"Far?" whispered the Jew with a catch in his voice. "Far from where?" |

| | |
|---|---|
| Leo Rosten: THE JOYS OF YIDDISH. New York: Pocket Books, 1970; p. 310. | Paris, 1939.<br>　Three weary German refugees stood in line, in the offices of a Relocation Committee.<br>　"Where would you like to go?" an official asked the first refugee.<br>　"London."<br>　"And you?" the official asked the second.<br>　"Switzerland."<br>　"And you?" he asked the third.<br>　"Australia."<br>　"Australia?" echoed the official. "Why so far?"<br>　The refugee said, "Far from where?" |
| Jan Meyerowitz: DER ECHTE JÜDISCHE WITZ. Berlin: Colloquium Verlag, 1971; p. 88. | Und dieser Emigranten "witz": "Wohin willst du auswandern?"<br>　"Nach Chile." "So weit weg?" "Weit weg – wovon?!" |
| Fritz Muliar: DAS BESTE AUS MEINER JÜDISCHEN WITZE- UND ANEKDOTEN-SAMMLUNG. Munich: Wilhelm Heyne Verlag, 1974; p. 91. | Nach dem Einmarsch der deutschen Truppen in Österreich geht Weichselbaum mit Thugut durch die Pazmanitengassae. Weichselbaum sagt: "Ich geh nach England, dor hab ich Verwandte, und du?"<br>　Antwortet Thugut: "Ich hab a Einreise nach Borneo!"<br>　"Borneo?" sagt Weichselbaum. "Is aber weit?"<br>　Traurig schaut Thugut ihn an: "Weit – von wo?" |
| POPECK RACONTE LES MEILLEURES HISTOIRES DE L'HUMOUR JUIF. Paris: Mengès, 1978; p. 133. | Au début de la guerre, tandis que les troupes allemandes déferlent, deux Juifs se retrouvent sur le quai d'une gare.<br>　– Où allez-vous? demande l'un.<br>　– A Varsovie … C'est loin …<br>　– Ah oui? Loin d'où? |

| | |
|---|---|
| Elizabeth Petuchowski: DAS HERZ AUF DER ZUNGE. AUS DER WELT DES JÜDISCH-EN WITZES. Freiburg: Herder, 1984; p. 113. | "Morgen reise ich fort." <br> "Wohin, Samuel?" <br> "Nach Brasilien." <br> "Das ist aber weit weg." <br> "Weit weg von wo?" |
| Ferruccio Fölkel: STORIELLE EBRAICHE. Milan: Rizzoli, 1988; pp. 176-117. | Avrom e Mendel viaggiano in treno. <br> "Dove vai, Avramole?" <br> "Vado lontano, Mendele." <br> "Ma vai lontano da dove, Avramole?" |
| Alan Dershowitz: CHUTZPAH. Boston: Little, Brown & Co., 1991; p. 5. | The concept of the "wandering Jew" gave rise to the old joke about the nineteenth-century Polish Jew from Warsaw, who tells his friend that he is moving to America. The friend exclaims: "But that's so far away." To which the rootless Jew responds: "From what?" |

17

# *The Ghost Army* (2013) and Deception as Performance

*Images and spoken text in the pre-title sequence of* The Ghost Army *are reproduced here with the kind permission of Rick Beyer.*

## Introduction

In a recent essay (Raskin 2017), I challenged the widely held view that all cinematic storytelling must be conflict-driven. As anyone familiar with the literature on screenwriting can confirm, a belief in the necessity of conflict is the very cornerstone of virtually every manual on the subject. Robert McKee, to name just one of the most highly respected commentators, elevates that principle to a "Law of Conflict," by which he means that *"Nothing moves forward in a story except through conflict"* (1997: 210, McKee's emphasis). In the face of this universally held view that there can be no storytelling without conflict, I invoked a statement made by the American politician Mo Udall in the mid 1970s: "If you can find something everyone agrees on, it's wrong" (cited by Wicker 1975).

217

Reasons for questioning the assumption that only conflict can capture and hold the viewer's interest in a cinematic narrative include the simple fact that even in a film involving a high-stake conflict between characters seeking to thwart each other's goals, there are scenes that are virtually conflict-free and yet hold the viewer's interest. There are also exemplary short films that are at no point conflict-driven, such as Unni Straume's *Derailment* (1993) and Marianne Olsen Ulrichsen's *Come* (1995). What is it, then, in those scenes or entire short films which are free of conflict, that keep the viewer glued to the screen?

It was in watching Rick Beyer's award-winning documentary film *The Ghost Army* that a viable answer to that question first came to mind. The resulting narrative model, developed in the recent essay mentioned above, will be mentioned here only cursorily since the purpose of the present discussion is to explain how it was inspired by Rick Beyer's film.

*The Ghost Army* tells the story of a secret U.S. Army unit officially designated as the 23rd Headquarters Special Troops – a unit which staged more than twenty deceptions designed to fool the German forces, from June 1944 to March 1945. The best possible introduction to the ways in which this unit operated – and to the documentary itself – is found in the film's three-minute long pre-title sequence, and with Rick Beyer's kind permission, a shot-by-shot breakdown of that sequence will now be provided, including all spoken text as well as stills from the film. It will be followed by a discussion of how this film inspired what might be called a performance-based narrative model, in contrast to the conflict-based models that have dominated screenwriting discussions for many decades. Closing this essay on *The Ghost Army* will be a new interview with Rick Beyer about the making of the film, and in which he responds to a final question concerning conflict and performance.

## The pre-title sequence

*The text in italics is the voice-over commentary spoken by Peter Coyote.*

*Images and text are reproduced here with the kind permission of writer/director Rick Beyer.*

Shot 1

Shot 2

Shot 3

Shot 4

Shot 5
*March, 1945*

Shot 6
*After nine months of bitter fighting, the Allies have driven the Germans across ...*

Shot 7
*... Europe to the Rhine River, ...*

Shot 8
*... the last natural barrier to the German heartland.*

Shot 9
*It is here that Allied generals expect the battered remnants of Hitler's once proud Army to mount their final defense of the fatherland.*

Shot 10
Stan Nance: Because the Germans had said "The Rhine River is going to run red with American blood." And they meant it.

Shot 11
*German reconnaissance planes take to the ...*

Shot 12
*... sky to ...*

Shot 13
*... pinpoint where the Allies will attack.*

Shot 14

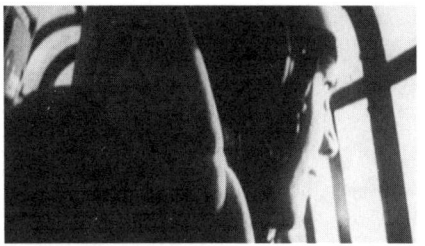

Shot 15

Shot 16
*Across the river from Dusseldorf, the view from the air reveals hundreds of American vehicles.*

Shot 17
*Intercepted Allied radio transmissions confirm the presence of two American divisions.*

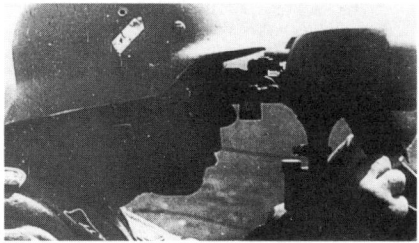

Shot 18
*German observation posts hear them ...*

Shot 19
*... moving in across the river.*

Shot 20
*All signs suggest the attack will come here.*

Shot 21a
*But the tanks ...*

Shot 21b
*... spotted from the air ...*

Shot 21c
*... are 93-pound inflatable dummies.*

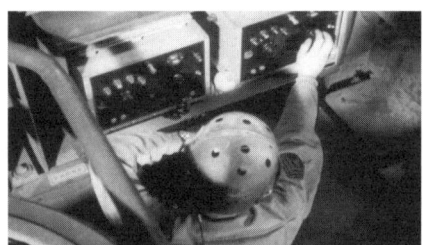

Shot 22
*The sounds ...*

Shot 23
*... come from loud speakers; ...*

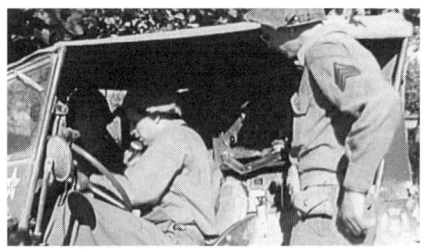

Shot 24
*... the radio transmissions from a script.*

Shot 25
Irv Stempel: It's amazing, the fakery that we were able to perpetrate upon the enemy.

Shot 26
*A group of hand-picked soldiers waging a secret war of deception was now trying to pull off one last …*

Shot 27
*… grand illusion. With thousands of American lives hanging in the balance. Including their own.*

Shot 28
Victor Dowd (off): I used to refer to us as the …

Shot 29
Victor Dowd: … Cecil B. DeMille Warriors.

Shot 30
*These "Artists of Deception" were also known as The Ghost Army.*

# From inflatable tanks to a performance-based narrative model

A belief in the necessity of conflict in all screenwriting is so firmly entrenched that conflict is generally defined loosely enough for it to be found anywhere one might look, in any story. Using the concept of "inner conflict," for example, can enable commentators to suggest that conflict is in play any time a character wants something that isn't instantly available (Phillips 2012; 57, 59), or – as I was told by the head of screenwriting at a major film school – whenever a character makes a choice, since one option is chosen at the expense of others. It is also common to confuse dramatic tension with conflict, in which case a character's experience of heightened excitement or anticipation can be mistakenly designated as an expression of conflict. With very few exceptions, the one form of conflict that is clearly identifiable as such in a film – and without requiring intellectual acrobatics to fit the definition – is *interpersonal* conflict, already defined above as a "high-stake opposition between characters who seek to thwart each other's goals" (and explained more fully in Raskin 2017: 29-30). Striking examples of conflict understood in this manner – which I believe is what most movie-goers would take the word 'conflict' to mean – are found in such films as *One Flew Over the Cuckoo's Nest* (Milos Forman, 1975), in which Jack Nicholson's McMurphy and Louise Fletcher's Nurse Ratched are locked in an increasingly bitter struggle; and in *Bad Day at Black Rock* (John Sturges, 1955), in which Spencer Tracy's Macreedy is pitted against the trio of racist villains played by Robert Ryan, Ernest Borgnine and Lee Marvin. These films are clearly conflict-driven.

War films are virtually by definition conflict-driven, involving interpersonal conflict elevated or magnified to a collective and international level. But although the setting for *The Ghost Army* is of course the armed struggle between the Allied and German forces, it is by no means that conflict in and of itself that holds our interest in this film, or that makes the operations of the secret U.S. Army unit so intriguing. Instead what it is that keeps us glued to the screen is the skill, resourcefulness and originality of the work performed a) by the filmmaker; and b) by the members of that secret army unit, as exemplified by their dreaming up and making effective strategic use of inflatable tanks in order to fool the enemy as to where the Allies were gathering their forces for an imminent attack. In other words, it is performance rather than conflict that captures and holds our interest here.

This is what came as a revelation to me when first seeing this film, and led to further thoughts about cinematic storytelling.

Even when conflict is in play, I would now suggest that what makes an event interesting to watch in a film is not the conflict itself but rather the skill, resourcefulness and originality of filmmakers' portrayal of the event and of the performance of one or both of the competing parties in waging the battle. In *Bad Day at Black Rock*, for example, when the bully played by Ernest Borgnine first grabs the one-handed Macreedy and a fight ensues, what fascinates us is the skill with which Macreedy uses his one hand to deliver judo chops that utterly overpower and flatten his bewildered opponent, while Macreedy himself remains unruffled, without even having to straighten his hat when the fight is over. And there are actually a number of conflated performances in play here, involving not only the character Macreedy's spectacular exploit, but also Spencer Tracy's acting in that scene, as well as the writer's thinking up of the event, the director's management of its staging, the cinematographer's framing of the characters, the editing of the shots, etc. All of these performances, each of which is deftly carried out, meld seamlessly into one coherent experience of the event.

Without denying that there is generally conflict at the heart of cinematic storytelling, I have learned from watching *The Ghost Army* that a genuinely engaging event or film is *performance-driven*, which also explains why conflict-free scenes and short films entirely free of conflict can hold our interest. This also means that cinematic and other kinds of storytelling appeal to us in essentially the same ways as painting, music and dance, in the sense that in all of these media, it is performance that captures and holds our interest. Conflict in itself can be tedious. A succession of shots of German and American troops simply shooting at each other can quickly become monotonous and dull. It is only when an impressive degree of performance is in play on the part of a fictional character, an actor, a filmmaker, or in the real-life exploits of, for example, a secret U.S. Army unit, that we can become spellbound.

For this and related realizations, I am indebted to Rick Beyer's *The Ghost Army*, which deftly – as a memorable performance in its own right – depicted the inflatable tanks, fake airfields, bogus radio transmissions and other deceptions that saved countless American lives on European battlefields in 1944-1945.

# An interview with Rick Beyer

*How and when did you first hear about the tactical deception unit known as the Ghost Army?*

I first learned about this unit in 2005, when my friend and former business partner Mark Tomizawa introduced me to a woman whose uncle served in the unit. Her name is Martha Gavin, and her enthusiasm was the spark that started the whole project. She was passionate that someone should make a film about this, and I became infected with her passion. Martha's uncle, John Jarvie, who turns 95 in a few days as I write in the spring of 2017, was one of my first interviews and one of the most appealing characters in the film.

By the time I met with Martha, I had already done a little research into the project, and found it appealing. I have always loved quirky history stories, the strange "can you believe it?" stuff. In fact, I've written an entire book series, *The Greatest Stories Never Told*, that focuses on just that. The idea that American soldiers in World War II went into battle with inflatable tanks and sound effects records was so bizarre, so contrary to every image from every war movie I've ever seen, that it immediately attracted my attention.

Then came the moment Martha walked into the coffee shop. She was carrying an armload of three-ring binders that turned out to contain her uncle's wartime artworks. That was when I really came to understand that many of the soldiers in the unit were artists, who used their spare time to paint and sketch what they saw on the battlefield. I was captivated with the way they presented such a unique and intimate perspective of the war. I came to realize this was an even more complex and multi-layered story than I thought. And that's how I got hooked.

Although it caused me some problems, I also loved the twin stories of deception and art. I say problems because funders and programmers like films that fit into an easily identifiable niche, and a film that is about both history and art is more difficult to categorize. The history people thought we were making a film about art, the art people thought we were making a film about history. Which may explain why we got no money from either the National Endowment for the Humanities or the National Endowment for the Arts. One TV executive actually told me that nobody was going to watch a film that was partly about WWII and partly about art. What I saw as something that raised the story to another level, this person saw as a reason to discard it. I think the finished film, and the response it has received, show who was right and who was wrong.

*There are four main components working together in the film: 1) archive footage and photos dating from the war; 2) new interviews you made with veterans of the unit; 3) the voice-over; 4) artwork done by men in the unit. Was that the basic concept for the film from the very start? Was the voice-over text written before, after or during the editing of the visual material and interviews?*

I knew from the very first that the interviews and archive material, including the art, would be the spine of the film. I love the veterans' stories with their great detail and texture and heart. I considered shooting re-enactment footage, but decided that it would distance us further from the reality of the story.

The editing and voice-over informed each other, and came together organically. I put the film together in segments. Usually I would start by assembling the sound-bites that I wanted to use, along with footage and images that were pertinent. I would do a rough assembly of this material, and see where we needed voice-over. Then there would be this back and forth – adjusting the voice-over, adjusting the edit, back and forth. Because the film came together over a period of years, there were a lot of changes, based on feedback from audiences and acquisition of new material.

*Was it difficult to find the archive footage and photos you used, and were you the one doing the research?*

We began by asking every veteran of the unit we came across to share photos and artworks. Sometimes they sent scans, sometimes entire scrapbooks showed up in the mail for us to scan and send back. Over time we built an archive of several thousand stills and artworks. That archive, by the way, is still growing 12 years later.

Initially I intended the veterans' photographs to form a much bigger part of the visual picture. Indeed, they did so in my first rough cut. I showed that cut to an executive producer at The History Channel, someone I considered (and still consider) a friend, to see what she thought. She told me the film was "visually stultifying." I was quite stung by that blunt assessment (you note that I have not forgotten!) but painful as her comment was, it turned out to be the single most useful piece of advice I ever received. I decided to replace every photograph I could with footage, and to use color footage whenever possible.

Of course there is almost no footage of the deception unit, because it was top secret. There is some footage of the sonic unit, and about 60 seconds of footage of inflatable tanks that was likely made in Britain in 1946. So this meant I had to find other footage that would illustrate what was going on in that moment. It was very important to me not to throw down generic WWII footage throughout the film … I wanted the shots to truly represent what we were talking about.

I made many trips to the National Archives in College Park Maryland, and also hired other researchers to search for footage. We made some great finds. One scene in the film takes place in the Normandy town of Trévières, near where the unit first bivouacked. We see the artists from the unit sketching in the bombed-out church. Amazingly, I was able to find U.S. Army footage shot inside that church the same week the Ghost Army soldiers were there, and to match shots from that film with paintings created by the soldiers. Through a film editor in Berlin, I was able to access rare footage of German aerial reconnaissance that he had bought in a Berlin antique shop.

Most of the color footage in the film comes from the Library of Congress, and was actually shot by famed Hollywood director George Stevens. He got his start directing films in 1930, his best known pre-war film being *Gunga Din*. Then he volunteered to head up a Signal Corps film crew that shot tons of footage of the fighting in Europe. Of course most of that is black and white. But he took with him a little bit of color stock, and a 16 mm camera, and shot maybe six hours of color footage. A lot of it is home movies of his crew. In fact, Stevens himself appears in numerous shots. His son, also named George Stevens, donated that color film to the Library of Congress, which gave us permission to access it for this film.

Stevens' most notable films came after the war: *Diary of Ann Frank*, *Giant*, and *A Place in the Sun*, the last two of which he won best Director Oscars for. Many critics have noted that the war changed his filmmaking style, from light comedic director before the war to a much darker style afterwards.

*Was it difficult to locate the veterans you interviewed? I imagine it didn't require much persuasion to get them to tell about their work in the Ghost Army.*

I got a great head start when I was invited to attend a reunion they held in Washington, DC, in 2005. It turned out to be the very last one. I interviewed six veterans in two days. They gave me the names of other veterans to contact, and we started building up a list. Over the last eight years I've probably spoken to 40 or 50 veterans of the unit, although I only interviewed 21 of them on camera.

Some men, especially those in the sonic deception unit, were told not to talk about it for 50 years after the war, and they took that very seriously. Having kept their mouths shut for so long, they were very happy to have a chance to talk freely about their experiences. For some of them it was the first time. I was blown away when a veteran named John Walker told me that his wife had died after they had been married for 40 years, and she never knew what he did during the war.

I didn't run into a single veteran who wasn't interested in telling his story. They were all delighted that this strange WWII escapade of theirs was finally getting some attention!

*Peter Coyote's delivery of the spoken text is superb. How did you decide on asking him to do the voice-over? And did it require much persuasion?*

As the rough cut neared completion, I consulted with my wife Marilyn, who was my partner in so many ways on this project. We put together a short list of candidates to narrate the film. At the top of the list were actors Peter Coyote and Chris Cooper. I was in the process of pitching the film to PBS, and I felt we needed somebody whose narration would enhance our film's credibility –make it more "PBS-like". And I could "hear" the script in the voice of each of those actors.

We sent both a packet with a rough cut, information on the unit and a letter asking him to narrate. Peter's assistant responded very quickly, within a day or two, and put us in touch with the agent who manages his narration activities. We paid a significant sum of money for his services, but I still suspect he gave us a great deal.

Peter was attracted by the way the film highlights the important role played by artists in carrying out these deceptions. He served on the California Arts Commission for a number of years, and feels very strongly that people need to understand the importance of the arts and art education. He saw how this fits right into that.

Before Peter recorded the narration, we showed the rough cut to many audiences, with my voice as a scratch track. After we added Peter's voice, people watching the film again told me how much they liked the new segments I added. "I haven't added any new segments," I replied. In each case, the segment was something that had been there before, but it took Peter's narration to make it really register. That seems to me a wonderful illustration of how important the choice of narrator is.

*Can you tell me how the production was funded? Was the film intended specifically for public service television?*

I originally pitched the film to The History Channel back in 2005. I had made other films for them, and I thought this would be right up their alley, but they were changing their business model and turned it down. So I decided to make it as an independent film with the idea of getting PBS to pick it up. I raised virtually all of the money for the film from individual donors. It took years, but eventually I had more than seven hundred donors who contributed $300,000. I pitched individual donors, held fundraising screenings, conducted a Kickstarter campaign, and did everything else I could think of to raise the money; I had never done this kind of fundraising before, and it was challenging.

Many filmmakers are put off by this kind of fundraising. They find it hard to ask people for money. I came to consider it a form of outreach. If you can communicate your passion, people want to help. I always say the best donor is the person who feels like you are doing them a favor by letting them be part of your project.

*Can you tell me in approximately how many countries it has been picked up by broadcasters? Was it also shown at film festivals? I imagine it has won some awards?*

The film premiered at the Salem Film Festival in Salem, MA in 2013. It was a memorable night: the film played to an SRO crowd during a blizzard! It eventually won the festival's audience award. We also played at about half a dozen other festivals. We had a very limited window because most festivals don't want a film once it has been broadcast on television. Sundance, Berlin and the other big festivals we entered all passed on the film – too bad for them!

Since the broadcast premiere on PBS in 2013, the film has been televised in about thirty countries. Interestingly enough, it has received an especially positive response in Germany. The film won a 2013 CINE Golden Eagle Award.

*Is there anything else you would like to add about the production, reception, or importance of this film?*

Filmmaking is a collaborative art. An enormous number of people contributed to this film, and I was lucky to have each and every one of them involved. While I hate to single anyone out, it's worth noting the role played by editor Jon Neuburger.

I edited the first rough cut of the film myself. It was very long, about an hour and forty-five minutes, and it had gotten a lackluster response from programming execs at PBS and elsewhere. I knew we needed to do another pass to sharpen it up.

Jon is a talented and experienced documentary editor, and we had worked together on another film, so we had good rapport. In the summer of 2010 he spent 6-8 weeks working with me to re-shape *The Ghost Army*.

He had already seen the rough cut, but we started by watching the film together. We stopped after every scene to discuss. It took two days, but at the end we had a plan for re-working the film. I went off to write a new opening, and John started attacking the edit. My initial rough cut was much more evenly divided between deception and art. Jon convinced me that the art had to be subordinate to the war story – that in fact every time we showed art it should move our war story along. That decision alone justified bringing him on, but in fact he did so much in that time to sharpen the storytelling. Many of the scenes of the original cut survived largely intact, but the overall narrative was *so* much stronger at the end of that summer. Without Jon's efforts, it would not be as good a film as it is.

This may also be a good place to note how much this film benefitted from the time it took to produce. Eight years went by from the time I started working on it to the time it premiered on PBS. The main reason it took that long is because of fundraising. And when you are going through that it seems like a drag. But in fact, it was a blessing. The fundraising required me to continually show partially finished versions of the film to people, who in turn provided incredibly valuable feedback. Spending years on the material also deepened my own understanding of the story, and allowed me time to tweak and finesse every detail. This was the absolute opposite of a rush job! And I think it shows in the final product.

*I'd like to tell you about a special meaning this film has for me and would then like to have your response. My own main field of research is short film storytelling and in that context, I have been arguing for some time that conflict – universally considered to be an absolute necessity in all cinematic storytelling – is merely optional and that other factors are what capture and hold the viewer's interest. While watching* The Ghost Army *I realized what those other factors are: the skill, resourcefulness and originality of the performances in play. In other words, though the backdrop for the story you tell is the conflict between the Allied and German armies, what makes it interesting is not the conflict itself but rather the brilliant deceptions performed by the American unit. On this basis, I am now developing a performance-based narrative model (focusing on character-performance as well as the performances of writer, director, actors, editor, etc.) as an alternative to a conflict-based model. Thanks to seeing your film. Does any of this make sense to you?*

Like any artist, I am delighted when my work inspires an unexpected line of thought or a new way of looking at things. That's the great thing about art – you never know what other people are going to take from it.

When I was making the film, I heard from some people that there wasn't a strong enough conflict at the core of it. That sounds silly – the film is about WWII and the titanic battle between the Allies and Nazi Germany. But you definitely don't get the sense of constant obstacles that they need to overcome. It's more like a journey with many interesting things to see along the way. Personally, I always found myself less interested in exactly how successful the deceptions were than the creative effort and attention to detail it took to mount them.

The response from audiences from around the world suggests that they agree, and that you may be on to something.

## *The Ghost Army*, principal production credits

| | |
|---|---|
| Director | Rick Beyer |
| Editor | Jon Neuburger |
| Director of Photography | Dillard Morrison |
| Narrated by | Peter Coyote |
| Screenplay | Rick Beyer |
| Music composed by | Matt Mariano |
| Sound mix, sound design | Richard Bock, Geof Thurber |

| | |
|---|---|
| Sound recordists | Ty Ford, Brian Buckly |
| Production Company | Plate of Peas Productions |
| Release, run time | 2012, 55 min. 39 sec. |
| Home page | http://www.ghostarmy.org |

# References

Forman, Milos (1975). *One Flew Over the Cuckoo's Nest*. USA, Fantasy Films.

McKee, Robert (1997). *Story. Substance, Structure, Style and the Principles of Screenwriting*. New York: Regan Books.

Phillips, Andrea (2012). *A Creator's Guide to Transmedia Storytelling*. New York: McGraw-Hill.

Raskin, Richard (2017). "On conflict in short film storytelling," in Pepita Hesselberth and Maria Poulaki (eds.), *Compact Cinematics*. Bloomsbury Academic US, an imprint of Bloomsbury Publishing, pp. 28-35.

Straume, Unni (1993). *Derailment/Avsporing*. Norway-France, Unni Straume Filmproduksjon and K-FILMS, France.

Sturges, John (1955). *Bad Day at Black Rock*. USA, MGM.

Ulrichsen, Marianne Olsen (1995). *Come/Kom*. Norway, Fikjonsfilm, Nordnorsk Filmsenter.

Wicker, Tom (1975). "The Fourth Law of Politics," *New York Times*, 4 May, section 4, 15.

# 18

# The King of Denmark and the Yellow Star: Changing Forms and Functions of an Irresistible Myth

*The immensely popular King Christian X
on his daily ride through Copenhagen,
unaccompanied by guards, 1940.*

## Introduction

When people outside of Denmark look back at the role that country played during the Second World War, there are two narratives that most frequently come to mind.

One of them is true: the miraculous rescue of nearly the entire Jewish population, smuggled on fishing boats to Sweden before they could be ar-

235

rested in October 1943, after Denmark's status changed from self-governing 'protectorate' to occupied territory under military rule.

The other narrative, involving a courageous symbolic gesture performed by King Christian X, never happened, in *any* form (Goldberger 1987: xvii; Levine 2001: 28-29; Berdichevsky 2013). In its initial version, this myth has the king making it known that *if* the Nazi occupying power should ever require that Danish Jews wear a yellow star, he himself would be the first to do so. This *hypothetical* or '*if*' version of the myth was circulated most widely from 1942 to 1944 in the U.S. and U.K. and according to Aage Bertelsen was "on everyone's lips" in Denmark in October 1943 (Yahill 1969: 443). The other main variant, which I will call the *American* version for reasons that will soon become clear, states that the Nazis ordered that all Danish Jews wear a yellow star, after which the king publicly donned one himself with the entire Danish population immediately following his example and giving the Nazis no choice but to rescind the order. This version was circulated mainly after the war was over, and promulgated widely by the Leon Uris novel and Otto Preminger film of *Exodus*, appearing in 1958 and 1960 respectively, and more recently by the award-winning children's book *The Yellow Star: The Legend of King Christian X of Denmark* by Carmen Agra Deedy, published in the U.S. in 2000.

In this essay, I will consider the functions likely to have been fulfilled by each of these versions of the myth.

# 1. THE HYPOTHETICAL OR 'IF' VERSION

When this mythical account appeared in American newspapers, the King reportedly made his promise or threat to don the yellow star either to a) a delegation from the Jewish community of Copenhagen; b) leaders of the Danish Lutheran church; or c) the Nazis themselves. Here are examples of each.

### a. an assurance to the Jewish community

The following article appeared in the Daily News Bulletin of the *Jewish Telegraphic Agency* dated October 11, 1942. (*Mogen David* refers to the Star of David, though it literally means Shield of David.)

**DANISH KING WILL DON MOGEN DAVID IF NAZIS FORCE JEWS TO WEAR YELLOW BADGES**
LONDON, Oct. 9. (JTA) – King Christian of Denmark, receiving a delegation of Copenhagen Jews on Sept. 27, on the occasion of his birthday, told them that if the Germans forced the Jews in this country to wear a yellow Mogen David badge, he would wear a yellow star upon his uniform in public and would order the entire royal household to follow suit, it was reported today by Danish sources here.

The delegation presented the monarch with a gold Mogen David on behalf of the Copenhagen Jewish community.

Bent Melchior, Chief Rabbi of Denmark from 1970 to 1996 and the son of Marcus Melchior, who was instrumental in saving the Danish Jews in 1943, kindly responded to my questions about the above report by writing (personal communication, 26 July 2017):

> My own reaction is that it is possible but in no way certain that a Jewish delegation went the day after the King's birthday to congratulate him. Having known the people, C. B. Henriques and Karl Lachmann, who were president and vice president of the community, it is most unlikely that they would have brought him a Magen David as a gift, gold or iron or any material. As far as the reported statement from the King is concerned, it is impossible to think that the delegation would not have shared it with other members of the community – as you yourself have concluded that the matter would have been reported through other sources than this telegraph service.

### b. a pledge to leaders of the Lutheran church

**REPORT DANISH RULER WILLING TO WEAR STAR DESIGNATING THE JEWS**
STOCKHOLM. – (AP) – King Christian of Denmark was quoted by a Danish refugee today as saying: "If the Germans want to put the yellow Jewish star in Denmark I and my whole family will wear it as a sign of the highest distinction." The refugee said that King Christian, who has protested against Germany's persecution of the Danish Jews, made the statement to leaders of the Danish Lutheran church.
*The Daily Times* (Davenport, Iowa), 11 October 1943, p. 15.

**KING CHRISTIAN DEFIES GERMANS** Same text as above
*Plain Speaker* (Hazelton, Pennsylvania), 11 October 1943, p. 1.

**DENMARK KING IN DEFENSE OF JEWS** Same text as above
*Honolulu Star Bulletin*, 11 October 1943, p. 3.

**DANISH KING WILLING TO WEAR JEWISH STAR, REFUGEE ANNOUNCES**
Same text as above but with "today" replaced by "yesterday."
*Troy Record*, 12 October 1943, p. 10.

## c. a threat made directly to the Nazis

**DENMARK'S KING IS AS FEARLESS AS HIS PEOPLE WILLING TO WEAR STAR**
[…] He warned the Nazis at the time that if they imposed their customary anti-Jewish regulations on Denmark he would personally lead all of his people in wearing the yellow Star of David insignia on their clothing exactly as prescribed for Jews under the Nazi anti-Semitic decrees. The only reason the Nazis were not able to drive roughshod over the wishes of the King from the beginning and not set up a Danish regime after the familiar pattern of Nazi puppet states was and is the tremendous popularity the monarch enjoyed among the rank and file of the Danish people.
Seymour Berkson, *The Courier-Journal* (Louisville, Kentucky), 31 August 1943, p. 7.

**DENMARK AND THE JEWS**
Instances are familiar of King Christian X's uncompromising manner and dignified bearing toward the German aggressors. Some of those instances relate to the King's response to the Nazi insistence upon introducing their anti-Semitic measures in Denmark. Thus, on one occasion his answer was: "We Danes do not consider ourselves inferior to the Jews; therefore, we do not have any Jewish problem in Denmark." …. And most recently, after the introduction of German military dictatorship in Denmark and their rounding up of Danish Jews, the King is reported to have declared: "If Jews in Denmark are required to wear a yellow badge, I and the Royal Family will also wear it as a sign of distinction."
Henrik von Kauffmann (ambassador), *The Jewish Ledger*, 12 October 1943 (Vilhjálmsson 2003: 103).

**KING CHRISTIAN'S ROYAL SPIRIT FANNED DENMARK'S DEFIANCE**
[...] Gen. von Hanneken saw Christian X and demanded anti-Semitic laws.
"No," said the king. "Since we Danes have never considered ourselves inferior to the Jews, I recognize no Jewish problem. And if you force the Jews of Denmark to wear the yellow Star of David, then I and my family will wear it also as a badge of honor."
George Creel, *The Minneapolis Star*, 21 Nov 1944, p. 10.
[Von Hanneken was supreme commander of the German forces in Denmark.]

**COURAGE IS THEIR BADGE**
Nazi: The Jews must wear the yellow badge.
King: If that is so then I shall wear the yellow badge myself and order that my entire house shall do the same.
Lisa Barrett Drew, NBC Radio Broadcast, 5 March 1944.

How these false reports in American newspapers and even a radio dramatization came about is a fascinating story in itself. As Vilhjálmsson (2003: 106-107), Goldberger (2006), Jespersen (2007: 439-440) and Bøggild and Fracapane (2013) have pointed out, once the U.S. had become engaged in the war, Denmark – and the king in particular – were characterized especially by right-wing American commentators as cowardly and spineless for having offered little resistance to the Nazi invaders and for being too compliant with them under the occupation. The one piece of evidence provided is from a quiz in *The Washington Post* on November 22, 1942, in which the reader is supposed to identify the ruler – Christian X shown in a photo – "whose nation put no armed might in the way of the Nazis" and thereby "made simpler the occupation of Norway" (Vilhjálmsson 2003: 107).

Based in New York at this time, a Dane named Caspar Hasselriis organized the *American Friends of Danish Freedom and Democracy* and distributed a Danish-American newsletter called *The Listening Post*, while working closely with the Danish ambassador to the U.S., Henrik Kauffmann. In 1940 Hasselriis hired Edward L. Bernays as a consultant; Bernays is known as "the father of public relations and spin" and described his own approach to the marketing of national policies as the "engineering of consent" (Bernays 1942: 241). These men, along with shipping magnate Hans Isbrandtsen, set out systematically to improve Denmark's image, one of their goals being "to insure its potential acceptance into the United Nations as an inherently Allied nation at war's ultimate end" (Goldberger 2016).

The idea for the reports cited above was presumably inspired by a cartoon Hasselriis included in *The Listening Post* on May 15, 1942. It was drawn by the Norwegian political cartoonist Ragnvald Brix, who signed it with his Swedish pseudonym Stig Höök. Scavenius, mentioned in the dialogue between Prime Minister Thorvald Stauning on the left and King Christian on the right, was Foreign Minister at the time and considered by many to be far too accommodating toward the Nazis.

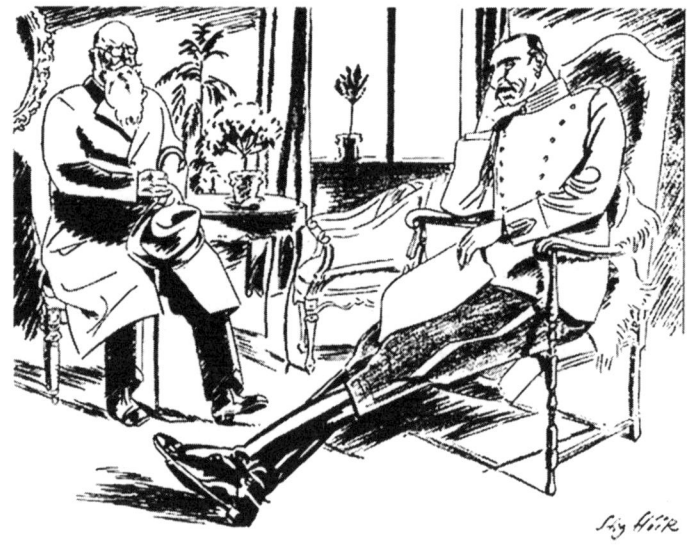

Reproduced here with the kind permission of
Göteborg Handels- och Sjöfartstidning.

– What shall we do, Your Majesty, if Scavenius succeeds in requiring our Jews to wear yellow stars?
– Then I suppose we will all have to wear yellow stars.[1]

---

1   The Swedish caption reads:
    – Vad ska vi göra, Ers Majestät, om Scavenius genomdriver att också våra judar ska gå med gula stjärnor?
    – Da får vi väl alla gå med gula stjärnor.

This cartoon had first appeared on January 10, 1942, in the Swedish newspaper *Göteborg Handels- och Sjöfartstidning*, and in 1975, folklorist Jens Lund was the first to identify the cartoon as a likely source of the myth we are discussing. What wasn't known until 2007, however, was that the cartoon had in turn been inspired by an entry the king had made in his diary on September 10, 1941, when describing a conversation with Finance Minister, then also acting Prime Minister, Vilhelm Buhl, whose words are cited at the beginning of this quotation (Jespersen 2007: 441-442):[2]

> Considering the inhuman treatment the Jews have been subjected to not only in Germany but also in other occupied countries, one begins to worry that one day this requirement may be made of us as well. If so, we would have to reject it outright in accordance with [the Jews'] protection under the Constitution. I stated that I would also not go along with such a demand made of Danish citizens. If a requirement of that kind were made, we would do best to deal with it by all wearing the Star of David. The Finance Minister added that that could always be a way out.

Word of Buhl's conversation with the king had apparently reached Brix, though Hasselriis and his fellow spin-doctors would not have known that when they devised their false reports to make Denmark and her king look their best. So they were probably unaware that their fabricated news had a substantial grain of truth at its core, though as far as we know, the king never shared this generous thought with a Jewish delegation, leaders of the Lutheran Church or the Nazis themselves.

It is true that the King made no secret of his protective attitude toward his Jewish subjects. In April 1933, he attended the service at the 100th anniversary of the Copenhagen synagogue. On December 31, 1941, he sent a personal handwritten letter to Rabbi Marcus Melchior, thanking him for a book sent as a new year's gift and expressing relief that a recent arson attempt had done little damage to the synagogue. And an early historian (Thaulow 1945: 174), reflecting at least popular beliefs at the time, de-

---

2   "Naar man saa den umenneskelige Behandling, Jøderne var Genstand for ikke blot i Tyskland, men ogsaa i de besatte Lande, begyndte man at være ængstelig for, at Kravet ogsaa en Gang blev stillet os, men det maatte vi pure afvise som følge af disses Retsstilling inden for Grundloven.
   Jeg udtalte, at jeg heller ikke vilde gaa med til et saadant Krav overfor danske Statsborgere. Hvis et saadant Krav rejstes, imødegik vi det bedst ved, at vi alle anlagde 'Davidsstjernen'. Finansministeren indskød, at det var jo altid en Udvej."

scribes one occasion on which Christian X reportedly responded to demands of the German authorities concerning the Danish Jews by thumbing through his papers and stating that there was no such provision in the conditions agreed to on April 9 (when the occupation began); and a subsequent occasion when the King is said to have assured representatives of the Jewish congregation that they could count on his full support. Several commentators have convincingly argued that even if Christian X never wore or made the threat or promise of wearing the yellow star, it's something that would have been in character for him to do (Yahill 1969: 63; Jespersen 2007: 443). And the King's entry of September 10, 1941 in his diary, quoted above, certainly confirms that view. With these factors in mind, I would suggest that even false reports of a statement Christian X never actually made may still have contributed to the Nazis' reluctance to introduce the use of the yellow star in Denmark in order not to disturb the delicate balance they had achieved in the peaceful functioning of the occupation, ensuring a steady flow of farm produce to German troops at a minimal cost of military might within Denmark. In order to preserve that delicate balance, the German plenipotentiary Werner Best repeatedly warned his superiors in Berlin against introducing measures against the Danish Jews (Lidegaard 2013: 49).

A point of this kind was made in a review of Bo Lidegaard's excellent book published in 2013, the English title of which is *Countrymen: How Denmark's Jews Escaped the Nazis*. The reviewer Michael Ignatieff wrote (2013, emphasis added):

> From very early on [...], the Danes, from the king on down, made it clear that harming the Jews would bring cooperation to an end and force the Germans to occupy the country altogether. The king famously told his prime minister, in private, that if the Germans forced the Danish Jews to wear a yellow star, then he would wear one too. Word of the royal position went public and even led to a myth that the king had actually ridden through the streets of Copenhagen on horseback wearing a yellow star on his uniform. The king never did wear a star. He didn't have to wear one, because, *thanks to his opposition*, the Germans never imposed such a regulation in Denmark.

Several commentators mention Victor Borge as a person who had a warm friendship with Hasselriis and who helped disseminate the story of the king and the yellow star through numerous radio and theatrical performances

(Paulsen 1967: 216-218; Bak 2001: 156; Goldberger 2016). However, no specific performances have been cited.

Up to this point, we have discussed the hypothetical version of the myth solely in relation to an American audience during the war years, where its function was to improve Denmark's tarnished image. The myth was also disseminated in the U.K. by a propaganda unit known as the Political Warfare Executive. This text, published in London's *Evening Standard* on October 13, 1943, might be a good example of that propaganda unit's eloquent handiwork (Vilhjálmsson 2003: 103-104):

> A NOBLE voice comes out of Nazi-occupied Denmark, a voice of tolerance and defiance, and of faith in humanity. "If the Germans want to introduce the Yellow Star for Jews in Denmark," announces King Christian, "I and my whole family will wear it as a sign of the highest distinction" …King Christian makes no empty gesture. His brave defiance expresses the call of conscience that humanity should be degraded no longer by crimes committed in the name of a false race theory and a wicked creed. Those Jews who perished in Warsaw, fighting Nazi panzers to the last, converted the Ghetto into a fortress. Now Denmark's King converts the Yellow star into a flame.

The goal of the Political Warfare Executive has been described as wanting to drive a wedge between the presumably German-friendly government and the resistance-minded population with the King as its spearhead: "to write up the King and to write down Scavenius" (Jespersen 2007: 440; Lidegaard 2013: 33).

## 2. THE AMERICAN VERSION

The earliest example I have been able to find of the version in which the King actually dons a Star of David dates from 1954, and is found in Sholem Asch's foreword to the American translation of Aage Bertelsen's *Oktober 43* (Bertelsen 1954: v-vi):

> This book is not the work of a single person. It was written by an entire people, from its highest citizen, old and noble King Christian X, who took from his head the glorious crown of Denmark and set it upon the blood-

stained head of the Jewish victim when he elected to wear the sign of death, the Jewish Shield of David, on his breast ...

But it was in Leon Uris' novel *Exodus* (1958) that this version of the myth found its first solid roots in American culture (Uris 1959: 75):

> From the German occupation headquarters at the Hotel D'Angleterre came the decree: ALL JEWS MUST WEAR A YELLOW ARM BAND WITH A STAR OF DAVID.
>
> That night the underground transmitted a message to all Danes. "From Amalienborg Palace, King Christian has given the following answer to the German command that Jews must wear a Star of David. The King has said that one Dane is exactly the same as the next Dane. He himself will wear the first Star of David and he expects that every loyal Dane will do the same."
>
> The next day in Copenhagen, almost the entire population wore arm bands showing a Star of David.
>
> The following day the Germans rescinded the order.

Well aware that this passage was at odds with historical fact, Julius Margolinsky, the librarian of the Jewish congregation in Copenhagen at the time, suggested that the passage simply not appear in the Danish translation of the novel and his advice was followed (Bak 2001: 158).

The mythical story was soon even more widely spread by Otto Preminger's feature film *Exodus* (U.S. release December 1960), for which Dalton Trumbo wrote the screenplay. In a memorable scene, a young idealistic Danish-American girl called Karen Hansen Clement (played by Jill Haworth) tells the story to the skeptical Dov Landau (Sal Mineo), with Haganah officer Ari Ben Canaan (Paul Newman) looking on and heightening the scene's gravitas:

KAREN: When the Nazis marched into Denmark, they ordered every Jew to wear a yellow armband with the Star of David on it. And when they ...
DOV: That's the worst thing that can happen?
KAREN: I said, listen! You don't know what you're talking about. The next morning, when every Jew in Denmark had to wear his armband, King Christian came out of Amalienborg Palace for his morning ride. And do you know something? He wore the Star of David on his arm.
DOV: But why should ...
KAREN: And you know something else? By afternoon, everybody was wearing Stars of David. Jews and Danes, and, well, just everybody.

When *Exodus* was released in Denmark (November 1961), that scene was singled out for special attention by several reviewers, who wrote, for example: "Embarrassment sinks over the audience and any dawning doubt about the film's general historic veracity intensifies" (Stegelmann 1961: 11).[3] Another reviewer described the scene as "Denmark-friendly in a way we could have done without" (Lind 1961: 11).[4]

And just as Danes who know it is untrue cringe when hearing the fabricated story retold, people from other countries sometimes become livid when told that the King never wore a Star of David. Former Chief Rabbi Bent Melchior stated in 2013: "I have made thousands of Americans furious, when

---

3  "*Flovheden sænker sig over salen, enhver gryende tvivl til filmens historiske korrekthed i det hele taget øges.*"
4  "*... det er en form for dansk-venlighed, man helst er fri for.*"

telling in lectures that [the story] wasn't true. But it wasn't, since the Jews in Denmark were never required to wear the yellow star" (Clausen 2013).[5]

A similar experience was reported by a member of the Danish-Israeli Association in Aarhus when around 1980 a reception was held for the Mayor of Beersheba (Berdichevsky 2016):

> who began his after-dinner talk in English by expressing the admiration of all ordinary Israelis for the "heroic action of King Christian … who put on the yellow star to save his Jewish fellow countrymen." I politely informed the mayor after observing the cringing faces of the assembled Danish audience in a whisper in Hebrew that the story was a myth and got an explosive reaction (in Hebrew) … "Of course it's true, we all know this in Israel."

The most recent revival of the legend came in 2000 with the publication of the children's book *The Yellow Star. The Legend of King Christian X of Denmark*, written by Carmen Agra Deedy, illustrated by Henri Sørensen and published by Peachtree Publications. It was translated into a dozen languages, with the Danish version appearing in 2004. The author had heard the story in 1996 or 1997 from an elderly stranger who sat next to her at a National Storytelling Festival (Deedy 2017). The illustrator, Henri Sørensen, hadn't heard the story before he was asked to illustrate the book. The publisher of the Danish Buster edition, Knud Pilegaard, whose father had been active in the Danish resistance and survived torture and imprisonment in Neuengamme, had heard the story many times and "had always been interested in history and fascinated by the destiny of the Jews" (Pilegaard 2017).

As told in this children's book, leaflets rained down on Copenhagen announcing the requirement that "all Jews must sew onto their clothing a yellow star which must be visible at all times." That night, while looking at a star-filled sky, King Christian realized that the best way to hide a star was to "hide it among its sisters." He did his daily ride on horseback the next morning wearing a yellow star on his tunic, and as they watched him his subjects knew what to do and followed his example.

---

5   "*Jeg har gjort tusinder af amerikanere rasende, når jeg i forbindelse med foredrag fortalte, at det ikke passede. Men det gjorde det jo ikke, fordi jøderne i Danmark aldrig blev pålagt at bære den gule stjerne.*"

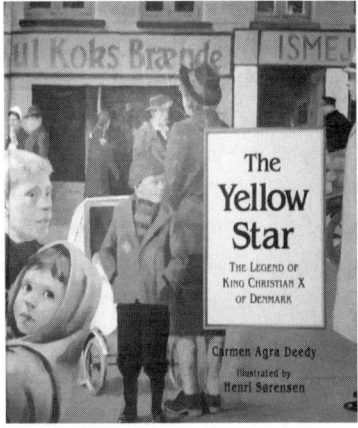

*First published in the United States under the title* The Yellow Star: The Legend of King Christian X of Denmark *by Carmen Agra Deedy and illustrated by Henri Sørensen. Text Copyright ©2000 by Carmen Agra Deedy. Illustrations Copyright ©2000 by Henri Sørensen. Published by arrangement with Peachtree Publishers and images used here also with the kind permission of Henri Sørensen.*

The book ends with an "Author's Note" stating that "there is no proof that the story ever happened," telling about the rescue of the Danish Jews, and concluding with a final reference to the story of the king and every Dane wearing the star in a "what if" mode, providing an inspiring example to follow.

## Conclusion

At the start of this study, I mentioned the two narratives generally associated with the fate of the Danish Jews during the Second World War: the true one about the rescue of nearly the entire Jewish population, smuggled on fishing boats to Sweden before they could be arrested, and the mythical one about King Christian donning a Star of David when the Jews were required to do so, or stating that he would if such a requirement were ever imposed on the Danish Jews.

I would like to end this discussion with a highly speculative thought for which I cannot muster a shred of evidence but which may help explain why long after the war was over, it was the narrative of the king and the star that was used in *Exodus* and a children's book, rather than the narrative of the rescue operation of October 1943.

The rescue narrative might begin with Werner Best, the German plenipotentiary in Copenhagen who, with a telegram sent to Berlin on September 8, 1943, set in motion the process leading to the arrest and deportation order of the approximately 7000 Danish Jews. The story then continues with the German diplomat Georg Ferdinand Duckwitz, who on Tuesday, September 28 leaked word of the impending arrest to the leader of the Danish Social Democratic party, Hans Hedtoft, with two other party leaders also present: H. C. Hansen and Alsing Andersen. Hedtoft in turn personally informed the head of the Jewish congregation, C. B. Henriques. Meanwhile a secretary of Alsing Andersen came to the apartment of Marcus Melchior to inform him of the situation. Marcus Melchior would be Chief Rabbi from 1947 to 1969, but in September 1943 he was not employed by the Jewish community. Because of a curfew in effect at the time, the first opportunity Marcus Melchior had to alert other people was at the morning service in the Synagogue on Wednesday, September 29. It was then that Marcus Melchior warned the congregation to go into hiding without delay and to spread word of the danger. Rosh Hashanah, the Jewish New Year, would start that evening but no services were held on Rosh Hashanah at the Copenhagen Synagogue in 1943 (Personal communication from Bent Melchior, 21 August 2017).

The story would then include the overnight creation of networks with the aid of the Danish resistance for the hiding and transportation of the Jews from Copenhagen, where most resided, to coastal towns such as Gilleleje, where they would again need hiding and arrangements with the captains of fishing boats for their passage to Sweden, not to mention arrangements made by Duckwitz and others with the Swedish authorities to accept this sudden influx of Jewish refugees. And the story would include the fact that of the nearly 500 Jews who were arrested, almost 90% survived thanks to food parcels delivered by the Danish Red Cross to all Danish prisoners at KZ camps.

The point I wish to make is that this narrative is exceptionally complex, involving many 'characters' and names to keep track of, many settings, logistical obstacles that had to be overcome, negotiations for hiding places in hospitals, churches and private homes, transportation by taxis, ambulances, etc. In contrast, the King and star narrative is easy to tell, involving one hero and just a few simple events. So in terms of storytelling challenges, the mythic narrative is a piece of cake while the true rescue story is cumbersome and difficult to tell.

Furthermore, the rescue story involves many events and layers as well as countless heroes, including a German diplomat, a Danish politician, a politician's secretary, a rabbi, resistance people, hospital staff, Lutheran ministers and church staff, friends and neighbors offering help, drivers, fishermen – the list goes on. In the Star of David narrative, there is one hero showing the way – not unlike certain Westerns in which a sheriff stands his ground against the villains and turns the tables on them. The appeal of that relatively simple but compelling dramaturgy needs no further explanation.

Americans and American Jews in particular in the post-war period were bursting with gratitude toward Denmark for having saved almost its entire Jewish population, in stark contrast to what had happened in many other occupied countries. To express that gratitude, the easily re-tellable narrative was chosen, as though it somehow also implicitly carried within itself the rescue story that involved too many storytelling challenges. This would be an essential celebrative function of the American version of the myth, just as improving Denmark's image was a main function of the earlier version.

Something of this very speculative claim is at least hinted at in this passage, which will provide a fitting last word to this discussion (Goldberger 1987: xvii):

> The story of how the Danes came to the aid of their Jewish population and successfully saved it from Nazi deportation is by now well known. Most have heard the legend of the Danish king who in protest and solidarity wore the Star of David. There is a variety of fanciful versions of the story, all of them untrue and yet almost impossible to eradicate from the received folklore of the Holocaust. One senses an almost pained, if not angry, resistance to attempts at demythologization.
>
> Obviously there is a strong element of wish-fulfillment at work here – as in all myths, sagas, and legends. People want the story to be true. Fortunately behind most sturdy myths a kernel of truth can be found. The story of the rescue of the Danish Jews is no exception, though I daresay that the measure of truth in this case is larger than a kernel, if allowance is made for symbolic transformation. Substitute the symbol of the king with the Danish people as a whole, and substitute further the wearing of a yellow star with the widespread and empathic compassion for the Jewish plight and you have the truth behind the myth.

# References and other consulted material

Adelson, Alan et al, reply by Istvan Deák (1989). "The Incomprehensible Holocaust: An Exchange," *New York Review of Books*, 21 December. http://www.nybooks.com/articles/1989/12/21/the-incomprehensible-holocaust-an-exchange-2/ Accessed 15 September 2017.

Bachman, Gideon (1961). "Exodus," *Film Quarterly*, vol. 14, no. 3, Spring, pp. 56-59. http://fq.ucpress.edu/content/14/3/56

Bak, Sofie Lene (2001). *Jødeaktionen oktober 1943. Forestillinger i offentlighed og forskning*. Copenhagen.

Barfod, Jørgen H. (1985). *The Holocaust Failed in Denmark*. Copenhagen: Frihedsmuseets Venners Forlag.

Berdichevski, Norman (2016). "A Tale of Two Kings: The Yellow Star Legend that Refuses to Die," *New English Review*, November. http://www.newenglishreview.org/custpage.cfm/frm/184593/sec_id/184593 Accessed 15 September 2017.

Berger, Paul (2013). "King Christian and the Yellow Star," *Forward*, 24 September. http://forward.com/opinion/184231/king-christian-and-the-yellow-star/ Accessed 15 September 2017.

Berkson, Seymore (1943). "Denmark's King Is As Fearless As His People," *The Courier-Journal* (Louisville, Kentucky), 31 August, p. 7.

Bernays, Edward L. (1942). "The Marketing of National Policies. A Study of War Propaganda," *Journal of Marketing*, vol. 6, no. 3, January, pp. 236-244.

Bertelsen, Aage (1954). *October 43*. New York: G. P. Putnam's Sons. Translated by Lilly Lindholm and Willy Agby, foreword by Sholem Asch. https://archive.org/details/october43aageber001971mbp Accessed 15 September 2017.

Bertelsen, Aage (1986). *Oktober 43*. Copenhagen: C. A. Reitzels Forlag. Orig. pub. 1952.

Christensen, Claus Bundgaard, Joachim Lund, Niels Wium Olesen and Jakob Sørensen (2015). *Danmark Besat. Krig og hverdag 1940-1945*. Copenhagen: Informations Forlag.

Christensen, Frits (2007). "Magtens fristelse," *Jyllands-Posten*, 4 November.

Christensen, John and Henrik Stevnsborg (2004). *Besat. Kampen mellem demotrati og diktatur i Danmark 1940-1945*. Copenhagen: Emil.

Clausen, Bente (2013). "Christian X var parat til at lade alle bære jødestjerne," *Kristeligt Dagblad*, 24 September.

Creel, George (1944). "King Christian's Royal Spirit Fanned Denmark's Defiance," *The Minneapolis Star*, 21 November, p. 10.

Crowther, Bosley (1960). "3 1/2-Hour Film Based on Uris Novel Opens," *New York Times*, 16 December.

*Daily Times* (Davenport, Iowa) (1943). "Report Danish Ruler Willing to Wear Star Designating the Jews," 11 October, p. 15.

Deák, István (1989/1990). See entries listed under Adelson and Lund.

Deedy, Carmen Agra (2000). *The Yellow Star. The Legend of King Christian X of Denmark*. Illustrated by Henri Sørensen. Text Copyright ©2000 by Carmen Agra Deedy. Illustrations Copyright ©2000 by Henri Sørensen. Atlanta: Peachtree Publishers.

Deedy, Carmen Agra (2004). *Den Gule Stjerne. Legenden om Kong Christian X af Danmark*. Illustrated by Henri Sørensen. Dyssegaard: Forlaget Buster. First published in the United States by Peachtree Publishers under the title *The Yellow Star. The Legend of King Christian X of Denmark*. Text Copyright ©2000 by Carmen Agra Deedy. Illustrations Copyright ©2000 by Henri Sørensen.

Deedy, Carmen Agra (2017). Personal telephone contact, 7 August.

Drew, Lisa Barrett (5 March 1944). "Courage Is Their Badge," NBC Purim Holiday Broadcast. https://www.genericradio.com/show.php?id=FMO39YT54 Accessed 23 October 2017.

E.U. (1961) "Exodus," *Information*, 4-5 November, p. 7.

Flender, Harold (1992). *Redningen i Danmark*. Dansk oversættelse Chr. C. Sørensen. Brøndby Strand: Forlaget Baruk. Orig. pub. 1963.

*Frihedsmuseet*. "King Christian and the Star of David." http://en.natmus.dk/museums/the-museum-of-danish-resistance-1940-1945/faq/king-christian-and-the-star-of-david/ Accessed 15 September 2017.

Goldberger, Leo, ed. (1987). *The Rescue of the Danish Jews. Moral Courage Under Stress*. New York and London: New York University Press.

Goldberger, Leo (2016). "The Origin of the King Christian Legend: The Ragnvald Blix Cartoon," *Scandinavian Jewish Forum*, 19 September. http://scandinavian-jewish.blogspot.dk/2016/09/ragnvald-blix-born-in-oslo-son-of-e.html Accessed 15 September 2017.

Grumberg, Jean-Patrick (2015). "Le roi du Danemark et l'étoile juive: un hoax qui date de 1942," *Dreuz.info*, 20 April. http://www.dreuz.info/2015/04/20/le-roi-du-danemark-et-letoile-juive-un-hoax-qui-date-de-1942/ Accessed 15 September 2017.

*History Watch* (n.d.). "Christian X og Jødestjernen." http://www.1sted.dk/2verdenskrig/danmark/kongen_stjernen.aspx Accessed 15 September 2017.

*Honolulu Star Bulletin* (1943). "Denmark King in Defense of Jews," 11 October, p. 3.

Ignatieff, Michael (2013). "One Country Saved Its Jews. Were They Just Better People?" *New Republic*, 15 December. https://newrepublic.com/article/115670/denmark-holocaust-bo-lidegaards-countrymen-reviewed Accessed 15 September 2017.

Jensen, Jacob Wendt (2014). *Victor Borge: Mennesket bag smilet*. Copenhagen: People's Press.

Jespersen, Knud J. V. (2007). *Rytterkongen: Et portræt af Christian 10*. Copenhagen: Gyldendal.

*Jewish Telegraphic Agency*, Daily News Bulletin (1942). "Danish King Will Don Mogen David if Nazis Force Jews to Wear Yellow Badges," 11 October, p. 3.

Jewish Telegraphic Agency (1972). "Danish Jews, Israelis Mourn King Frederik IX; Was Friend of Jews," vol. 39, no. 11, pp. 2-3. http://www.jta.org/1972/01/17/archive/danish-jews-israelis-mourn-king-frederik-ix-was-friend-of-jews

Kauffmann, Stanley (1969). "Double feature," review of *Exodus*, *The New Republic*, 19 December, pp. 21-22.

Kirchhoff, Hans (2005). *Gads Leksikon. Hvem var hvem. 1940-1945.* Copenhagen: Gad.

Kirchhoff, Hans (2013). *Holocaust i Danmark*. Odense: Syddansk Universitetsforlag.

Kirchhoff, Hans (2015). *At handle med ondskaben. Samarbejdspolitikken under besættelsen.* Copenhagen: Gyldendal.

Kurzweil, Aryeh (1960). "Bag Exoduss kulisser," *Jødisk Samfund*, vol. 31, no. 9, pp. 14-17.

Levine, Ellen (2001). *Darkness Over Denmark. The Danish Resistance and the Rescue of the Jews.* New York: Scholastic.

Lidegaard, Bo (2013). *Landsmænd. De danske jøders flugt i oktober 1943.* Copenhagen: Gyldendals Bogklubber.

Lind, Mogens (1961). "Stor film om Israel – med skarp tendens," *Berlingske Aftenavis*, 4 November, p. 18.

Lund, Jens (1975). "The Legend of the King and the Star," *Indiana Folklore*, vol. 8, no. 1-2, pp. 1-37.

Lund, Jens, reply by Isván Deák (1990). "The Legend of King Christian: An Exchange," *New York Review of Books*, 29 March. http://www.nybooks.com/articles/1990/03/29/the-legend-of-king-christian-an-exchange/ Accessed 15 September 2017.

Melchior, Marcus (1963). *Levet og oplevet. Erindringer.* Copenhagen: Hirschsprungs Forlag.

Melchior, Marcus (1973). *Darkness Over Denmark. A Rabbi Remembers.* London: New English Library.

Melchior, Bent (2017). Personal email communication, 26 July.

Mikkelsen, David (2000/2016). "A Star is Borne," 5 July 2000/18 November 2016. http://www.snopes.com/history/govern/yellowstars.asp Accessed 15 September 2017.

Paulsen, Frank M (1967) *Danish-American Folk Traditions: A Study in Fading Survivals.* PhD dissertation, Indiana University.

Pilegaard, Knud (2017). Personal email communication, 18 August.

*Politiken* (2013). "Christian X var parat til at lade alle bære jødestjerne," 24 September. http://politiken.dk/indland/art5471400/Christian-X-var-parat-til-at-lade-alle-bære-jødestjerne Accessed 15 September 2017.

Rasmussen, Bjørn (4 Nov 1961). "Premingers 'Exodus,'" *Aktuel*, 4 November.

*Reno Gazette-Journal* (1943). "The Courageous Danes," 31 March, p. 4.

Stegelmann, Jørgen (1961). "Den lange vej. Imperial's premiere på Otto Premingers filmatisering af Leon Uris' 'Exodus,'" *Berlingske Tidende*, 4 November, p. 11.

Sørensen, Henri (2017). Interviewed by the author on August 7.

Terkelsen, T. M. (1944). *Front Line in Denmark*. London: Free Danish Publishing Company.

Thulstrup, Irmeline (1961). "Filmromantik og virkelighed," *Kristeligt Dagblad*, 4 November, pp. 11-12.

Togeby, Sigurd (1945). *Kongen morer sig. 100 Historier om Kongen*. Copenhagen: Thorkild Bechs Forlag.

*Troy Record* (1943). "Danish King Willing to Wear Jewish Star, Refugee Announces," 12 October, p. 10.

Uris, Leon (1959). *Exodus*. London: Allan Wingate. Orig. pub. 1958.

Uris, Leon (1959). *Exodus*. Danish trans. by Mogens Boisen. Copenhagen: Grafisk Forlag.

Vilhjálmsson, Vilhjálmur Örn (2003). "The King and the Star. Myths created during the Occupation of Denmark," in *Denmark and the Holocaust*, edited by Mette Bastholm and Steven L. B. Jensen. Copenhagen: Danish Center for Holocaust and Genocide Studies, pp. 102-117.

Vilhjálmsson, Vilhjálmur Örn and Bent Blüdnikow (2006). "Rescue, Expulsion, and Collaboration. Denmark's Difficulties with its World War II Past," *Jewish Political Studies Review*, vol. 18, no. 3-4, Fall. http://www.jcpa.org/phas/phas-vilhjalmsson-f06.htm Accessed 15 September 2017.

Vilhjálmsson, Vilhjálmur Örn (2010). "Christian X og jøderne. Hovedrolleindhavere i dansk krigspropaganda," *Rambam. Tidsskift for jødisk kultur og forskning*, no. 19, pp. 68-85.

Weissbrod, Rachel (1999). "*Exodus* as a Zionist Melodrama," *Israel Studies*, vol. 4, no. 1, pp. 129-152.

*Wisconsin Jewish Chronicle* (1942). "Danish King Will Don Mogen David," 16 October, p. 5.

Yahil, Leni (1969). *The Rescue of Danish Jewry. Test of a Democracy*. Translated from the Hebrew by Morris Gradel. Philadelphia: Jewish Publication Society of America.

# Acknowledgments

I am grateful to a number of journals for permission to reprint the following articles: "Casablanca and United States Foreign Policy," *Film History*, 4:2 (1990), 153-164; "*Le Chant des Partisans*: Functions of a Wartime Song," *Folklore*, 102:1 (1991), 62-76; "Far from Where? On the History and Meanings of a Classic Jewish Refugee Joke". *American Jewish History* 85:2 (1997), 143-150. © 1997 American Jewish Historical Society. Reprinted with permission of Johns Hopkins University Press; "Camus' Critiques of Existentialism," *Minerva – An Internet Journal of Philosophy*, 5 (2001); "Two Marseillaise scenes: From *Casablanca* to *West Beirut*," *Canadian Journal of Film Studies*, 16:2 (Autumn 2007), 112-118; "The Moth in *Merry Christmas, Mr. Lawrence*," *Asian Cinema*, 18:2 (2007), 281-287; "From Leslie Howard to Raoul Wallenberg: the transmission and adaptation of a heroic model" first appeared in *P.O.V. – A Danish Journal of Film Studies*, 28 (December 2009), 84-104; "Five explanations as to who named Malta's Gloster Gladiators 'Faith', 'Hope' and 'Charity' in 1940-1941," *Journal of Maltese History* 4:2 (2015). Henri Sørensen's Illustrations from Carmen Agra Deedy's *The Yellow Star: The Legend of King Christian X of Denmark* are published here by arrangement with Peachtree Publishers and with Henri Sørensen's kind permission.

Thanks are also due to: Aarhus University Press, for permission to print an English translation of my interview with Alain Resnais, which appeared in French in *Nuit et brouillard by Alain Resnais: On the making, reception and functions of a major documentary film* (1987, pp. 47-63) and for permission to reprint a portion of "The photo in context" from *A Child at Gunpoint. A Study in the Life of a Photo* (2004); to Praeger Books for a publishing agreement enabling me to include here "*Bad Day at Black Rock* and the overcoming of evil" which originally appeared in *A History of Evil in Popular Culture: What Hannibal Lecter, Stephen King, and Vampires Reveal about America* (2014), Vol. 1, pp. 281-294; to Sandrew Metronome and Kjell Grede for permission to use stills and dialogue from *Good Evening, Mr. Wallenberg* (1990); to Ziad Doueiri for permission to use several stills from *West Beirut* (1998); to Johan Oettinger and Aarhus University Press for permission to use the shot-by-shot breakdown of *Seven Minutes in the Warsaw Ghetto* (2012) that appeared in *Seven Minutes in the Warsaw Ghetto and With Raised Hands. A film ebook*, Aarhus University Press (2013), 14-26; to Rick Beyer for permission to do a shot-by-shot breakdown of the pre-title sequence of *The Ghost Army* (2013); to Bernard Serf for permission to use Barbara's handwritten notes for the song, *Göttingen*; and to Patrice Grelet at the Musée de la Légion d'honneur et de la chevalerie for permission to use the handwritten notes for the *Le Chant des Partisans; to* Matt Jacobsen, editor of Oldmagainearticles.com for providing a copy of "Bad Time at Honda" in *American Magazine,* January 1947; and to Mary Engel for her kind permission to use Ruth Orkin's photo, "Jewish Refugees."

## Publication histories of the chapters in this book

### 1. *Casablanca* and United States Foreign Policy

This study appeared in a slightly longer form in my dissertation, *The Functional Analysis of Art. An Approach to the Social and Psychological Functions of Literature, Painting and Film* (Aarhus: Arkona, 1983), pp. 277-304. A shorter version was subsequently published in *Film History*, 1990, vol. 4, no. 2, pp. 153-164. That journal has kindly given permission for the inclusion of this essay in the present volume.

### 2. Bogart's Nod in the *'Marseillaise'* Scene: A Physical Gesture in *Casablanca*

This essay first appeared as an article in *P.O.V. – A Danish Journal of Film Studies*, no. 14 (December 2002), pp. 136-142.

### 3. A Note on a Wartime Function of the Bogart Image

This note first appeared in *The Functional Analysis of Art. An Approach to the Social and Psychological Functions of Literature, Painting and Film* (Aarhus: Arkona, 1983), pp. 305-308.

### 4. Two *'Marseillaise'* scenes: From Michael Curtiz's *Casablanca* (1943) to Ziad Doueiri's *West Beirut* (1998)

This essay first appeared in the *Canadian Journal of Film Studies*, vol. 16, no. 2 (Autumn 2007), pp. 112-118, and is included here with the kind permission of that journal. The stills from *West Beirut* are used with the kind permission of Ziad Doueri.

## 5. From Leslie Howard to Raoul Wallenberg: The Transmission and Adaptation of a Heroic Model

This study originally appeared in *P.O.V. – A Danish Journal of Film Studies*, no. 28 (December 2009), pp. 84-104. Stills and dialogue from *Good Evening, Mr. Wallenberg* are used with kind permission from Sandrew Metronome and Kjell Grede.

## 6. Interview with Alain Resnais on *Night and Fog*

Recorded in Paris on February 18, 1986, this interview appeared in French in my book *Nuit et Brouillard by Alain Resnais. On the Making, Reception and Functions of a Major Documentary Film* (Aarhus University Press, 1987), pp. 47-63. Here it is published in English for the first time, in my translation from the French.

## 7. Reflections on Art and the Holocaust: Elie Wiesel versus Alain Resnais

This essay has not been previously published. It does, however, build upon and further develop thoughts proposed in "Art and the Holocaust: positioning *Seven Minutes in the Warsaw Ghetto*," *Short Film Studies*, 2014, vol. 4, no. 2, pp. 223-226.

## 8. An Iconic Holocaust Photo in Context

This essay was a chapter in my book, *A Child at Gunpoint: A Case Study in the Life of a Photo*, published in 2004 by Aarhus University Press, and included here with the kind permission of that publisher. The introductory note, added here in order to provide necessary background information, is from another book, *Seven Minutes in the Warsaw Ghetto and With Raised Hands. A film ebook*, published in 2013 by Aarhus University Press and also used here with permission.

## 9. *Bad Day at Black Rock* and the Overcoming of Evil

This essay appeared as a chapter in *A History of Evil in Popular Culture: What Hannibal Lecter, Stephen King, and Vampires Reveal about America*, ed. Sharon Packer and Jodie Pennington. Santa Barbara: Praeger, 2014; vol. 1, pp. 281-294. It is included here in accordance with Praeger's generous publishing agreement. I wish to thank Matt Jacobsen, editor of Oldmagazinearticles.com for providing a copy of "Bad Time at Honda," *American Magazine*, January 1947.

## 10. The Moth in *Merry Christmas, Mr. Lawrence*

This essay first appeared in *Asian Cinema*, vol. 18, no. 2 (2007), pp. 281-287, and is included here with the publisher's kind permission.

## 11. The Role of the Birds in *Seven Minutes in the Warsaw Ghetto*

This essay has not been previously published.

## 12. '*Le Chant des Partisans*': Functions of an Underground Song

This essay appeared in *Folklore*, vol. 102, no. 1 (1991), pp. 62-76, and is included here with the kind permission of that journal. An earlier version appeared in my Danish dissertation, *The Functional Analysis of Art* (1983), pp. 168-190. Monsieur Patrice Grelet at Musée de la Légion d'honneur et des ordres de chevalerie kindly supplied copies of the handwritten manuscript for the song.

## 13. On Barbara's Need to Write the Song *Göttingen*

This essay has not been previously published.

## 14. Camus' Critiques of Existentialism

This essay first appeared in *Minerva – An Internet Journal of Philosophy*, vol. 5 (2001) and is included here with the kind permission of that journal.

## 15. Five Explanations for the Naming of Malta's Gloster Gladiators 'Faith,' 'Hope' and 'Charity' in 1940-1941

This essay appeared in the *Journal of Maltese History*, vol. 4, no. 2, 2015, and is included here with the kind permission of that journal.

## 16. Far from where? A Classic Jewish Refugee Joke

This essay first appeared in *American Jewish History*, vol. 85, no. 2 (1997), pp. 143-150. © 1997 American Jewish Historical Society. Reprinted with permission of Johns Hopkins University Press. It has also appeared as a chapter in the 2nd edition of my book, *Life Is Like a Glass of Tea. Studies of Classic Jewish Jokes* (New Orleans: Quid Pro Books, 2015).

## 17. *The Ghost Army* (2013) and Deception as Performance

This essay has not been previously published.

## 18. The King of Denmark and the Yellow Star: Changing Forms and Functions of an Irresistible Myth

This essay has not been previously published.

    I am deeply indebted to Former Chief Rabbi Bent Melchior who was most generous with his time and help in connection with this essay. I would also like to thank historian Bo Lidegaard, author Carmen Agra Deedy, illustrator Henri Sørensen, publisher Knud Pilegaard, former colleague Aage Jørgensen and librarians Lisbeth Raahauge Karlsson and Ken Nielsen for their help.